M000247709

RETIREMENT PLANNING

QuickStart Guide®

RETIREMENT PLANNING

QuickStart Guide®

The Simplified Beginner's Guide to Building
Wealth, Creating Long-Term Financial Security,
and Preparing for Life After Work

Ted D. Snow, CFP®, MBA

Copyright © 2021 by ClydeBank Media LLC

All rights reserved. No part of this publication may be reproduced, distributed, or transmitted in any form or by any means, including photocopying, recording, or other electronic or mechanical methods, without the prior written permission of the publisher, except in the case of brief quotations embodied in critical reviews and certain other noncommercial uses permitted by copyright law. For permission requests, write to the publisher, addressed "Attention: Permissions Coordinator," at the address below.

ClydeBank Media LLC is not associated with any organization, product or service discussed in this book. Although the author and publisher have made every effort to ensure that the information in this book was correct at press time, the author and publisher do not assume and hereby disclaim any liability to any party for any loss, damage, or disruption caused by errors or omissions, whether such errors or omissions result from negligence, accident, or any other cause.

Trademarks: All trademarks are the property of their respective owners. The trademarks that are used are without any consent, and the publication of the trademark is without permission or backing by the trademark owner. All trademarks and brands within this book are for clarifying purposes only and are owned by the owners themselves, not affiliated with this document. The QuickStart Guide chevron design mark is a registered trademark of ClydeBank Media LLC.

Disclaimer: The purpose of this book is to provide the public with accurate, simplified information. This information should not constitute "financial advice," "legal advice," "retirement planning advice," or "investment advice." Please consult your attorney, financial adviser, or another licensed professional for advice tailored to your financial needs and objectives. When it comes to funds and other investments, past performance in no way guarantees future performance. ClydeBank Media LLC does not in any way guarantee or promise any specific threshold of financial return or immunity from loss resulting from investments made in the funds featured in investment information articles.

Editors: Bryan Basamanowicz, Marilyn Burkley
Cover Illustration and Design: Katie Poorman, Copyright © 2021 by ClydeBank Media LLC
Interior Design & Illustrations: Katie Poorman, Brittney Duquette, Copyright © 2021 by ClydeBank Media LLC

First Edition – Last updated: July 4, 2023

ISBN-13: 9781636100043 (paperback) | 9781636100050 (hardcover) | 9781636100067 (eBook) | 9781636100074 (audiobook) | 9781636100241 (spiral bound)

Library of Congress Control Number: 2021931797

Author ISNI: 0000 000 46456 9247

Publisher's Cataloging-In-Publication Data
(Prepared by The Donohue Group, Inc.)

Names: Snow, Ted D., author.
Title: Retirement planning QuickStart Guide : the simplified beginner's guide to building wealth, creating long-term financial security, and preparing for life after work / Ted D. Snow, CFP®, MBA.
Other Titles: Retirement planning Quick Start Guide
Description: [Albany, New York] : ClydeBank Finance, [2021] | Series: QuickStart Guide | Includes bibliographical references and index.
Identifiers: ISBN 9781636100043 (paperback) | ISBN 9781636100050 (hardcover) | ISBN 9781636100241 (spiral bound) | ISBN 9781636100067 (ePub)
Subjects: LCSH: Retirees--Finance, Personal--Handbooks, manuals, etc. | Retirement income--Handbooks, manuals, etc. | Retirement--Planning--Handbooks, manuals, etc.
Classification: LCC HG179 .S66 2021 (print) | LCC HG179 (ebook) | DDC 332.024/014--dc23

For bulk sales inquiries, please visit www.go.quickstartguides.com/wholesale, email us at orders@clydebankmedia.com, or call 800-340-3069. Special discounts are available on quantity purchases by corporations, associations, and others.

Copyright © 2021
ClydeBank Media LLC
www.quickstartguides.com
All Rights Reserved

ISBN-13: 978-1-636100-05-0

OVER
850,000
READERS **LOVE** QuickStart Guides.

Really well written with lots of practical information. These books have a very concise way of presenting each topic and everything inside is very actionable!

– ALAN F.

The book was a great resource, every page is packed with information, but [the book] never felt overly-wordy or repetitive. Every chapter was filled with very useful information.

– CURTIS W.

I appreciated how accessible and how insightful the material was and look forward to sharing the knowledge that I've learned [from this book].

– SCOTT B.

After reading this book, I must say that it has been one of the best decisions of my life!

– ROHIT R.

This book is one-thousand percent worth every single dollar!

– HUGO C.

The read itself was worth the cost of the book, but the additional tools and materials make this purchase a better value than most books.

– JAMES D.

I finally understand this topic ... this book has really opened doors for me!

– MISTY A.

Contents

PART I – DESIGNING YOUR RETIREMENT

PART II – TRANSITIONING INTO RETIREMENT

PART III – LIFE AFTER RETIREMENT

BEFORE YOU START READING, DOWNLOAD YOUR FREE DIGITAL ASSETS!

 Portfolio Asset Allocator Workbook

 Long-Term Care Need Calculator

 End-of-Life Planning Guide

 Cash Flow/Budget Calculator

TWO WAYS TO ACCESS YOUR FREE DIGITAL ASSETS

Use the camera app on your mobile phone to scan the QR code or visit the link below and instantly access your digital assets.

or — go.quickstartguides.com/retirement

📱 SCAN ME   🖥 VISIT URL

Introduction

As in all successful ventures, the foundation of a good retirement is planning.
— EARL NIGHTINGALE
American author

Whether you are on the verge of retiring or still years away from it, you may have some ideas about what your retirement might look like. Maybe you dream of spending days on the golf course or teaching your grandkids to fish. Perhaps you'll tour the world, go back to school, or volunteer in your community. Maybe you're interested in starting a small business or writing your first novel.

Regardless of what you plan to do, you'll need financial resources to achieve a secure and sustainable retirement. You'll also need trustworthy information to help you manage those resources—a commodity that can be hard to come by. It's not that information is unavailable; there's plenty of it out there. Search the internet for just about any financial topic you can think of, and you'll find numerous sites offering facts, opinions, and special deals, all geared toward you. The challenge is in separating the reliable information from that which is not trustworthy. While many people heading into retirement rely on advice from a professional financial advisor, others prefer to handle their finances on their own. Wherever you fall on that spectrum, this book will provide information you can trust and rely upon. I have tried to write in a manner that is clear and accessible, and I trust that the content offered will be useful.

Having been a CERTIFIED FINANCIAL PLANNER™ practitioner for many years, I have my own opinions about money management, and you will read those opinions as you go through the book. I assure you, however, that the opinions and advice I offer are the same that I would give to my clients and are always geared toward your best interests. I simply want to help you cut through all the chatter and get to the information you need.

Writing this book was especially important to me, and something I realized I needed to do. It's been a journey, and I hope you choose to travel it with me. Let me tell you about myself, my story, and the purpose I have found for my life.

My Story—My "Why"

Ever since I was five years old, I've been intrigued with how money works. I remember going to the Main Street bank in my small hometown of Magna, Utah, to deposit my one-dollar weekly allowance into an old passbook savings account. The day I read the numbers in the passbook and noticed I had saved thirty-five dollars, I thought to myself, "Wow! That's a lot of money!"

When I was in sixth grade at Webster Elementary, the school set up a little "city" called Websterville on the third floor of our school building. There was a general store, a café, a clothing store, and other businesses, all operated by students who seemed to fit the role of proprietor. I, of course, was chosen to be the banker, depositing the financial gains of other business-minded youngsters and helping my fellow students make withdrawals for the purchase of Laffy Taffy and Blow Pops at the general store.

When we graduated sixth grade to move on to junior high, we were able to cash in our Websterville dollars for real money. As a sign of my future calling, I broke the record for the highest bank account balance Websterville had ever seen. I was extremely excited to cash in my Websterville fortune and claim my real-money reward! Ripping open the envelope that contained my hard-earned profits, I was dismayed to discover that what amounted to two hundred dollars in Websterville money had shrunk to just twenty dollars. It was my first harsh lesson in currency exchange.

Survivors of the Great Depression, my parents instilled in me a spirit of conservation when it comes to spending and saving. Our family's needs were met, but certainly not all our wants. And yet, I was content in the secure love of my parents and the ways they provided for us. My life was simple—playing basketball and baseball and riding bikes, never thinking about the money we didn't have. With college on the horizon, I started a serious path to saving. At sixteen years of age, working summer construction and stocking shelves, I saved 100 percent of the cost of my associate degree at Snow Junior College, and with my additional savings I pursued my dream of majoring in business and minoring in economics at Utah State. I finished my degree and still had $4,000 in my pocket and no school debt.

Landing my first professional position at Fidelity Investments, my starting salary was a whopping $15,000 a year. Through my time at Fidelity I gained valuable experience in investing and money management, while personally applying my newfound knowledge by maximizing my 401(k) investments every year. With a move to Dallas at age twenty-eight, I saw an increase in salary to $30,000, and my 401(k) portfolio finally reached $100,000. I celebrated with Mexican food and margaritas. Life was good.

Then, in April 1994, our family experienced tragedy with the death of my father. All in one day, my mother lost her husband and his $35,000-a-year pension that provided for her. Because of some poor financial advice from a wealthy friend, my dad unwittingly left my mother in poverty. On his pension paperwork there were two choices: a "life only" benefit that pays out while the retiree is alive, and a "joint-and-survivor" payout that would have taken care of my mother following my father's death. My father's friend had advised my dad to check the "life only" pension box, leaving my mother without a pension, and social security as her only source of income.

The stark reality of how many people make ill-informed and financially devastating decisions fueled a passion in me to start my own financial planning practice. I was seventeen years old when my father made a bad decision that resulted in such terrible consequences for my mother. I was thirty when he died, and there was nothing I could do to change my mom's situation. From my Dallas Fidelity call center cubicle, I suddenly realized the importance of advising people face-to-face and earnestly counseling clients on a wide breadth of practical and often critical financial decisions, not just the narrow path of investment options and limited advice that Fidelity allowed.

Still haunted by my father's mistake and its consequences, and firmly motivated to steer my career in a more meaningful and personal direction, I completed my MBA in personal financial planning at the University of Dallas in 1995, and in 1997 I took a leap of faith away from the comforts of my salaried position at Fidelity to start my own practice. Armed with excellent client servicing skills, investing experience, an MBA, a $20,000 severance, and now close to $250,000 in my portfolio, I started as an advisor with Principal Financial Group, with a commission-only income and zero clients. Yet God had a plan for my life.

I am writing this book for everyone. Regardless of your religion or lack of religion, political views, or family background, I believe the value of a financial education is universal and essential. That said, it would be disingenuous for me to share my personal experience with you if I omitted the profound role my faith has played in my personal approach to money management, as well as the approach I take with clients in my practice. The Bible has a lot to say about money and how it should be handled. It offers lessons regarding living within your means, debt management, preparing for the future, providing for yourself and others, and sharing resources with those who are in need. Many clients have opinions that are different than mine, but over the years a substantial number have come to share my belief that money is a tool, a means to an end. We don't serve money. We let money serve us, so we can accomplish that which is good.

How Giving Changed My Practice and My Life

The first years of building my business were exciting but, truth be told, often anxiety-provoking as I worked hard to establish a clientele and save money needed to grow my company. My beautiful wife, Mary, whom I married when I was thirty-six, has been an unfaltering partner as my company has expanded and thrived. She currently serves as its client services director, and, together, we are living out God's plan for our lives, a key component of which is giving. In my view, giving and money management are inextricable. Moreover, I view the practice of bold, enthusiastic, "radical" giving as a gratifying, spiritually enriching response to the abundance brought on by success in one's financial life.

As my business became well established and increasingly profitable, I began to reexamine my giving practices. I had the opportunity to personally witness the vast needs of poorer and marginalized people around the world. From journeying to China, where I practiced conversational English in Beijing and Guangzhou, to traveling to Honduras, where my missionary work led me to build homes for those living in poverty, my experiences in these countries opened my eyes to the pressing needs of many people and how much I took for granted in my comfortable life in the United States. It became clear to me that I needed to engage in more radical giving.

Mary and I took time to discern the way we wanted to share our resources, then committed to a variety of poverty-focused ministries we believe are important and worthwhile. Last year our donations totaled 13 percent of our income, an amount we feel is sustainable with the possibility of future increases. We contribute to village schools in Pakistan, Africa, and Haiti; supplemental food programs; local homeless and campus ministries; and safe houses for troubled youth in the United States and abroad.

Giving to these ministries has greatly increased the meaning and purpose of the money I earn. Purposeful working and earning to have resources to share is a principle I pass along to clients and one that characterizes my financial planning practice. I advise my clients about financial matters with a broader lens in view, above and beyond communicating and managing the intricate steps of wealth management. I view my work as a ministry of helping and financially serving clients, their families, and the causes they care about. I believe that by leaning on experience, sound research, continuing education, and, most importantly, prayer and scripture for wisdom and support, I have been able to build a successful practice and provide clients with a sense of peace as they become less fearful and more secure and confident in their financial lives. Many of my clients have been with me since the inception of my practice, giving me the opportunity to serve two, or even three, generations.

What began as a childlike fascination with the growth of money in Websterville and deepened into a conviction about prudent financial decision making from my mother's experience has landed me in a life-impacting profession.

When to Start Retirement Planning

Like most worthwhile endeavors, planning for your retirement will require time, effort, and patience. It's a marathon, not a sprint, and it should begin well in advance of the day you leave work behind you. Planning for your retirement, in fact, is a practice that should begin when you land your very first job.

I talk to all my clients, regardless of age, about retirement planning. Whether they are just getting started in a career, building a career, or getting ready to end one, I believe it is imperative that each has a vision of what they'd like their retirement to look like, and an understanding of the steps they will need to take to achieve that vision. When you are in your twenties and thirties, retirement can seem extremely far off in the future. Trust me, though, the years go fast, and retirement approaches quickly.

No two people plan for retirement in the same way, and that's okay. But one thing I've learned is that planning is a practice—a discipline of sorts. About ten years ago, I decided it was time for me to lose some weight. I realized that a lot of pounds had crept onto my frame over the years and it was at the point where the extra weight was beginning to negatively affect my health, making it difficult for me to participate in activities I enjoyed and perhaps raising some risk factors for disease.

Once I had made a conscious decision to lose weight, I had to come up with a plan for how to move forward, and then establish new practices: a different eating plan and plenty of additional exercise. It was difficult at first, as old habits die hard, but it got steadily easier. About a year after I started, I realized my healthier lifestyle had become ingrained. I enjoyed healthy foods that I probably would not have eaten in the past and was rediscovering outdoor activities in which I hadn't participated for years. Losing fifty pounds not only eliminated strain on my heart and joints, it provided a sense of overall happiness and well-being. I felt that I had accomplished something good and worthwhile, not only for myself, but for my wife and clients and friends.

Frankly, I can't see myself ever reverting to that former lifestyle, because the new one is so much better. But, without a plan and lots of practice, it's likely I never would have lost those fifty pounds. The same is true for retirement planning. At some point, you need to make a conscious decision to begin, and then establish financially healthy practices that will become lifelong habits. Retirement planning often begins by default. As soon as you start making contributions to an IRA or a 401(k) plan, you've started planning for retirement. Active planning, however, is preferable to passive planning, so in addition to contributing to a retirement fund, you could be thinking about establishing a health savings plan, buying some stocks and bonds, looking into insurance plans, having the correct and up-to-date legal estate documents drafted, and making sure you're sticking to your budget. In short, strive to develop and adhere to the following twelve habits of financially healthy people. I often provide a list of these habits to my clients (figure 1).

12 HABITS
Of Financially Healthy People

 Practice generosity

 Learn as much as you can about issues affecting your finances

 Act with discernment

 Work hard to generate maximum income

fig. 1

 Take measured risks

 Invest well, with the intent of generating income

 Stick to a budget

 Work together as a family

 Be a saver

 Establish a reward system

 Include your spouse or partner when making financial decisions

Set financial goals to keep yourself on track

If you have not already done so, the best time to start planning for your retirement is now. How you plan may vary depending on your age, but remember, it is a process, not an event.

Retirement on Purpose

While this book deals primarily with financial matters, it also touches on some of the psychological aspects of retiring. We know that major life events, regardless of what they are, can cause significant stress. Make no mistake about it, retirement is a major life event. Unless you can figure out a way to transition from full-time to part-time employment, chances are your work life will come to an abrupt halt, either because you've chosen to leave work or you've been told you'll have to leave. And then what? I've known individuals who have crafted elaborate retirement plans, and others who figured they would just let retirement happen. My feeling is that those with a plan—those who retire on purpose and with a purpose—generally do better in retirement than those who do not.

Instead of retiring from a job, why not determine to retire to something more purposeful for you? Make time your friend, not something to just be endured. Think of things you've always wanted to do but never found time for. Write them down and start dreaming. They don't have to be grand adventures, like embarking on a trip to China or setting out to climb the Matterhorn. Maybe you'd like to visit all fourteen presidential libraries, take in some Broadway shows, or finally master the art of fly fishing. Perhaps you have a shelf lined with books you've never taken time to read. Retirement, if planned well, can offer you freedom that simply didn't exist while you were working. Rediscover your lost love of camping, or get out the guitar that's been in your closet for years. You'll finally have time to discover new adventures and pastimes, or rediscover old ones.

A few ideas and suggestions for retirement:

» Work through a reputable organization to arrange a "home exchange." These organizations can facilitate, for example, a couple in Ohio exchanging their home for one in Ireland for three months.

» Volunteer to tutor students who need extra help with reading, math, or another subject.

» Take some classes. Learn a new language or explore the history of ancient civilizations.

» Get a National Parks senior pass and decide which ones you'd like to visit.

» Build something, even if you never have before. You can find online instructions for building flower boxes, a bench, or a bookcase.

» Join a local theater group and audition for a play, or volunteer to help construct or paint scenery.

» Volunteer to help at your grandchild's school.

» Take up a hobby such as photography, bird watching, or brewing your own beer.

The Fit Retiree

Regardless of what age you are when you retire, it is important to take care of yourself physically, mentally, and spiritually. It's not something most of us like to think about, but our bodies change as we get older. For many people, it takes a little longer to get going in the morning. You might wonder what is causing that pain in your lower back, or why walking up the steep hill behind your house is harder than it used to be.

Your mental health also may change with aging. The Centers for Disease Control and Prevention estimates that 20 percent of Americans aged fifty-five and older experience some sort of mental health concern, most commonly depression, anxiety, bipolar disorder, or severe cognitive impairment. We know that older men have the highest suicide rate of any age group, and that many older adults suffer from loneliness, loss of identity, and other concerns.

Just as with your physical and mental health, it's possible you'll notice changes in your spiritual health. You may find that activities that were important to you no longer seem to matter as much. Maybe you have stopped making time to help with your local Habitat for Humanity effort or no longer deliver food for Meals on Wheels. You may feel spiritually bereft or have a sense of emptiness.

Staying fit physically, mentally, and spiritually can be challenging, but it is well worth the effort if you want to lead an active and satisfying life.

After retiring from a career with the Texas state police, Bruce, sixty-one, and his wife, Marcia, sixty-three, spent six months training to get into great physical condition and then hiked the Appalachian Trail from Georgia to Maine. After being on the trail for five months, they returned home and discovered they needed something to do. They were in great shape physically, but their spiritual lives were unfulfilled. They found a spiritual calling through volunteering in their community, serving meals, helping senior citizens with projects such as hanging ceiling fans or mowing lawns.

In December they helped with a food and clothing drive for underserved families. When asked about his desire to serve, Bruce said he remembered something he had learned long ago in his church's Sunday school.

"The first third of your life you serve yourself—education, job, and growing up," Bruce quoted. "The second third you serve your family—a career to raise your kids. The last third, you need to serve others."

There are dozens of ways to stay active and physically fit. Activity in the form of something you enjoy should be part of your daily schedule, whether it's walking with a friend, joining an exercise class, bicycling, or lifting weights. You'll thank yourself as you experience increased energy and a healthier body. Maintaining good physical health can also have positive effects on your mental health. Researchers have found that a healthy lifestyle including exercise, a well-balanced diet, sufficient sleep, and stress management can help prevent the onset or worsening of some mental health conditions, in addition to keeping you fit physically.

You can take steps to stay mentally sharp by engaging in activities like working crossword puzzles, listening to stimulating podcasts, reading books, and taking online classes. You could join a book discussion group or learn how to play bridge and join a bridge club. Socialization is important at every age, but perhaps particularly so for older people.

While working to maintain your physical and mental health, also keep an eye on your spiritual health. Research suggests that people who engage in spiritual practices tend to live longer, cope better with stressful situations, find greater enjoyment in life, and even recover more quickly from illness or surgery. There is no right or wrong way to discover spiritual connections. You can be involved with a congregation, practice spirituality through volunteer work in your community, or participate in mission trips like the ones that changed my life.

The fit retiree works to make and maintain connections with others. She remains physically active, controls her stress, maintains good eating habits, pays attention to any emotional or mental concerns, and remains spiritually engaged. If you have experienced problems or have concerns about your physical, mental, or spiritual health, don't hesitate to reach out to your primary caregiver, a mental health professional, a clergy member, or a trusted family member or friend.

Manage Your Money, Don't Let It Manage You

I know people who constantly worry about their finances, despite the fact that they are well off. They fret and move money from one account to another, worrying all the time that they won't have enough for the trip they're planning or the work they want to do on the house. My heart goes out to these people. They are not managing their money—their money is managing them.

If you have and adhere to a sound financial plan, then you should be able to sidestep a lot of the worrying. Of course, you need to keep an eye on your portfolio, and in chapter 10, I'll show you how to do that without stressing yourself out. Meanwhile, you can take charge of your finances by doing the following:

» Establishing and adhering to a workable budget
» Setting up retirement accounts and funding them to take full advantage of employer matches
» Getting your debt under control and paying off your mortgage before retirement if possible
» Making sure you have the different insurance coverages you need
» Adding stocks and bonds to your portfolio
» Planning for what you will need in retirement
» Making sure your portfolio remains balanced and diversified
» Planning for retirement income
» Creating your estate planning legal documents and making changes to them as your life changes
» Living within or well below your means

Establishing and living in those ten habits can go a long way toward you controlling your money instead of your money controlling you, and be assured that you will learn throughout this book how to accomplish all of those goals. Your spending and saving habits will greatly affect your overall financial picture and, ultimately, how you will be able to live in retirement. For now, however, I want to call your attention to the first task mentioned: establishing and adhering to a workable budget.

I've never fully understood why so many people bristle at the idea of a budget. I have repeatedly watched a client's anxiety level skyrocket when I begin talking about how important it is to have a budget in place and get into the habit of sticking with it. A budget is simply a plan for how you will save, give, and spend your money. It gives you control over your money, helping to ensure that you are saving enough, avoiding debt, and not overspending.

A good working budget is a foundational piece of your financial plan and a baseline practice for so many other critical retirement planning activities, like saving, investing, and paying down debt. It doesn't have to be scary, and it's an easy first step to take to ensure you are managing your money and not the other way around.

You can access the "What Is My Current Cash Flow" budgeting calculator, along with several other helpful and free tools, in your Digital Assets. Visit go.quickstartguides.com/retirement.

You've already read how important giving is in my life, but I am certainly not alone in that conviction. We know there are many benefits to giving as generously as you are able, and research is revealing more all the time. It's been found that the act of giving lights up the part of the brain that produces oxytocin, a hormone that, among other things, promotes social bonding. Giving bolsters positive emotions and reinforces thoughts of the world being a good place.

Dr. Martin Seligman, a scholar and author who is known as the "father of positive psychology," identified five important concepts that promote happiness and well-being. Called the PERMA model, the concepts are: positive emotion, engagement, relationships, meaning, and accomplishment.

According to Seligman, all these core concepts can be achieved by doing just one thing: giving. When you give, it not only helps others but provides tangible benefits to you. In fact, Seligman asserts, the act of giving can contribute to one's overall success in life.

Choosing a cause that's important to you and supporting it generously can keep your heart soft and make you feel that you're a part of something bigger than yourself. I mentioned my trips to Honduras and China where I encountered people who had very little—practically nothing in some cases. Nonetheless, with only their basic needs met, they were able to find joy in their families and communities. I was struck by their happiness, despite their profound poverty. The attitudes I witnessed in those places caused me to examine how I was living, burdened with possessions that disproportionately claimed my time, attention, and financial resources. I freed myself of many of those possessions, including my home. Mary and I now live in a beautiful, low-maintenance apartment. We have more free time to do the things we're passionate about. We also have more financial resources, which we use to support causes that are important to us and others. Stepping up the giving of our time, talents, and treasure has affirmed our faith and given us the satisfaction that comes from sharing generously for a good cause.

When deciding where you would like to direct your giving, think about what is important to you—what resonates with you. Perhaps you experienced a rocky childhood and feel pulled to support an organization like a boys and girls club that provides after-school programs and other activities intended to keep kids involved in healthy ways. Maybe you could cook and serve meals at a community shelter, work to ensure people have safe housing, contribute to an environmental cause, help at an animal shelter, or support your local library. There are thousands of worthy organizations and charities you can get involved with and support.

NOTE

If you are new to giving and not sure where you would like your support to go, you can learn a lot about charitable organizations and what they do from Charity Navigator, a nonprofit that assesses and evaluates charities in the United States. The organization posts listings of charities in categories such as "ten charities with the most consecutive four-star ratings."

THE 5 USES OF MONEY

GRAPHIC

fig. 2

1 — Giving

2 — Saving

3 — Taxes

4 — Debt

5 — Living Expenses

The five uses of money, in order, are giving, saving, taxes, debt, and living expenses. I believe that employing money in this order creates a healthy, sustainable financial plan.

I feel so strongly about the importance of giving that I place it first in what I call "The Five Uses of Money" (figure 2). When I think about how money is used, five key areas come to mind. You might argue for others, but for me, the five uses of money are, in order of importance, giving, saving, taxes, debt, and living expenses. I understand that the idea of giving as the most important use of my money may sound radical, but bear with me as I explain.

There's no question that saving money—starting as early as possible and maximizing your savings as you are able—is important to your future financial health, because it gives time for your money to compound and work for you. Paying taxes, which I cite as the third use of money, is not an option, although I'll offer some advice on how to minimize the amount of tax you must pay.

Some people would place paying off debt higher up on the uses-of-money list, and there may be times when it's appropriate to pay off debt in place of, or in addition to, saving. If you have debt on a high-interest credit card, for instance, it might be smart to get that paid off while temporarily reducing the amount of money you save. It makes no sense to be paying 20 percent interest on credit card debt while your investment is earning 8 percent. However, if the interest rate on your student loan debt is 4.6 percent and your investment is earning 10 percent, it might make more sense to pay off your debt slowly while continuing to save and invest.

The fifth use of money, paying for your living expenses, is an area over which you have some control. Living expenses, in my opinion, fall into two categories. There are expenses like mortgage payments, electric bills, and the cost of groceries that you must pay. Those are true living expenses. Others, like vacations, pricey electronics, or eating in restaurants all the time, are discretionary—you can control the extent to which you spend. Taking control of how you spend your money gives you power, and when you put that power into practice, you take charge of your money and are able to control how it is used.

When you exercise a bit of frugality with regard to your living expenses—maybe you cook dinner instead of going out, or you decide you can live without the newest version of the iPhone for several years—it frees up some money. And, sure, you could deposit that extra money into your savings or use it to pay down some debt. But I would encourage you to consider that donating to a cause you care about may be the best use of that money. Because when you do that, it not only benefits the cause, but you reap the rewards identified in the PERMA model, and the win–win effect of giving is achieved.

Let's be clear that when I claim giving as the most important use of money, I'm not suggesting it must, or even should, be your largest expenditure. Obviously, most people don't give more to charity than they pay in rent or mortgage expense. The extent and magnitude of one's giving, just like one's motivation for giving, is personal. While my giving amounts and motivation are faith-driven, yours may spring from a commitment to justice, concern for the hungry, or a desire to make a difference in your community. When I say

I believe that giving should be the first use of money, I mean it should be the most important and significant manner of spending. Whether you give ten dollars or a thousand, know that your decision to give is meaningful.

How This Book Is Organized

This book is intended to teach you about a variety of topics and issues that pertain to retirement, regardless of how far along your career path you have progressed. From setting up your first retirement account, to investing in the stock market, to considering when to start collecting Social Security, you will learn how the decisions you make and the actions you take at various stages of your life will affect your financial future.

It is my life's work to educate people about their finances and help them plan for their futures. Ideally, I get to work with a client long term, working together to achieve financial success and secure a well-planned and much-deserved retirement. I would like this book to help you chart a course to that same objective.

The book is divided into three parts. The first part, "Designing Your Retirement," focuses on setting up retirement accounts that will work for you for many years, letting you take advantage of the great power of compound interest. You'll learn about stocks and securities, indexes, and mutual funds, and you'll achieve a better understanding of what types of insurance are important at different stages of your life. We'll explore what expenses you should anticipate in retirement and glance at what life could look like when you are no longer working. We'll also explore the concept of financial independence and how some individuals are saving and investing at a breakneck pace to be able to stop working long before the traditional retirement age.

Part II, "Transitioning into Retirement," is intended to help you fine-tune your retirement plans. We'll explore topics such as Social Security, pensions, and annuities. We'll consider how you might generate income after retiring, through portfolio withdrawals, real estate, or perhaps starting a new business. We touch on the increasing problem of fraud and cybercrime, offering some advice on efforts you can take to avoid becoming a victim. You'll also learn why it's so important to keep an eye on your portfolio to keep it balanced and manage your taxes.

The third part of the book, "Life After Retirement," examines some of the psychological aspects of retirement and what you might do to adjust to and embrace this stage of your life. It also takes a dive into Medicare, a subject that can be a bit daunting to figure out. We'll look at some issues concerning estate planning, including wills, trusts, and powers of attorney.

By the time you finish reading, I hope you will feel confident in your ability to plan for your retirement.

Chapter by Chapter

» PART I: Designing Your Retirement

» Chapter 1, "Key Retirement Accounts—It's Never Too Early to Start," explores different types of 401(k)s and individual retirement accounts (IRAs) and the advantages and downsides of each. You'll read about health savings accounts (HSAs), which offer some significant tax benefits while enabling you to save money for future medical expenses. And you'll learn about different types of financial advisors and the importance of choosing the right one.

» While establishing retirement accounts is your first step, it's also important to understand the benefits and risks involved with other types of investments, including stocks, bonds, and real estate. Chapter 2, "Investment Strategies," explores those topics and can help you begin to build a diversified and balanced portfolio.

» Insurance is an important aspect of financial planning, and chapter 3, "Insurance," explains how insurance fits into the larger financial picture. You'll learn about various types of insurance and which are most important during certain stages of life. We'll pay special attention to the subject of disability insurance, which provides vital protection if you are not able to produce an income for an extended period.

» Chapter 4, "Understanding Your Retirement Needs," helps you to understand what your expenses in retirement might look like and why a sound budget is such an important tool in managing those expenses. I'll urge you to take a hard, honest look at what you have, what you are likely to need, and whether you'll be able to meet your expenses while maintaining as much of your retirement savings as possible. We'll also begin to look at the risk of outliving your retirement savings and what your post-retirement life might look like.

» Chapter 5, "Accelerating Your Retirement Timeline," explores an ongoing movement known as FIRE, which stands for Financial Independence, Retire Early. The movement has been around for decades but has recently picked up steam thanks to a growing number of people who have decided that working until they are sixty or seventy is not for them. Not everyone can save large amounts of money while they are young, of course, and that is a key component of FIRE. Everyone, however, may be able to benefit from scaling back on spending when possible and, as a result, be able to save, give, and invest more.

» **PART II: Transitioning into Retirement**

» As you begin part II, you'll learn about the traditional "three-legged stool" of retirement income: Social Security, pensions, and personal savings. Chapter 6, "Social Security and Pensions Are Nice, But Not the Whole Picture," looks at the dangers of over-reliance on Social Security and explains that pensions have largely been replaced by retirement accounts such as 401(k)s. We'll explore the timing of taking Social Security and, if you do have a pension, whether it makes sense to take it in monthly payments or as a lump sum.

» In chapter 7, "Annuities," you will learn about different kinds of annuities and what type might be best for your financial situation. Annuities, which are a much-debated financial tool, can provide income to supplement Social Security, making them a sound investment decision for some retirees. They can be a complex financial product, though, and it is usually best to get some advice regarding which type to purchase.

» Chapter 8, "Reaping the Rewards of Sound Retirement Planning," discusses options for helping to fund your retirement, which of course is the reward of years of careful planning, saving, and investing. If you have stocks that pay dividends, you might choose to use them to generate income. Or you could begin to withdraw money from your retirement funds, even if that entails paying taxes on that money. Other means of generating income might include starting a business with low start-up and overhead costs or renting property you own.

» Chapter 9, "Fraud," contains a cautionary tale, as fraud and scams have increased dramatically in the past few years and can threaten to derail your sound retirement planning and your ability to reap the benefits of that planning. It is important to be aware of some common methods employed to trick people into revealing sensitive information or enabling cybercriminals to access online accounts. Although fraud frequently occurs online, it can also be conducted over the phone, by mail, or in person. The good news is that there are tools available to help you avoid scams and fraud.

» In chapter 10, "Managing Your Portfolio," you will read about the importance of asset allocation and rebalancing your portfolio as needed. We will discuss the need for staying the course during a market downturn, a rule I cannot stress enough, because letting emotions run their portfolio has been the ruin of many investors. This chapter also deals with the advantages of using dividend reinvestment to keep your portfolio diversified and discusses strategies you can employ to minimize the taxes you have to pay.

» **PART III: Life After Retirement**

» Moving into part III, chapter 11, "Retiring from Work and Into Life," explores some of the psychological aspects of leaving a job and a career. You may have to "reinvent" yourself, letting go of the identity that was associated with your work. We'll consider how your retirement might affect not only you, but also family members. You will read about individuals who have started new careers after retiring or have used that time to go back to school or travel. Looking at retirement not as the end of something, but the beginning, can help assure you of a positive experience.

» Chapter 12, "Managing Your Health Plans," deals with the high cost of health care and the importance of choosing the right plans. We take a deep dive into Medicare, about which entire books have been written, to help you better understand how to navigate that system. You'll read a little about Medicaid and who can benefit from it. Health insurance can be a complicated topic, but it's important, and I want you to get a feel for what is available and what to consider when choosing your plans.

» Planning for how your affairs will be handled after you die is also important, and chapter 13, "Estate Planning," will lead you through the basics of wills, trusts, powers of attorney, and other aspects of planning. It also touches on the subject of end-of-life care and some of the important decisions you should be thinking about in advance of that time.

DESIGNING YOUR RETIREMENT

| 1 |

Key Retirement Accounts
It's Never Too Early to Start

Chapter Overview
» The Advantage of Time
» Key Accounts
» Financial Advisors

Compound interest is the eighth wonder of the world. He who understands it, earns it. He who doesn't, pays it.

– ALBERT EINSTEIN

If you are reading this book in your twenties or thirties, I really like your chances for a successful retirement. Using time to your financial advantage is a key element of investing, and if you have already started thinking about how to accomplish your financial goals while putting money away for retirement, then you are definitely on the right track.

The reason is that the earlier you start investing, the more time your money has to grow and the more you benefit from *compound interest*, which is interest paid on your initial deposit plus the interest you earn on that deposit. Compound interest might not seem like a big deal when you are just starting to save and invest your money, but it becomes important over time.

Let's say you invest just $250 in an account that earns 6 percent annual interest, and then you invest $50 a month for five years. Over five years, your total contribution to the account will be $3,250. At the end of five years, however, thanks to the beauty of compound interest, you will have $3,826. I know that does not seem terribly impressive, but you earned $576 in five years just by having your money invested.

But what if you invested $2,500 at 6 percent annual interest and added $100 a month for five years? At the end of the five-year period you would have invested $8,500, but your investment would be worth $10,349—$1,849 more than you had put into the account. And if you leave the money where it is and keep adding $100 a month, in five more years (assuming you continue to earn 6 percent interest compounded annually), your account will be worth $20,936. You get the idea, right?

NOTE

My company website has a compound interest calculator that is easy and fun to use and provides a clear illustration of the power of compound interest. You can find it, along with many other practical calculators, at snowfinancialgroup.com/resource-center/calculators.

There are a lot of formulas that tell you how much you should invest each year and how much you should have saved by various points in your life in order to ensure you will meet your retirement goals. The fact is that many people have no idea how much money they will need to retire.

Bankrate, a personal finance company, conducted a survey in 2018 asking participants how much money they personally would need to save to fund their retirements. A startling 61 percent of all the age groups surveyed said they did not know. But here's the thing: when it comes to your financial future, knowledge is power. When that knowledge is coupled with discipline and a sound investing strategy, the future gets even brighter.

MY TAKE

Investors make many mistakes, some resulting from carelessness, others from bad advice, and others from a lack of understanding. The three biggest mistakes I have watched investors make over the course of my career are these:

1. Starting to invest too late, thereby losing out on the advantages of compounding.

2. Not investing enough. Contribution to investments every month should be a fixed expense in your budget.

3. Becoming conservative with their investment selections too soon. Sure, it is good to tilt your portfolio to less risky investments as you get close to retirement, to protect your assets in the event of a downturn. Being too risk-averse, however, can limit your earnings potential to the point where it will be difficult to keep up with inflation and meet your financial goals (you will read more about inflation in chapter 2).

If you are in your forties or fifties, or even your sixties, and are just starting to plan for retirement, your work will be a little harder. But coming late to the game is way better than not coming at all. So, regardless of what age you start planning for retirement, you need to know about some key accounts that can help you work toward meeting your goals.

Key Retirement Accounts to Start Building Now

When you are in your twenties, thirties, or forties, saving for retirement can seem like a daunting task. *Forbes* reported recently that 44.7 million people in 2020 were carrying $1.56 trillion in student debt, with an average of $32,731 per person.

Even if you have college debt under control, you might be looking to buy a home or a condo, or finally trade in the old Honda you've been driving since high school. If you get married and have a couple of kids, that presents another set of challenges, along with all the joys, as you are probably thinking about getting a college fund started.

You can work all that out using discipline and a well-thought-out budget, which you read about in this book's introduction. Keep the five uses of money—giving, taxes, savings, debt, and living expenses—in mind; live within or, preferably, below your means, and make it a priority to get as much money as you can into some key accounts.

As you read in the introduction to this book, a good budget can help you avoid the financial traps of too much debt, too little savings, and too much spending. You can find good budget worksheets online or with a subscription to Microsoft Excel 365, or you can go to my website link noted earlier in this chapter. You may find that some budgeting tools are tailored to different age groups.

401(k) Plans

Until about forty years ago, *defined benefit pension plans*, usually just referred to as pensions, were common for employees in both the public and private sectors. Pensions, which provide retired workers with fixed incomes throughout their lifetimes, are still offered to many government workers, but are far less common today in the private sector. You will read more about pensions in chapter 6. A big reason for the decline of pensions, at least among private sector workers, is the advent of 401(k) plans, which are *defined contribution plans*. A defined contribution plan is one in which an employee—not an employer—contributes a portion of every paycheck to an account set up to fund retirement. Unlike a pension plan, distributions are not predefined or guaranteed but depend on how long the account value remains intact. There are other types of defined contribution plans, but 401(k) plans are by far the most popular and common.

These plans got their start in 1978, when Congress changed the tax code with legislation titled the Revenue Act. A provision in that act—Section 401(k)—gave employees an opportunity to channel money from bonuses or *stock options*, a form of compensation giving employees the right to buy shares of their company's stock, into what amounted to a tax-deferred retirement savings account. Ted Benna, who was a benefits consultant at the Johnson Companies, championed the plan and eventually became known as the "father of the 401(k)."

In 1981 the IRS announced that, in addition to bonus or stock options money, employees could start contributing to their 401(k)s through salary deductions. Employers applauded the 401(k) because it was less expensive to fund than defined benefit pension plans. Employees, who were told 401(k)s could help them meet their financial goals, also embraced them. Millions of Americans currently have about $5.7 trillion invested in 401(k)s.

When you invest in a 401(k) plan, the contributions you make go into a mix of investments that you determine. These are most commonly mutual funds that contain domestic and international stocks, money market funds, and bonds. Your employer, the plan sponsor, works with a third-party administrator (TPA) and a record keeper, who is the investment provider, to make sure the plan remains in compliance and your money is invested according to your wishes. The TPA can also offer information about the plan and answer any questions you have.

The Beauty of the 401(k) Plan

Though still subject to the whims of the market, there is a lot to like about 401(k) plans. They are easy to access, especially if you work for a large company, many of which enroll employees in plans automatically. Smaller companies can offer auto-enrollment, but not all do, so be sure to ask about getting into a plan when starting a new job.

Another plus for 401(k) plans is that your contributions are deducted from your paycheck before they are taxed. Contributions are systematically taken from your paycheck and automatically deposited into the 401(k) account. For a lot of people, this is an easier and less painful way to invest, as the decision of whether to contribute each pay period is already made. When you leave a job for another one, you have the option to take your

401(k) plan with you, leave it where it is, or roll it over into an individual retirement account (IRA).

Even better than easy access and automatic deductions is the employer match to a 401(k). Most employers (but not all) contribute money to their employees' 401(k)s, usually based on the employee's wage compensation. This happens in different ways.

Normally, an employer will match a percentage of an employee's compensation, up to a certain amount. In 2019, the average match by employers was 4.7 percent, the highest amount ever. Let's think about that for a minute. If your goal is to invest 10 percent of your annual salary, an employer match of 4.7 percent means the burden of saving on your part falls to 5.3 percent—a significantly lower level. Put another way, you are getting an instant return on your personal investment of nearly 100 percent before the money is even invested into any mutual fund, just by virtue of making your contribution. Then once the money is invested, it earns compound interest on the employer match and your contributions.

Any amount of matched contribution is good. If your company offers a 50 percent match on up to 6 percent of your pay, you should make every attempt to contribute at least 6 percent to take advantage of the maximum match. That's a win–win, in that while you are investing money on your own, you're also getting a bonus from your employer.

The maximum amount that an employee can contribute to a 401(k) is indexed each year. For 2020 it was $19,500, a $500 increase from the previous year. The Internal Revenue Service (IRS) reviews the maximum contribution amount each year and decides whether to adjust it. The amount increased from $18,000 in 2015 to $19,500 five years later.

If you are fifty or older, you can make catch-up contributions to your 401(k) on top of your regular contributions. This rule benefits older workers who have not saved as much as they would have liked, but who now are able to contribute larger amounts. The catch-up amount is also indexed every year. For 2020 the limit was $6,500, an increase of $500 from the previous year. So, if you were fifty or older in 2020, you could contribute up to $26,000 to a 401(k) plan, certainly a significant amount, and an important move if you are not yet close to your savings goals. Add in your employer's matching power and these catch-up contributions can provide you with a serious boost.

NOTE

The amount that your employer contributes to your 401(k) does not count toward your employee yearly contribution; it is in addition to your contribution. A general rule of thumb is to try to save 10 percent of your salary when you are starting out. If you can save 10 percent on your own and get the employer match on top of that, you will be moving in a direction to meet your retirement goals.

Another benefit of contributing to a 401(k) plan is that it reduces your taxable income. Your contributions are made on a pretax basis, which means the amount you contribute is deducted from your annual income for tax purposes. If you earn $75,000 and contribute 6 percent to a 401(k), your taxable income is reduced by $4,500, meaning you will pay taxes on $70,500 instead of $75,000. You will, however, need to pay income tax on any pretax money you withdraw from the plan when you retire.

A variation of a traditional 401(k), which is what has been discussed up to this point, is a ***Roth 401(k)***. The difference between the two is that contributions to a Roth 401(k) are taxed up front, meaning the contributions do not reduce your taxable income. The attractive thing about a Roth 401(k) is that, under current law, assuming that certain criteria have been met, you pay no tax on the money when you take it out of the account, no matter how much your account grows.

If your employer offers both, and you need to choose between a traditional and a Roth 401(k), consider this: A Roth 401(k) makes sense for anyone who currently is in a low tax bracket but expects to move to a higher tax bracket and remain there as the money is withdrawn from the 401(k) account. It would be less beneficial to someone whose income and tax bracket will be lower when the money is withdrawn from the account.

MY TAKE

Gauging what your tax bracket will be during retirement is not easy, as it is dependent on a variety of factors such as the amount of your savings, how much taxable income you withdraw from accounts, and other considerations. A CERTIFIED FINANCIAL PLANNER™ practitioner can help you get a sense of where you can expect to be, tax-wise, and what type of 401(k) makes the most sense.

NOTE

A traditional 401(k) makes sense for anyone who wants to reduce their taxable income today. However, you can contribute to both a traditional and a Roth 401(k) to get the best of both worlds.

If you change jobs, you have some choices about what to do with your 401(k). If your former employer's plan allows you to maintain your account, you can simply leave your 401(k) where it is. Just be sure to continue monitoring it. If your new employer offers a plan that includes a better variety of investments or other advantages, then you can transfer your prior 401(k) to the new plan. Be sure to get help filling out the paperwork so that the transfer is completed without tax consequences and/or penalties.

Some employees who move from job to job are not attentive to their 401(k)s and end up having several accounts, sometimes in different states. Reports indicate that Americans misplace billions of dollars a year when they switch jobs or financial institutions and leave money behind. Be sure to consider your 401(k) options when you change jobs and do not assume that it will be taken care of for you. If there's a possibility that you could have funds in old 401(k) accounts, use a resource like www.unclaimed.org, which enables you to check for assets in any state in which you have lived or worked.

IN PRACTICE: I often encourage my clients to consolidate their old 401(k)s into one account for ease of administration and cost savings.

Another option is to roll over the money in the 401(k) to a traditional or a Roth IRA. Despite annual contribution limits for IRAs, there is no limit to the amount you can directly roll over from a 401(k). You could also cash out your 401(k) when changing jobs, but, unless you desperately need the money, this should not be considered, or at most, viewed as a last resort. A cash-out is counted as income on which you will be taxed, you will face a penalty for early withdrawal if you are under fifty-nine and a half, and, most important, your potential to earn returns on your money will end.

Depending on your job sector you may encounter variants of the 401(k) plan, such as 403(b) plans and 457(b) plans, which were designed for government workers, not-for-profit employees, and educators.

Downsides to a 401(k) Plan

As I said previously, 401(k) plans are not perfect. If you want to access your money before you are fifty-nine and a half, you will have to pay income tax that was deferred, plus a 10 percent penalty. Some plans allow for a hardship withdrawal, which would enable you to withdraw money in the event you became sick or disabled. In that case there would be no penalty, just taxes due.

Also, depending on the type of plan you have, the employer contribution share of your 401(k) may not be available to you until you have been with the company for a certain amount of time. The money taken from your paycheck and invested, and your employer's matching funds, are all yours from the start, but if there is a profit-sharing component to your 401(k), meaning that your employer sets aside a portion of pretax profits to contribute to employees' retirement plans, then that money may not be available until you have worked for the company for a specific amount of time.

When employer contributions are available to you depends on your company's **vesting schedule**. With some organizations, employer contributions to an employee's 401(k) are available immediately. This is called **immediate vesting** and, obviously, is a nice perk.

Another type of vesting is **cliff vesting**, in which the employer's contributions become available to an employee only after a certain amount of time, up to three years. If your company has a two-year cliff vesting schedule, for instance, you could work there for one year and eleven months and receive none of the contributions your employer made to your 401(k) if you leave. Work for the extra month, and 100 percent of employer contributions are yours.

A common vesting schedule is **graded vesting**, which enables an employee to take ownership of employer contributions gradually (figure 3). A typical graded vesting schedule is six years, with the amount of ownership increasing by 20 percent every year starting at the end of the second year.

If you are participating in a 401(k) plan through work, try to get a handle on what kind of fees are being levied. You can ask your plan's TPA or your human resources representative to explain the cost structure. As a participant of the plan, you are entitled to receive annual updates to the plan that include the cost structure. It is good to know this because 401(k) plan costs vary, and you could be charged with fees that are higher than normal.

YEARS OF SERVICE	GRADED VESTING	CLIFF VESTING
1	0%	0%
2	20%	0%
3	40%	100%
4	60%	100%
5	80%	100%
6	100%	100%

When employer contributions come by way of profit share and vesting periods are used, either graded or cliff vesting may be applied.

CAUTION

Smaller 401(k) plans often incur higher fees than larger plans. That is something to be aware of if you work for a small company that offers a 401(k).

A sticking point for some people regarding 401(k)s is that the plans do not offer enough investment options. The average large 401(k) plan in 2016 offered twenty-seven investment options. Though the trend over the years has been for 401(k)s to offer fewer and fewer options, a countertrend has emerged recently in the form of the growing popularity of an investment option called the *self-directed brokerage window*.

The Self-Directed Brokerage Window Option

A brokerage window is an option within a 401(k) plan that gives you many more investment options than you'd find in an ordinary 401(k). If your employer offers this option, then you can buy and sell securities through a brokerage platform. You simply move money from the fund side of your 401(k) plan to the brokerage window, in which you can invest in individual stocks, bonds, and other securities.

The brokerage window option has been around for a while but has recently become more popular among employers and employees (figure 4).

NOTE

A self-directed brokerage window option is not the same as a true self-directed 401(k), which enables you to choose from investments including real estate, tax lien certificates, foreign currencies, energy investments, and others. To have a true self-directed 401(k) you must have your own company.

INVESTMENT OPTIONS

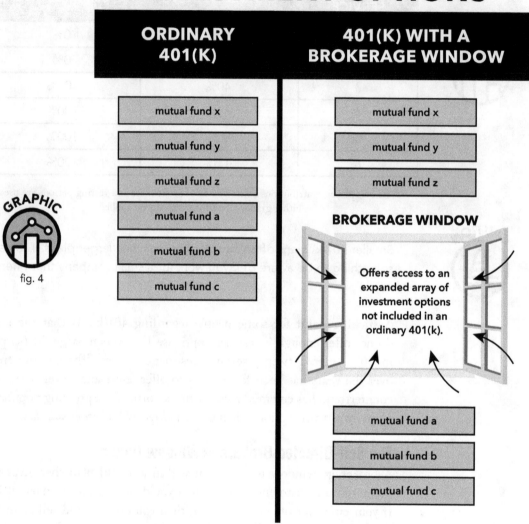

fig. 4

ORDINARY 401(K)	401(K) WITH A BROKERAGE WINDOW
mutual fund x	mutual fund x
mutual fund y	mutual fund y
mutual fund z	mutual fund z
mutual fund a	**BROKERAGE WINDOW**
mutual fund b	Offers access to an expanded array of investment options not included in an ordinary 401(k).
mutual fund c	mutual fund a
	mutual fund b
	mutual fund c

Individual Retirement Accounts

If you don't have access to a 401(k) plan, or if you are contributing enough to your 401(k) to get the full match from your employer and are looking for another type of retirement fund, then consider opening an *individual retirement account*, or IRA. It is not unusual to have a 401(k) and an IRA, and both give you the advantage of reducing your taxable income, which is always a good thing. You should know, however, that IRAs have income limitations. If your income is too high, your ability to make IRA contributions may be limited.

An IRA is simply an account you set up with a financial institution. Getting an account set up is not difficult, and you do not need a lot of money to get started. In fact, there typically is no fee to open an IRA, and many brokerages let you start an account with any amount of money you can contribute. You can open an IRA at most banks and credit unions, but those institutions tend to offer IRA *certificates of deposit (CDs)*, which are more like savings accounts than other types of investments. You'll do better setting up an IRA through a *mutual fund provider* or an *online broker*, both of which offer investments that have the potential for far higher returns.

About the only requirement for opening an IRA account is that you must have *earned income*, either from an employer or from being self-employed. If you do not have earned income but your spouse does, you can open a *spousal IRA*, to which your husband or wife can contribute money on your behalf.

EARNED INCOME

INCLUDES	EXCLUDES
• Wages	• Rental property
• Salaries	• Alimony
• Tips	• Child support
• Bonuses	• Social Security
• Commissions	• Unemployment benefits
• Money earned through self-employment	• Interest and dividends

GRAPHIC

fig. 5

A requirement of starting an IRA is that you have earned income. Some sources of income do not qualify as earned income.

Many investors like IRAs because they allow you to choose your own investments. You can mix stocks, bonds, mutual funds, exchange-traded funds (ETFs), and other investments in a combination that makes sense for your risk tolerance and financial situation. Or you can choose a ready-made collection of investment options. You will read more about *asset allocation*, or how to balance your investments based on various factors, in chapter 2.

Like a traditional 401(k), a traditional IRA is tax-deductible, meaning you can reduce your taxable income, and *tax-deferred*, meaning that your contributions and any earnings will not be taxed until the savings are withdrawn. The 2020 contribution limit to an IRA was $6,000, or $7,000 for those fifty or older. That amount, of course, is much less than you can contribute to a 401(k), and IRA contributions will not be matched by your employer, so be sure to fund your 401(k) account first.

Normally, you cannot withdraw from a traditional IRA account until you are fifty-nine and a half without incurring a penalty. Any money you take out before that age is, under normal circumstances, considered taxable income and there is a 10 percent penalty on it, courtesy of the IRS. There are exceptions to that rule, however. Under certain circumstances you can withdraw money early without penalty: if you become permanently disabled; if you need the money to pay for medical expenses; or if you use the money to pay for higher education for yourself, your spouse, a child, or a step-child or step-grandchild. You also can take out up to $10,000 without penalty if you are purchasing a home for the first time.

Remember that beginning to invest money as early as possible results in huge benefits later in life. Investing even a small amount each month adds up to big results. A classic example of the benefits of saving early is the story of the investor who starts saving at age 25 and the investor who starts saving at age 35:

Christine, who works as a veterinary assistant in a large practice, decides at age 25 to open an IRA to supplement her employer-sponsored retirement plan. By giving up her five-days-a-week latte and making a few other concessions, she can save enough to contribute $100 a month to her IRA, and her money compounds at an annual 5 percent rate of return.

Christine's brother, Kevin, works as a public relations specialist and has an employer-sponsored retirement plan. Kevin, however, is not inclined to give up anything he enjoys; he spends his twenties and early thirties traveling, learning the ins and outs of fine wines, and upgrading his sports car every two or three years. At age thirty-five Kevin meets the woman of his dreams, gets engaged, and decides that it is time to supplement his 401(k) with an IRA. He opens an account and starts contributing $100 a month, which compounds at the same annual rate as Christine's savings.

Life happens, and Christine and Kevin are now both in their sixties and looking toward retirement. When age sixty-five rolls around, Christine's

IRA account is worth $162,000, and Kevin's is worth $89,000. By starting to invest ten years earlier, Christine was able to save $73,000 more than her brother, while investing just $12,000 more (figure 6).

CHRISTINE VS. KEVIN

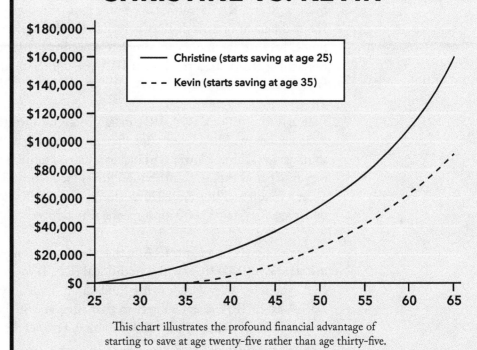

GRAPHIC

fig. 6

This chart illustrates the profound financial advantage of starting to save at age twenty-five rather than age thirty-five.

MY TAKE

One of the wisest decisions of my life was made at the ripe old age of twenty-two. As a new employee of Fidelity Investments, I decided to take advantage of their generously matched 401(k) offering. Within a few years, I was regularly contributing the maximum allowable amounts. The company matched my contributions and I benefited tremendously from the robust market growth that ensued in the 1980s and 1990s. My decision to begin working toward a financially healthy retirement at a young age was the key to my being where I am today. Thanks in large part to that same 401(k), I've accumulated enough wealth that I no longer need to ever worry about my retirement assets.

Having read some general information about IRAs, let's have a look at a couple of variations on the traditional IRA and consider the advantages and disadvantages of each.

Roth IRA

Roth IRAs are like traditional IRAs, except for the way they are taxed. Just like a Roth 401(k), a Roth IRA is funded with money you have paid taxes on, so the contributions do not reduce your taxable income. Like traditional IRAs, one's ability to participate in and derive tax advantages from a Roth IRA is subject to restrictions for high-income earners. The real benefit of a Roth IRA is realized when you start withdrawing funds, because the money is completely tax-free under current tax law. Remember that with a traditional IRA you are required to pay income tax on the money you withdraw.

Like a Roth 401(k), a Roth IRA makes sense for investors who believe their tax rate will be higher after they retire than it is currently. If you think you will be in a lower tax bracket after you retire, a traditional IRA may be a better choice. Contribution limits for a Roth IRA are the same as for a traditional IRA; in 2020 the limits were $6,000 for an individual under age fifty and $7,000 for someone fifty or over.

A nice thing about a Roth IRA is that there are no *required minimum distributions* (RMDs), as with a traditional IRA. If you have a traditional IRA, you must start withdrawing funds from it when you turn seventy-two. A Roth IRA is not subject to that rule, and if the money is not needed it can remain in place until the account owner dies, at which time it can be passed along to heirs.

Another benefit of a Roth IRA is that you can withdraw your contributions from the account at any age without penalty. However, if you end up taking out investment earnings before age fifty-nine and a half, you may be charged a penalty. Let's say that you have $80,000 in a Roth IRA. If $60,000 is from your contributions and $20,000 is money your contributions have earned, you can only withdraw $60,000 without risking a penalty. If you take out the entire $80,000, you risk paying a penalty on $20,000 of it.

SEP IRA

If you are a self-employed small business owner, you might consider a *simplified employee pension (SEP) IRA*. A SEP IRA enables business owners to make pretax contributions for themselves and their employees. A self-employed person who does not have employees, like an Uber driver, a freelance writer, or someone who has a child-care business, can also save with a SEP IRA.

SEP IRAs were designed to encourage employers who might not otherwise do so to establish retirement plans for employees. They are easy to set up; do not cost much to administer; and are accessible to sole proprietors, partnerships, and corporations. Another advantage of a SEP is that contributions are tax-deductible. Like traditional IRAs, they are also tax-deferred.

SEP IRAs have much higher contribution limits than traditional or Roth IRAs. In 2020, employers could contribute $57,000 or up to 25 percent of an employee's gross salary (whichever is less) into a SEP account. A self-employed person could contribute up to 20 percent of their net income.

If you are self-employed and would like to know exactly how much you can contribute to your SEP plan, check out my "Self-Employment Retirement Plan Maximum Contribution" calculator. Find it in your Digital Assets at go.quickstartguides.com/retirement.

An employer can determine the amount to be contributed to each eligible employee's SEP account, including her own. However, the same percentage of salary must be contributed for each employee. SEP accounts are employer funded; employees cannot make contributions. The amount contributed can change from year to year, which is an advantage to the owner if the company's cash flow is not predictable. An employer who contributes money to an employee's SEP IRA does not decide how the money gets invested—that is up to the employee. While SEP accounts are employer funded and employees cannot contribute on their own behalf, some SEP plans allow employees to make traditional IRA contributions to their SEP accounts, if the maximum annual limit is not exceeded.

Health Savings Accounts

You can think and say whatever you want about health care in America, but most people agree that it is expensive. In 2018, national health spending was $3.6 trillion, or $11,172 per person, according to the Centers for Medicare & Medicaid Services. That health spending cost accounts for 17.7 percent of the nation's *gross domestic product* (GDP), which is the total value of all goods and services produced within the country's border during a specific time period. And it is predicted that national health spending will continue to grow at an average rate of 5.4 percent a year.

It is difficult to predict what health care will look like and how much it will cost in the future, so it might be a good idea to consider a *health savings account* (HSA), which enables you to save money for future medical expenses. You can only open an HSA if you have an HSA-compatible *high-deductible insurance plan*. That type of plan, which has lower *premiums* and higher *deductibles*, has become increasingly common and is the only type of plan some employers offer.

A high-deductible plan means that you must pay for a certain amount of health care services before your insurance kicks in. If your deductible is $4,000, for instance, you'll need to pay $4,000 out of pocket before the insurance company will start picking up the tab. Certain services deemed necessary by federal law or by the insurer, such as an annual physical exam or a mammogram, may be covered even if you have not yet reached your deductible.

If you are young and healthy, a high-deductible plan might make sense because you won't need many health care services. If you have a high-deductible plan and you require a lot of services, an HSA can help you cover the cost of those services until you meet your deductible. You contribute money to an account you set up for the specific purpose of paying for health care. Because the money in the account can be invested, it can grow over time.

Several factors make HSAs advantageous:
» The money you put into an HSA is not taxed.
» There is a maximum amount you can contribute (subject to change every year) but not a minimum, so you get to choose how much to save.
» You control the money in the account.
» You don't have to spend all the money within a calendar year; any money left rolls over indefinitely.
» You can invest the money in mutual funds or other types of investments.
» Earnings from investments in an HSA also are tax-free.

The HSA is one of the only things in the financial world that is "triple tax-free." Your contributions are not taxed, the growth of the money in the account is not taxed, and when you spend the money on health care, it is not taxed. Take advantage of HSAs when you can.

You will read more about HSAs in chapter 12, "Managing Your Health Plans." For now, just remember that an HSA is another important account to consider when looking ahead to your retirement.

On Your Own or with an Advisor?

Whether to seek out the services of a financial advisor to manage your investments and accounts is a tricky question. It becomes even trickier when it is asked of a financial advisor. I have clients who take great interest in all aspects of their finances. These clients take the time to educate themselves on all aspects of their financial lives. They count on me for advice and some direction, but they take ultimate responsibility for their money, because it is their money, not mine.

Then there are the clients who just want me to manage their money and make sure it keeps growing. They do not have the time or interest to spend hours comparing investments or combing through financial reports. They do not want to learn about online brokerages and investment accounts; they just want to feel confident that someone they trust is handling their money in a competent manner.

If you're in your twenties or thirties and contributing to an employer-sponsored 401(k) and maybe putting some money into an IRA and/or an HSA, you may not want a financial advisor right now. If you're getting closer to retirement age and your financial situation has become more complex, with multiple investments, insurance policies, estate distribution plans, etc., you may start thinking about the help you need to ensure that all parts of a financial plan are coordinated properly and there are no major tax, estate, or planning "gotchas" lurking down the road. I liken a CERTIFIED FINANCIAL PLANNER™ practitioner to a coach. Regardless of how astute you are regarding your accounts and investments, it cannot hurt to have a professional overseeing the larger financial plan, making sure everything is organized, and coordinating the handling of all the different aspects. Even elite athletes—the absolute best of the best—have coaches to keep them on track and provide support.

So, that is my pitch for finding a financial advisor—one you like and trust and with whom you can build a relationship. There are a couple of categories of advisors:

» **A CERTIFIED FINANCIAL PLANNER™ practitioner is** a professional who has earned national certification requiring a fiduciary relationship with their clients. A *fiduciary relationship* is a legal relationship between an advisor and a client that establishes ethical guidelines and rules.

  - A CFP® practitioner completes a rigorous exam process.
  - A CFP® practitioner must hold at least a bachelor's degree.

- A CFP® practitioner must have at least three years of experience in a field related to finance.
- A CFP® practitioner is required to pursue thirty hours of continuing education every two years to keep current and informed about the industry.
- A CFP® practitioner deals in the areas of investments, estate planning, business planning, retirement planning, tax planning, insurance planning, and everything in between.

» **Registered investment advisors (RIAs)**, who, in accordance with the Investment Advisers Act must be registered with the Securities and Exchange Commission (SEC), also must report their own personal assets.

- Not all RIAs are CFP® practitioners. RIAs are not required to complete continuing education to hold their licenses, nor are they required to complete a rigorous certification exam.
- Like CFP® practitioners, RIAs are fiduciaries. They are legally required to act in accordance with their clients' best financial interests.
- RIAs generally help their clients with investments and financial planning. They usually do not sell commission-based insurance products.

MY TAKE

I may be biased, but I strongly recommend limiting your search for fiduciary advisors to CFP® practitioners and RIAs. There are other players in the field—stockbrokers and insurance agents—who solicit retirees or near-retirees. Many of these brokers and agents are not fiduciaries, are limited in their scope of services and products, and are not subject to the same continuing education requirements as CFP® practitioners.

Many people use online brokerage accounts that not only serve as trading platforms but can provide limited advice and analysis, online education, and other services. Most, but not all, online investment services offer phone support, but many do not have brick-and-mortar locations.

Robo-advisors are online services that use sophisticated software and computer algorithms to analyze, build, and manage your investments based on a risk assessment evaluation and a survey of your investment objectives. These have become increasingly popular, particularly among younger, do-it-yourself investors.

While there is value in online advisors and robo-advisors and they are important tools for investing, they are not specific to retirement planning because they assist only with your investments, not other aspects of your financial life such as estate planning or insurance planning. For more information about online advisors and robo-advisors, see appendix I of this book. You can also learn a lot more about these types of advisors in my sister book, *Investing QuickStart Guide*.

Chapter Recap

» Key retirement accounts include a fully matched 401(k), an individual retirement account (IRA), and a health savings account (HSA).

» The sooner you begin saving, the more your money can grow and compound.

» Choosing a financial advisor is a personal decision that should be carefully considered.

| 2 |
Investment Strategies

As in all successful ventures, the foundation of a good retirement is planning.
– EARL NIGHTINGALE
American author

If you find yourself with a reliable source of income, an **emergency fund** to fall back on, debt that is under control, and the ability to donate generously to a charity of your choice, then before you do anything else, give yourself a pat on the back. You have taken great strides to help shore up your financial future and are most certainly ready to take the next step! Once you have established and are funding the accounts discussed in chapter 1, it's time to start thinking about some investment strategies.

Most experts advise that you have enough money in an emergency fund to cover three to six months of expenses. To determine an amount, add up your monthly living expenses, which include food, housing, health insurance and health care costs, utilities, debt, and personal expenses. Multiply that figure by four or five to get an idea of how much money you'd need to sustain your normal lifestyle amid a financial emergency. If the number you come up with looks intimidating, don't panic. Keep in mind that in most cases you will be able to decrease your personal expenses when you go into "emergency mode." For example, if you lose your job, then you may no longer be paying day care expenses, which can be hefty. As you refine your "emergency budget" and eliminate spending on nonessential shopping, restaurants, entertainment, and so forth, what do your revised monthly living expenses look like? Multiply these revised expenses by four or five and see if you can create a savings goal more imminently attainable. Make sure to keep your emergency fund in an account where you can easily get to it if you need to. A money market, checking, or savings account will not pay much interest, but your money will be readily available. Shop around for the account that offers the best deal. You can compare interest rates and terms on money market bank accounts at www.bankrate.com.

So, it is time to start thinking beyond IRAs, HSAs, and 401(k)s, which logically leads us to stocks, bonds, and real estate. Burton Malkiel, an economist and writer who is most famous for his classic book *A Random Walk Down Wall Street*, asserted that the only relevant categories of investments are cash, stocks, bonds, and real estate. Cash might not seem like an investment, but think about it for a minute. Cash enables you to buy things you need, such as a car or a refrigerator. It can be used to purchase a home or land, which may increase in value. Cash also creates a margin of safety in your financial plan, so that you're not one financial setback or crisis away from total catastrophe. Margin also allows you to take advantage of market opportunities, should they arise. If a great stock shows up on the market at a low price, then having margin allows you to load up on shares. There are many types of investments within Malkiel's four silos, and you'll be reading more about some of those as we proceed through this chapter.

Regardless of how you invest, it is important not to limit yourself to 401(k)s, IRAs, and the other specific retirement savings vehicles discussed in chapter 1. By supplementing your retirement accounts with other investments, such as individual or joint brokerage accounts, real estate investments, or cash, you are building a more durable nest egg and will enjoy greater peace of mind and flexibility, now and in retirement. I will tell you right now that if you think you will do okay living on Social Security or pension benefits only, you may be mistaken. Let's have a look at two threats to every retirement: inflation and longevity.

Inflation

Inflation is not a huge issue while you are earning a paycheck, because most people get pay increases that enable them to deal with it. But in retirement, inflation, which averages 3 percent annually, can be a big problem if you do not have income sources beyond Social Security or a pension. Social Security and, in limited cases, pension benefits, include *cost-of-living adjustments (COLAs)*. You cannot be sure that those adjustments will keep pace with inflation. And, with Social Security, increases are not guaranteed. You will learn more about Social Security and how those COLAs are formulated in Chapter 6, so for now I will just tell you they don't automatically occur, and they are not always enough to make up for inflation. You can see from the chart in figure 7 how COLA rates have varied from year to year over the past decade.

THE INCONSISTENCY OF COLAs

fig. 7

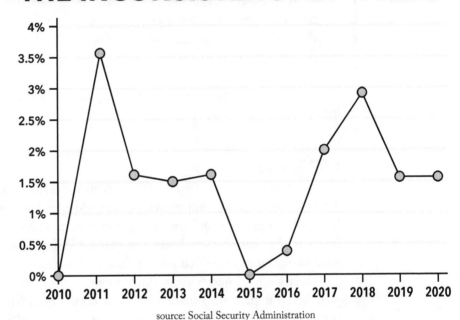

source: Social Security Administration

Social Security cost-of-living increases between 2010 and 2020

Though 3 percent is the historical average, inflation can rise far beyond that. Consider that in 1980, due to a major worldwide recession and other factors, the inflation rate in the United States rose to nearly 15 percent. If you are counting on a fixed income and there is a big jump in inflation, then you are going to be negatively impacted. Long-term investment in stocks and appreciable securities gives you a fighting chance to keep up with inflation.

Living on a fixed income, you lose purchasing power every year you are alive. At a 3 percent inflation rate, it would take twenty-four years for your purchasing power to be cut in half. In other words, if you need $75,000 today to live, in twenty-four years you will need $150,000 just to maintain your same standard of living.

— TED SNOW

I know it is depressing to think about, but you need to keep inflation in mind when planning how to invest your money, and to understand that the total amount of the money you save will not be worth the same as it is today.

Tom starts saving $5,000 a year in 2020 at age thirty-five. With average stock market returns of 7 percent, in 2050 Tom will turn sixty-five and his savings will total $505,365. That is great for Tom, but the not-so-great thing is that, assuming a yearly inflation rate of 3 percent, the purchasing power of his savings will be less than half of its 2020 value. By 2050, Tom's nest egg would be worth only about $208,000 in 2020 dollars, irrespective of taxes.

Building a range of investments can help you build the savings and income you will need to live.

Longevity

It seems counterintuitive to think about longevity as a negative quality. After all, who doesn't want to live to a ripe old age? The question is, can you live well to a ripe old age? Can you get to a point where you will not be too much of a burden on your children or friends? Will you have the income you need to pay for any care that may become necessary?

These are hard questions to think about, but consider this. It is easier to plan for an unpleasant situation before it occurs than when you are in the throes of it and then must react when it may be too late. Typically, when you put off dealing with potential life events, it limits your options and causes you to make quick and often poorly thought-out decisions when an event occurs.

According to the **Social Security Administration (SSA)**, someone who is sixty-five years old can, statistically, expect to live for about another twenty years. And, according to the SSA, one-third of people who are sixty-five now will reach ninety, and one in seven will live to be ninety-five or older. That is good news, except for a few big concerns.

The big risk is outliving your money.

– KEITH BERNHARDT

vice president of retirement income solutions for Fidelity Investments

While it is great to have additional years doing things you enjoy with the people you love, living to be ninety or even older means that you will need more money than if you live to be only eighty or eighty-five. Living longer also increases the chance that you may encounter hefty health care costs; you may even need to pay for assisted living or skilled nursing care, for which the costs can be staggering. According to the 2019 Genworth Cost of Care Survey, released by Genworth Financial, the median cost of long-term care in the United States ranges from $1,625 a month for adult day care to $8,625 a month for a private room in a nursing home. In-home care by a health care aide averages $4,385 per month.

Having investments in place beyond your retirement accounts can help you accumulate enough assets to cover the cost of inflation, as well as the cost of living a long life. Let's start by having a look at how stocks and bonds can be important pieces of your retirement portfolio.

Stocks and Bonds

Stocks and bonds are both classes of assets, and both are used as tools by a company or other entity to raise money. The difference between stocks and bonds is that having **stocks** is considered ownership in a company and **bonds** are considered a loan to the company. When you buy stock, you buy a little piece of a company. When you buy bonds, you are loaning your money to a company, government, or other entity with the understanding that it will likely be paid back to you—with interest—at an agreed-upon time called a maturity date.

NOTE

Our discussion in this book regarding stocks and bonds is brief. I highly recommend that you read my previous book, *Investing QuickStart Guide,* for more in-depth information about investing.

Stocks are bought and sold on a **stock exchange**, and bonds are traded on the OTC, or over-the-counter **bond market**. There are **primary markets** and **secondary markets**. A primary market is where stocks and bonds are offered for the first time, such as stock that is offered in an **initial public offering (IPO)**, and a secondary market is one where investors buy assets from other investors on an exchange instead of from issuing companies.

Both stocks and bonds are important pieces of an investment portfolio. Although you have greater potential for higher returns with stocks, they usually carry more risk than bonds. That is why it is important to rebalance your portfolio (but not go overly conservative) as you move closer to retirement. A mistake that young investors sometimes make is to be too conservative with what they buy. Before you invest your money, determine your **tolerance for risk**, and understand that risk and reward are always linked. The higher the risk, the greater the potential for reward. Consider your age, your current financial situation, and your risk tolerance, then buy accordingly.

More about Stocks

All stock represents ownership. You buy a piece of a company and hope that its stock will increase in value. The more shares of stock you own in a company, the greater your share of ownership is. Let's have a look at some different classes and categories of stock.

Common stock vs. *preferred stock.* While common and preferred stock both represent ownership in a company, there are several differences between the two, many of which will be discussed later in this chapter. The most notable difference is that shareholders of common stock generally have voting rights, and holders of preferred stock do not. Voting rights entitle shareholders to weigh in on issues affecting the company, such as who should be named to the board of directors. If you own common stock, the company will send you a ballot or notify you electronically about an upcoming vote. Don't miss out on your chance to vote.

It is important to understand that a company can issue both common and preferred stock—it is not limited to one or the other. Common stock, however, is the most widely traded of any corporate security.

Stocks issued by various companies are categorized differently according to the nature of the companies themselves. These categories include *growth stock, value stock, income stock*, and *penny stock.*

Growth stock, as the name implies, is the stock of a company that is expected to have higher-than-average increases in revenue and earnings, because they plow earnings back into the company to grow it. Value stocks are those that are undervalued compared to the stock of similar companies. The price of a stock can fall for many reasons, including an internal event that affects the company. If a company is hurt by a scandal, for instance, the price of its stock might temporarily drop and then come back up as memory of the scandal fades. The period during which the price is lower may be a good time to buy that stock, but be sure to do your own research before purchasing.

Income stock is stock that carries a relatively high dividend payout relative to its price. A penny stock is a low-priced stock, usually traded at less than five dollars a share and sometimes traded outside of the major stock exchanges. Another category is *blue chip stock*, which is the stock of large, successful companies that have proven growth characteristics and consistent dividend payments over time.

Stock is also categorized by size. Large capitalization, or *large-cap stock*, is that of companies with very high *market capitalization*, which is the total value of all the company's outstanding shares at current prices. Small capitalization, or *small-cap stock*, is that of companies with a small business value.

Stock can also be categorized as either defensive or cyclical. *Defensive stock* is a class of stock that is not easily affected by the overall condition of the economy. Generally, discount retail, health care, and food supply are sectors that fall into this category. *Cyclical stock*, on the other hand, is stock that is negatively affected by downturns in the economy. Generally, it includes sectors such as travel and tourism, home appliances, and auto manufacturing.

You can earn money from common stock when the value of the stock increases and you sell it for more than you paid for it. Or you can earn money if the company pays *dividends*. Many companies, although not all, pay dividends. Preferred stock normally carries a fixed dividend, meaning that stockholders will receive a fixed amount, usually on a quarterly basis. Dividends paid on preferred stock tend to be higher than those paid on common stock, and preferred shareholders are paid before common shareholders. Understand, however, that dividends are never guaranteed.

Usually, a company experiencing tough times will cut dividends paid on common shares before preferred shares and will repay preferred stockholders for dividends withheld during a downtime before repaying common stockholders. And if a company fails completely, preferred stockholders get preference in payment when the company liquidates.

NOTE

Some companies are notable for dependable dividend payments. According to *U.S. News & World Report Money*, these companies have paid dividends continuously for more than fifty years: California Water Service Group, Coca-Cola, Colgate-Palmolive Company, Farmers & Merchants Bancorp, Genuine Parts Company, Hormel Foods Corporation, Johnson & Johnson, Lowe's Companies, and Stanley Black & Decker.

The likely payment of dividends on preferred stock makes it attractive to some investors. But there is a downside, and that is a limited potential for appreciation of your share price. Preferred stock is a hybrid between a stock and a bond. The price of preferred stock is determined by the company that issues it and is usually twenty-five dollars a share. That price tends to remain even. So, while preferred stock is more likely to pay dividends and tends to be less volatile than common stock, there is less room for price appreciation.

Some people engage in researching companies and stocks before deciding what to buy. Other people shoot from the hip, follow gut hunches, or hire advisors to make decisions for them. Deciding what stocks to buy and how to buy them is a personal decision and depends on many factors, including your time frame, risk tolerance, and the amount of time you are willing or able to spend on market research and keeping track of your portfolio.

What is important when choosing stocks is to diversify and to be prepared to ride out highs and lows of the market. Balance defensive stock with cyclical stock, large-cap stock with small-cap stock, and value stock with growth stock. There is an astounding amount of information available about assessing and buying stock. Some of it is sound, and some is not. Stick to reputable sources and do not get hung up on trying to digest and apply every bit of information you come across.

More About Bonds

Whereas stocks may be the hotshot daredevils of your portfolio, bonds are more predictable over time. As you know, bonds are a lending instrument. You loan money with the expectation that you will get it back, with interest, at a specified time. There are, however, different types of bonds issued by different types of entities. Bonds can be held for various periods of time. Bonds held for longer periods typically pay higher interest than those held for short periods.

US Government Bonds

The US government is the world's largest seller of bonds, issuing them online at monthly auctions. Called Treasury bonds, or T-bonds for short, they are sold in multiples of one thousand dollars. You can buy them directly from the government on the primary market, or from a bank or broker on the secondary market.

You can agree to loan your money to the government for anywhere between one month and thirty years. The longer you agree to let the government hold onto your money, the higher an interest rate you will get. Interest rates on T-bonds also vary due to supply and demand. If investors are clamoring for Treasury securities, which are considered a safe but not terribly profitable investment, it usually means that there is unease about the stock market. Buyers are wary that the stock market may be in unstable territory, and they move their money to bonds instead. That demand allows the government to lower the interest it pays on the bonds. Conversely, if the demand for T-bonds goes down, the government is forced to up its interest rates to attract buyers.

People talk generally about Treasury bonds or Treasuries, but there are actually three phrases that refer to these securities. If the **term**, or length of time the bond is issued for, is one year or less, the security is called a Treasury bill, or T-bill. If the security is issued for a term of two to ten years, it is called a Treasury note, or T-note. Only when a security is held for more than ten years is it called a Treasury bond, or T-bond.

TALK THE TALK

Term of the Treasury Security	Referred to as
≤ 1 year	Treasury bill or T-bill
2–10 years	Treasury note or T-note
> 10 years	Treasury bond or T-bond

GRAPHIC

fig. 8

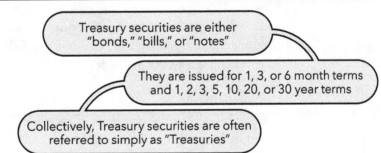

Treasury securities are either "bonds," "bills," or "notes"

They are issued for 1, 3, or 6 month terms and 1, 2, 3, 5, 10, 20, or 30 year terms

Collectively, Treasury securities are often referred to simply as "Treasuries"

What to call a Treasury security

While Treasuries are considered safe, they do come with some risk. If interest rates go up after you buy a Treasury security, then your bond, bill, or note will be worth less on the secondary market than what you paid for it. You will still receive your one thousand dollars upon maturity, but that means you are forced to wait out the term of the bond. Because Treasuries carry less risk over time than stock investing, there is less potential for reward.

Bonds are generally considered to be safe investments, but there is a reason they play second fiddle to stocks. Studies have shown that stocks outperform Treasuries most of the time, regardless of the amount of time for which you compare the two. A famous study by economists Eugene Fama and Kenneth French revealed that over a one-year period, stocks outperform T-bills 69 percent of the time. Over fifteen years, stocks win 96 percent of the time.

Government Agency Bonds

Government agency bonds are issued by a department of the federal government or a government-sponsored agency, rather than directly from the US Treasury. The Federal Housing Administration, the Government National Mortgage Association, and the Small Business Administration are examples of government agencies that issue bonds. These bonds typically pay a little more interest than Treasuries, but some are not fully guaranteed. They generally are exempt from state and local taxes, but, as with all bonds, they carry interest rate risk when interest rates fluctuate.

When interest rates go up, the price of a bond falls.

Municipal Bonds

Municipalities raise money for major projects or purchases by selling bonds. They are considered safe because there is a low default rate; plus, the interest you earn is not subject to federal and state taxes, and sometimes not subject to local tax.

Corporate Bonds

Companies also offer bonds as a means of generating cash. Bonds issued by large, reputable companies are called *investment-grade bonds*, and they have a low chance of default. Bonds issued by less reputable companies are more prone to default and are known as *high-yield bonds* or *junk bonds* (figure 9).

fig. 9

MOODY'S		S&P		FITCH			
Long Term	Short Term	Long Term	Short Term	Long Term	Short Term		
Aaa		AAA		AAA		**PRIME**	INVESTMENT-GRADE
Aa1		AA+		AA+		**HIGH GRADE**	
Aa2	P-1	AA	A-1+	AA	A-1+		
Aa3		AA-		AA-			
A1		A+	A-1	A+	A-1	**UPPER MEDIUM GRADE**	
A2		A		A			
A3	P-2	A-	A-2	A-	A-2		
Baa1		BBB+		BBB+			
Baa2	P-3	BBB	A-3	BBB	A-3	**LOWER MEDIUM GRADE**	
Baa3		BBB-		BBB-			
Ba1		BB+		BB+		**NON-INVESTMENT GRADE/ SPECULATIVE**	HIGH-YIELD/JUNK
Ba2		BB		BB			
Ba3		BB-	B	BB-	B		
B1		B+		B+		**HIGHLY SPECULATIVE**	
B2	Not Prime	B		B			
B3		B-		B-			
Caa		CCC+				**SUBSTANTIAL RISKS**	
Ca		CC	C	CCC	C	**EXTREMELY SPECULATIVE**	
C		CC-				**IN DEFAULT** (with little prospect for recovery)	
/				DDD			
/		D	/	DD	/	**IN DEFAULT**	
/				D			

Bonds are graded by ratings agencies to determine the risk of default.
The higher the letter, the better the quality.

Finding the Right Stock-to-Bond Ratio

Stocks and bonds make up a major portion of the portfolios of many investors, either as individual investments or as part of a *mutual fund, index fund*, or **exchange-traded fund** (ETF), all of which are explained later in this chapter. Most advisors recommend that you shift the makeup of your portfolio away from stocks and more toward bonds as you get older and closer to retirement. A more bond-focused portfolio may help reduce the pain of market downturns and preserve more of your savings. However, focusing your portfolio on bonds too soon can backfire.

The ratio of stocks to bonds in your portfolio is called **asset allocation**; this is simply a method used to balance different types of investments to ensure diversification and manage risk (figure 10). For years, a common rule of asset allocation has been to hold a percentage of stocks that, when added to your age, equals one hundred. So if you are thirty, your stock-to-bond ratio would be 70 percent stocks and 30 percent bonds or other "safe" investments. At age forty, the ratio would be 60 percent stocks to 40 percent bonds, and so on.

fig. 10

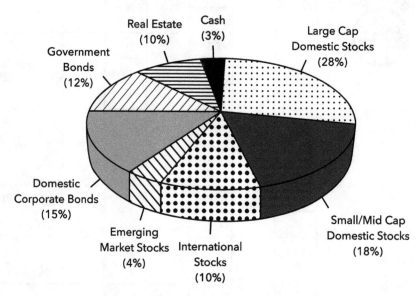

A sample model for allocation of assets in a portfolio

In recent years, however, many advisors have refined that rule, noting that retirees are living longer, and bonds may not generate enough income to keep up with inflation. The key to asset allocation is finding a strong mix of assets that are diversified and make sense for your situation. Thankfully, there is a wide variety of investments available, and many ways to build a healthy and profitable portfolio over the long term. You will learn more about asset allocation in chapter 10, "Managing Your Portfolio."

Mutual Funds and Indexes

Most retirement accounts include mutual funds, so if you have an IRA or a 401(k), it is likely that you are already familiar with this type of investment. A mutual fund is an investment in which investors pool their money. A fund manager uses the money to buy a variety of investment vehicles, likely including stocks, bonds, cash equivalents (like T-bills), and real estate.

Most people consider the diversity offered by mutual funds their primary advantage. Plus, they are professionally managed, which means you are not responsible for choosing and rebalancing securities. Unlike the share price of stocks and ETFs, which goes up and down during the day, the value of mutual fund shares is calculated once at the end of each day, using *net asset value* (the value of the fund's assets less its liabilities divided by the number of shares outstanding).

There are thousands of mutual funds from which to choose. Generally, they can be broken down into four broad categories: stock funds, bond funds, *money market funds*, which are funds that purchase short-term securities such as cash or cash-equivalent securities, and *balanced funds*, which contain both stocks and bonds.

Another distinction is between *open-end mutual funds* and *closed-end mutual funds*. Open-end funds have no size limit, meaning they can continually issue shares in response to demand. Closed-end funds, on the other hand, issue a limited number of shares. Once they're all sold, new prospective buyers will need to wait for someone to sell their shares. The price will then be determined by supply and demand for the shares.

An *index fund* is a type of mutual fund (or ETF) that tracks the performance of a market index, such as the Dow Jones Industrial Average or the S&P 500. It does this by buying and holding some or all of the securities of companies listed in an index. When the value of stocks in the index goes up, the value of the fund increases. When the price of stocks in the index declines, the value of the fund goes down. An advantage of index funds is that they are "passively managed," which means that the securities in the fund are not extensively traded throughout the year by well-paid fund managers. The securities may be automatically reconfigured to ensure they continue to align with their target index, but such reconfiguring does not require "active management." Actively managed funds, by contrast, are comprised of securities that are traded throughout the year by fund managers, who are constantly on the lookout for their next great stock pick. The costs associated with operating a passively managed fund are understandably lower than those of an actively managed fund.

Cost vs. Value

Cost is certainly something to watch for when choosing investments. There are plenty of costs associated with investing, many you may be unaware of. For instance, when you buy a mutual fund you are charged an *expense ratio*, which is the percentage of the full value of the fund that is used to pay for expenses associated with the fund (figure 11). Those expenses include administrative costs, taxes, legal expenses, accounting fees, management fees, marketing costs, auditing fees, and others. All those expenses add up, and over time you can end up paying a lot of money. It's a good idea to learn as much about the expenses you are charged as possible. Don't be afraid to ask what expenses are associated with a particular investment, as some are not as readily disclosed as others.

GRAPHIC

fig. 11

$$ER = \frac{\text{Total Fund Costs}}{\text{Total Fund Assets}}$$

Expense ratio formula. The percentage of the value of a fund used to pay for administrative and other costs is the expense ratio.

Keep in mind, however, that though there are costs associated with investing, those costs serve the purpose of ensuring an investment is managed properly, which brings value to that investment. While there may be higher costs associated with an actively managed fund than with one that is passively managed, active management may well add value to the fund that more than makes up for the costs.

MY TAKE

I know many people who have lost money in the market because they did not have the right investments or investment advice. Human beings act out of emotion, and fear is a powerful motivator. There are many studies—most notably Dalbar's yearly report called "Quantitative Analysis of Investor Behavior"—that chronicle the destructive tendency for investors to add investments when markets rise, then sell them when markets fall. Being confident in your investments and having the benefit of a trusted advisor can add great value to your portfolio, which, in the long run, reduces cost to you.

Exchange-Traded Funds

ETFs are an interesting investment in that they are something of a mixture between a stock and a mutual fund. They are a pool of assets, like mutual funds. Unlike mutual funds, they trade on the open market and their value goes up and down as they are bought and sold throughout the day. A lot of investors like ETFs because many are passively managed and generally come with lower expenses than most mutual funds. According to the investment research and management firm Morningstar, some passively managed ETFs charge less than 0.5 percent, while the average fee for actively managed funds is 0.67 percent.

ETFs, which were introduced in 1993, exploded in popularity following the Great Recession. Upset that their actively managed mutual funds lost a significant portion of their value after Lehman Brothers, one of the largest investment banks in the world, filed for bankruptcy in 2008, many investors turned to lower-fee ETFs. In the decade following the collapse of Lehman Brothers, US money invested in ETFs increased from $531 billion to $18.75 trillion, according to software company Statistica. That investment is still far less than the money invested in mutual funds, but the increase has been impressive.

Mutual funds, index funds, and ETFs are popular investment vehicles, and each brings advantages and disadvantages. When choosing funds, consider your investing strategy and what you need. Consider expenses, ease of buying and selling, tax implications, risk, the level of management, your investing timeline, and your investment budget before selecting.

Knowing your current asset allocation is an important step in building a retirement plan. Enter the investments you currently hold into the Asset Allocator Tool Workbook to discover your portfolio position. See if you need to make changes to get on track for retirement. Visit go.quickstartguides.com/retirement to find the workbook in your Digital Assets.

Real Estate Investments

While you are correct in thinking that an investment in real estate means purchasing a beach house to rent out to vacationers or buying a home to fix up and flip (hopefully making a profit on the deal), you can also invest in real estate without ever purchasing a property. In fact, the most common way to invest in real estate is through a real estate investment trust, or REIT (pronounced "reet").

A REIT operates similarly to a mutual fund or exchange-traded fund, in that it pools money from investors. Rather than using those funds to purchase stocks and bonds, however, they are used to buy real estate assets. That real estate is leased, and the income collected is distributed as dividends to shareholders. REITs can be targeted toward specific types of real estate, like hotels, cell towers, office buildings, and self-storage, to name a few. They can also target real estate in a particular part of the world.

REITs vary in how they are traded. Some have high liquidity and are traded often in public markets, while others, known as non-traded REITs, do not. Non-traded REITs are public securities, but they often come with conditions such as income and net-worth requirements for investors. Non-traded REITs also tend to be less transparent and are generally not available to sell for about five to seven years or longer.

In my opinion, traded REITs are preferable. Not only are they more liquid, they are also more transparent than non-traded REITs. Additionally, non-traded REITs may contain covenants that limit liquidity. Finally, in my experience, the upside potential for traded REITs has been superior.

Information regarding real estate investment is limited in this chapter, but you can learn all the ins and outs in the *Real Estate Investing QuickStart Guide*, written by Symon He.

Investors make money from real estate in several ways. REITs are generally easier and more passive, but many retirees pursue direct real estate investment through the acquisition of rental properties. Rental property ownership can generate a stream of income. The amount of income will vary depending on the type, size, and location of the property, but renting can be lucrative if handled properly and under the right circumstances. You can also make money if your property value increases, although that is not guaranteed. Or you can turn a profit from business activity related to the property, such as charging hotel patrons to park in a parking garage.

Real estate adds diversification to your portfolio with low correlation to other asset classes. That means the value of the real estate may not be impacted as much by news or events that affect the stock market or other investments. And people who own, rent, or manage real estate get several tax breaks and deductions that can result in tax savings, as well as cash flows from depreciation.

The 1031 Exchange

If you are thinking about purchasing one or more properties as part of your retirement plan, be sure to familiarize yourself with the 1031 exchange concept that allows you to exchange one investment property for another and defer capital gains taxes. If you own a piece of land, for instance, you can exchange it for a multiunit apartment building that can generate income. Even if you sell the land for more than you pay for the apartment building, under the 1031 exchange you will not have to pay capital gains tax until you sell the building for cash.

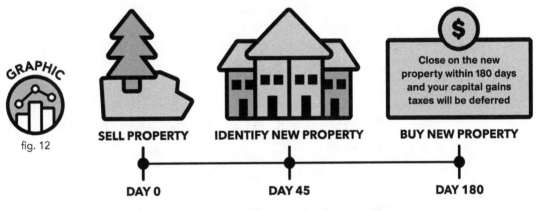

GRAPHIC

fig. 12

SELL PROPERTY **IDENTIFY NEW PROPERTY** **BUY NEW PROPERTY**

Close on the new property within 180 days and your capital gains taxes will be deferred

DAY 0 **DAY 45** **DAY 180**

How a 1031 exchange works

There are a lot of regulations that apply to the 1031 exchange, so be sure you have a full understanding of it before you attempt to use it. Both properties must be located in the United States, and you must sell and purchase properties within a particular time frame. The replacement property must be identified within 45 days from the sale of the first property, and the acquisition of the replacement property must be complete within 180 days of the sale (see figure 12). If you're careful to dot all your i's and cross all your t's, then the 1031 exchange can really work in your favor as far as your taxes are concerned.

An investment in real estate, either through a REIT or by purchasing property, can be a smart addition to your portfolio. As with all forms of investing, however, it entails risk, so be sure to educate yourself before you buy. Managing property and tenants can be problematic, so understand all the legal implications prior to such an undertaking. We'll talk more about how to legally structure your purchase of real estate and how to protect your real estate assets in chapter 8, "Reaping the Rewards of Sound Retirement Planning."

Chapter Recap

> » Inflation and longevity can compromise your retirement plan if not considered and planned for.

> » Stocks and bonds are two major asset classes, with stocks proving to be more profitable over time.

> » Mutual funds and ETFs share similarities, but ETFs offer additional flexibility.

> » You can invest in real estate without ever buying property. Real estate trusts, or REITs, can help you diversify your portfolio.

| 3 |
Insurance

An ounce of prevention is worth a pound of cure.
— BENJAMIN FRANKLIN

Insurance contracts, in my humble and professional opinion, are asset preservation tools. If you view them as just another bill, you may not see the value they represent for you and your family.

Many people buy insurance reluctantly, just because they "have to." But, when you think about it, insurance is about protecting those who are dear to you and what you have worked hard to attain. I look at buying insurance the way I view paying taxes. I pay taxes on income I have earned, and that is a good thing. I buy insurance as an asset protection mechanism because there are people in my life whom I cherish and things I own that I value.

You can insure your cell phone, your dryer, your vacation, and, if you are a piano player (according to a variety of published reports), your hands. But the insurance you really need is that which protects your family, your health, your home, your savings, and your lifestyle—either the one you have currently or the one you hope to achieve in the future.

Insurance companies provide customers with access to something especially important called *leverage*. Leverage is the idea that small amounts of money can be used to exert control over larger amounts of money. In the world of insurance, customers contribute small amounts of money in exchange for access to large benefit pools that can compensate for loss.

Historians tell us that humans have been using insurance in some form or another since ancient times. Early farmers donated grain to a public stockpile to be shared in the event of famine. Sea traders found ways to protect their goods, ships, and lives. In America, insurance got its start during Colonial times in Philadelphia, often called the birthplace of our nation.

The British had employed property insurance since the founding of Lloyd's of London, an esteemed insurance company, in 1688. During a time when houses were built close together and constructed almost entirely of wood, fires were commonly caused by, among other things, cooking over open flames. When parts of Philadelphia, then one of the largest cities in the new nation, began encountering a similar situation, town leaders, including Benjamin Franklin, formed The Philadelphia Contributionship for the Insurance of Houses from Loss by Fire in 1752.

Several years later Franklin and others founded a life insurance company called the Presbyterian Ministers' Fund, and, during the Industrial Revolution (1790s through the 1830s), firms were formed to provide business and disability insurance. The Traveler's Insurance Company got into the game in 1864 by selling accident insurance, and later instituted policies to insure automobiles.

Today, there are thousands of insurance companies operating across the country, with 2.8 million people employed in the industry. In 2018, Americans paid insurance premiums totaling $1.22 trillion, according to the Insurance Information Institute, an organization that seeks to teach consumers about insurance.

We all know that life does not always go as planned, and that the unexpected can sometimes happen. Many families in the US are one event away from a financial crisis. A car accident, an unexpected death, a serious illness, a house fire, a business lawsuit, and other unplanned events are reasons for which we need insurance. Like other strategies I have already discussed, the insurance coverage needed varies according to the risks associated with various seasons and stations of life. If you are single with no dependents and do not own a home, for instance, you will require less insurance than someone who is married with three teenagers (two of whom drive), and owns a home, a boat, three cars, and a small business. As you near retirement age, it is smart to reevaluate all your policies and assess whether there might be some you no longer need or perhaps others you should add.

Disability Insurance

LIMRA, an association of insurance companies and financial services organizations, conducted a survey in 2017 polling people on their thoughts about disability insurance. Sixty-five percent of those who responded expressed the view that most people need disability insurance. Only 48 percent, however, said they needed the insurance for themselves, and only 20 percent of respondents said they had disability insurance. The "it can't happen to me" mentality causes many people to put off buying disability insurance, putting themselves and their dependents at great financial risk (figure 13).

fig. 13

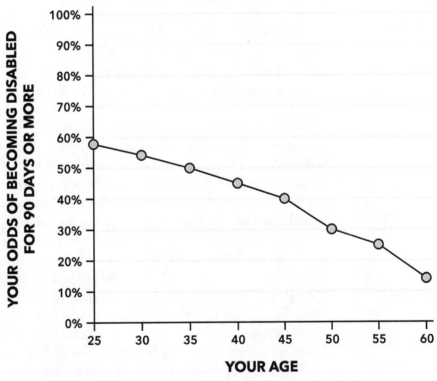

WHAT ARE YOUR CHANCES OF BEING DISABLED?

source: Commissioner's IDA Morbidity and Commissioner's SO Mortality Tables, Society of Actuaries

The likelihood that you will suffer from a debilitating event may be greater than you think.

According to Community Educators, an Iowa-based organization that develops and delivers continuing education courses for insurance and financial professionals, more than 375,000 Americans become totally disabled each year. Other data show the following:

» Just 2 percent of foreclosures on conventional mortgages occur due to the death of the homeowner; 46 percent of foreclosures are the result of a disability.

» If you have saved 10 percent of your income each year, being disabled and unable to work for one year would eat up ten years of savings.

» There is a 50 percent chance that someone who is thirty-five will become disabled for a three-month period or longer before turning sixty-five.

» About one in seven workers between thirty-five and sixty-five will become disabled for five years or longer.

These are sobering statistics, to be sure, and I hope that they have caught your attention and caused you to think about whether you would be prepared in the event of a disability. When you buy disability insurance, you are ensuring your ability to meet your everyday living expenses until you turn sixty-five.

In my experience as an advisor, I've seen firsthand the value that disability insurance can provide during exceedingly difficult times. One of my clients, a self-employed IT contractor, was only thirty-five years of age when the onset of ocular histoplasmosis left him blind in one eye. Fortunately, since only one eye was affected, he was able to continue working. Nevertheless, he made a partial claim on his disability insurance and received a $45,000 lump sum payment. That same contract will come into play again should the disease progress to his other eye and render him wholly incapable of working. I hope it never comes to that, but if it does, the policy will pay out a monthly benefit through age sixty-five equal to approximately 65 percent of his income. And while that amount may seem like a steep reduction in income, at his income bracket 65 percent is a fair reflection of what his take-home pay would be were he to continue working, once taxes and other deductions were factored in.

I have another client who was tragically diagnosed with cancer at age 45. Though she had disability insurance through her employer, I brokered a supplemental plan for her that provided more extensive coverage. Following her diagnosis, the supplemental plan paid benefits on top of what she received from her employer's plan, and those benefits persisted until the doctor gave her the "all clear" to go back to work. No one should have to worry about money when battling a deadly disease. I'm grateful that the added coverage helped my client navigate through that difficult time.

MY TAKE

If there is one takeaway I hope you get from reading this book, it's knowing the importance of disability insurance. If you earn $75,000 a year and your career is cut short at age forty, then you have lost the ability to earn an additional $1,875,000 by the time you turn sixty-five, not taking into consideration potential raises and bonuses.

NOTE

IN PRACTICE: Before you invest, buy disability insurance. I encourage my clients to get as much coverage as their budget will allow, whether it's through a group plan, a personal plan, or a combination of both. Long-term loss of income due to disability is a risk you cannot afford to take. Get your disability insurance in place, followed by an emergency fund, and then concentrate on investing.

Some employers, but not all, offer group disability insurance as part of their compensation package. Large companies are more likely to offer it than smaller ones, although some small firms offer modest plans that employees can choose to upgrade for more coverage. Though I've not known it to be a common occurrence, an increasing number of employers are offering disability as a voluntary benefit, meaning the employee must pay the entire premium. Typically, disability insurance through an employer is at least partially paid for by the employer and combined into a package of multiple benefits. If your employer is offering voluntary disability insurance as a stand-alone employee-funded product, then you should absolutely take it, given its importance to your overall financial well-being. If your employer does not offer group insurance, you will need to purchase an individual policy through a broker.

NOTE

A sobering statistic from the Social Security Administration says that one out of four twenty-year-olds will become disabled before reaching retirement age.

CAUTION

When making a disability claim through Social Security, prepare to be patient. Claims can take years to be approved and may require three or four attempts. Therefore, I recommend having your own personal policy or one through your employer's group plan. I don't mean to discourage you from submitting a claim through Social Security. On the contrary, if you have a valid claim, then you should submit it. I just want you to know what you might be up against in terms of processing time and probable application rejections.

Should you find yourself in a position where you need to pay for your own disability insurance, don't despair. There is a bright side. If you buy the insurance yourself with after-tax dollars, 100 percent of the benefits you receive if you become disabled will be tax-free. If the insurance is paid for by your employer, then you will pay taxes on any benefits that are attributed to your employer's contributions. If you have group disability insurance through your employer, be sure you know the conditions of the plan and what it would provide if you became disabled. Understand how the plan defines a disability and what percentage of your salary you would receive. If you do not think the plan would continue to support you and your dependents, then investigate getting a personal supplemental policy through a broker.

Portability is another factor to consider if you have group disability insurance through your employer; if you change jobs, the policy will no longer cover you. Individual policies typically cost more than group policies but tend to offer portability and often better benefits. On the other hand, it is more common for an individual policy to limit coverage eligibility due to a preexisting condition, whereas group policies tend to cover all employees regardless of their health status. For instance, if you become disabled at age thirty due to a back problem that resulted from a fall from a horse when you were a teenager, then you may not be covered under an individual plan. Be sure you understand the terms of the policy before purchasing.

Short-Term Vs. Long-Term

Disability insurance comes in two flavors: short-term and long-term. Just as you would think, short-term policies provide benefits for a short period—from several months to a year. Long-term plans pay for longer periods—most until you reach age sixty-five, and some even longer.

Short-term plans have a shorter waiting period. With a short-term plan your benefits typically start somewhere between zero and fourteen days of when you become disabled. With a long-term policy, ninety days is a widely used waiting period, but some are shorter and some longer. If you have a long-term policy, it is important that you plan for how to cover your expenses until the benefits start.

Recall the information in chapter 2 regarding the importance of having an emergency fund. This importance becomes clearer in the event of a disability where no earned income is flowing to get you through the ninety-day waiting period.

Disability insurance plans will cost between 1 and 3 percent of your income. Short-term plans are generally less expensive. Regardless of how old you are, claims made on long-term plans will be paid out for at least a year and possibly up to age sixty-five (retirement age), after which you can qualify for Medicare. How much you'll pay in premiums depends on a variety of factors, including your age, sex, the type of work you do, and the amount of income you want to protect in the event you become disabled (figure 14).

GRAPHIC

fig. 14

	SHORT-TERM INSURANCE	LONG-TERM INSURANCE
How much does it cover?	Up to 100% of your salary, depending on the plan	Usually between 50% and 60% of your salary
How long does it last?	Usually 3–6 months, but depends on the policy; it can last up to one year	At least one year or longer if your disability continues
How much does it cost?	1–3% of your yearly income	1–3% percent of your yearly income
How soon would you get your first payout?	Usually two weeks from when the doctor confirms you have a disability	The month following the end of your waiting period

Differences between short-term and long-term disability insurance in a group plan

CAUTION

Group plans only cover base salary. They do not cover commissions or bonuses. If much of your income comes from commissions or bonuses, then you should consider a personal plan to supplement your group plan.

Other Factors to Consider

Disability insurance policies can hold *any occupation* or *own occupation* definitions. An "any occupation" definition is more restrictive. If you are disabled but your employer can move you to another job within the company, then benefits won't be paid. The policy may only provide benefits if you are totally unable to work in any type of job, even a lower-paying or less physically demanding one. Most group plans become "any occupation" plans after two years of paying a benefit. For an "own occupation" plan, you will pay more; however, it will be less restrictive. Benefits are paid under "own occupation" plans based on your inability to do precisely what you were hired to do.

If you were hired as a supervisor of high-rise building construction and your disability limits you from fulfilling the duties of that occupation, then you will not be asked to work in the office if you hold an "own occupation" plan. You will be at home receiving benefits.

Employers usually structure their group plans as "own occupation" for a period of two years before they revert to "any occupation" status.

Something important to consider is whether a plan is written as a *guaranteed renewable* plan. That means that so long as you continue to pay your premiums, you will not lose coverage. Your premiums can increase, but your coverage must continue. A *noncancelable policy* also means your policy must be renewed, but you get the added advantage of being able to renew the policy each year without an increase in your premium or a reduction in your benefits.

Some insurers offer policies that enable you to upgrade your plan and to do so without any additional underwriting qualifications. These *additional purchase options* can be important as your salary increases. For instance, a policy that comes with a cost-of-living adjustment means that your benefits will increase over time as the cost of living goes up. Another policy provision could include the ability to increase your coverage in the event your income increases beyond a certain percentage. Plans with additional purchase options are generally more expensive than those that do not include that benefit, but they may also be exactly what you need for your family.

Depending on the insurer, you may be able to find a policy that would allow you to return to work part time, or even in another occupation, but still collect your benefits.

A surgeon who loses the use of their hands may be paid as a lecturer or consultant while still receiving disability benefits.

Most plans waive your premium after you become disabled, and others will return a portion of your premiums if you do not have any claims within a specified time frame.

As you can see, there are a lot of factors to consider when thinking about disability insurance. I understand it may not seem like a high priority when you are in your twenties or thirties, but if, God forbid, you suffered an accident or your health failed so that you could no longer work, having disability insurance would ease at least some of the consequences.

MY TAKE

Your earnings potential over your lifetime is the most valuable asset you have. Insure the risk of not having an income if you become too sick or too hurt to work. Your retirement depends on it.

Life Insurance

If you are single with no dependents, you probably don't need life insurance. If you have enough saved to meet your debts and pay for your final expenses, there is no compelling reason to buy life insurance, except for locking in your insurability. When you have family members who depend on you financially, life insurance becomes far more urgent. It is not a pleasant exercise, but think of the consequences if you die young, leaving behind children and a spouse. Could they afford to keep their home? Would they have to downgrade their standard of living? Would there be money to pay for your children's college? Could your spouse retire without having to worry about being impoverished?

Life insurance protects those you love in the event of your death. One thing that became exceedingly obvious during the time I was writing this book is that life comes with no guarantees. The COVID-19 virus was on a rampage, sickening and killing vast multitudes. People became very aware of the fragility of life. I found myself underwriting more life insurance policies than I'd ever written before in any one year.

The amount of life insurance you should have depends on your circumstances and the lifestyle to which your family is accustomed. You should craft a policy that provides enough to pay off any debts, such as a mortgage, car loans, or student loans. It also will need to replace your income, or at least a portion of it, for several years.

NOTE

If you are a smoker looking for an incentive to quit, consider this: *Forbes* published an online article in March 2020 comparing average life insurance rates for nonsmokers versus smokers.

The average yearly premium for a 30-year-old male nonsmoker was $303, compared to $828 for a 30-year-old who smokes. The gap gets even wider for 40-year-old males, going from $397 for a nonsmoker to $1,531 for a smoker. The difference was slightly less for women smokers and nonsmokers, but not much.

A rule of thumb is that you should have life insurance that is worth ten to fifteen times your current salary, so go ahead and do the math. You may need to adjust that number based on your family's needs. You can find all sorts of online calculators to help you determine an appropriate amount of life insurance. One method used frequently is called DIME, an acronym that stands for debt, income, mortgage, and education expenses. You simply find the total of those categories to determine what your policy should provide as a death benefit, your "base number" (figure 15).

GRAPHIC

fig. 15

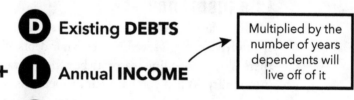

D Existing **DEBTS**

+ **I** Annual **INCOME** → Multiplied by the number of years dependents will live off of it

+ **M** Remaining **MORTGAGE** Balance

+ **E** Estimated Future **EDUCATION** Costs

___

= YOUR BASE NUMBER

The DIME method is one of several methods that can be used for calculating life insurance needs.

The cost of your policy is based on your life expectancy, which is determined using factors such as your gender, overall health, age, and whether you engage in dangerous activities, like hang gliding or driving a motorcycle. Cost is also determined by the type of policy you buy—term or whole life. You may be required to get a paramedical exam when you apply for life insurance and may be asked to submit significant information regarding your health and lifestyle.

Term Life Insurance

Term life insurance is just what it sounds like: insurance that you buy for a certain period. You typically buy term life insurance for ten, fifteen, twenty, twenty-five, or thirty years. If you get a *convertible term policy*, then you will be able to convert your policy to a whole life policy without providing *evidence of insurability*, which is proof of good health.

Term insurance is like renting a house or apartment, whereas *whole life insurance* is like owning a home with equity. As you pay premiums on your whole life policy, you accumulate a cash value in the policy that can be accessed prior to your death. Premiums paid on term insurance secure coverage for a fixed period but do not build any cash value. The premiums are lower when you are younger and healthier, and they increase as you get older. If you keep paying the premiums, the insurance will provide a predetermined death benefit to your beneficiaries. The *death benefit* is 100 percent income-tax-free regardless of the amount and can be taken as a lump sum or spread out over time.

Term life insurance is straightforward and usually significantly less expensive than whole life insurance, which is a permanent form of insurance. Term life policies are well suited for people living on slimmer budgets who need coverage to ensure that significant ongoing financial obligations will be met. Term life holders are often those raising children, paying for college, and paying off a mortgage, and these obligations, unfortunately, will not dissolve in the event of untimely death. If there is still a need for life insurance later in life, after these midlife obligations have been met, then it is possible to convert a portion or all of a term policy into a whole life policy for lifetime protection.

About 90 percent of term policies never pay a death benefit. There are two reasons for this. One is that the policy expires, or "terms out," before the policyholder dies. The other is that the person simply stops paying the premiums and does not convert the policy into a whole life policy.

A downside is that if you reach your sixties and seventies and still need the financial safety net that life insurance provides, it may be hard at that point to find an affordable whole life policy when your term expires.

Whole Life Insurance

Whole life insurance is a form of permanent insurance, meaning if you keep paying your premiums, your policy will never expire. That is a plus because it eliminates the possibility of having a term policy expire and finding out that you are no longer insurable. Moreover, there are certain attributes of whole life insurance that allow policyholders to achieve a greater array of savings and other financial objectives.

NOTE

I'm going to give you a rundown of the various unique investment-like attributes of whole life insurance. However, before I do that, I want to state plainly that life insurance is, first and foremost, insurance. The savings and investment-like components are secondary. I don't advise anyone to purchase a policy as a savings vehicle if they are not in need of insurance coverage.

A by-product of whole life insurance is a cash value component that builds up in the policy. A portion of each premium you pay goes into a tax-deferred "savings" account (the cash value account), on which you will earn some interest. How much you save each month and how much interest you earn are determined by the terms of your policy. Many whole life policies also provide "dividends"—technically a small return of premiums—if the company's profitability in terms of investments, claims paid, and expenses is better than expected.

In addition to these dividends and providing a predictable way to save money on a regular basis, the earnings on your savings in your whole life policy can be tax-free if you structure your distributions properly. In addition, you can borrow against the cash value of the policy; this gives you the advantage of something known as *infinite banking*, which effectively enables you to become your own bank to finance personal and business transactions.

If the cash value of your whole life policy is $40,000 and you decide to buy a $35,000 vehicle, you can borrow the money for the car from the insurance company. Because your loan is collateralized against your accumulated cash value, you are not taxed when you do this. Once you buy the car, you can start paying back the money you borrowed from the insurance company. With infinite banking you do not have to qualify for a loan, as you are effectively underwriting your own debt. Another beautiful thing about the infinite banking concept is that the interest rate on the money you borrow is typically less than the interest rate you are earning in the account.

Some people employ the infinite banking concept throughout their lives—irrespective of their credit score—and upon their death, the policy pays a death benefit less any loans outstanding. Infinite banking can create a type of family bank, providing financial independence and eliminating the need to borrow money from other sources.

MY TAKE

I have employed infinite banking for myself and about two dozen of my clients. It is a great way to self-finance your future purchases, while building equity, retirement income, and having life insurance protection all at the same time.

Premiums for whole life insurance are higher than those for term life insurance, so you will have to consider this in your budgeting. There are some compelling reasons why most people buy term life insurance, but whole life policies do make sense for certain financial situations.

Long-Term Care Insurance

Long-term care insurance (LTCI) is important for several reasons, not all of which are related to your financial future. If you have ever been a caregiver to someone suffering from a serious condition like cancer, Alzheimer's disease, or heart failure, you understand how grueling it can be. I have witnessed the health of caregiving spouses decline as they attempt to care for their sick partner.

Watching a beloved caregiver struggle can cause guilt and anxiety in a patient, who often feels responsible. A long and loving relationship can ultimately become frayed by the stresses of caregiving.

In addition to that harsh reality, paying for long-term care can wreak havoc on your financial plan. You read some statistics in chapter 2 about the cost of long-term care, but I think this is worth a reminder: Genworth Financial, in its 2019 Cost of Care Survey, announced that the national median cost of care for a private room in a nursing home was a whopping $103,500 a year. In-home care by a health care aide averaged $52,620 a year.

There are several ways to pay for long-term care. One is to use your savings and investments, which no one wants to do. At the amounts described above, your savings could be used up quickly if you needed nursing care for several years. If not carefully planned for, these costs can cause great financial devastation for the surviving spouse. Another way to pay for long-term care is to self-insure, which means you would earmark investments intended to pay for that care.

Those with low incomes and virtually no assets may be eligible for **Medicaid**, which is the largest public payer of long-term care. Or you can purchase long-term care insurance, which transfers your risk to the insurer.

IN PRACTICE: When my clients express concern about the cost of long-term care insurance, I tell them that, in my opinion, they have a choice. They can make a little mistake, which is to spend some of their hard-earned money to purchase the insurance, or they can make a big mistake and choose not to buy it. The "little mistake" refers to the prospect of spending some money for an insurance plan you end up never needing. The "big mistake" refers to the prospect of losing a huge portion of your retirement portfolio to long-term care costs if you are not insured, and of potentially leaving your surviving spouse with a severely reduced retirement account. I'd rather make the little mistake any day!

The US Department of Health and Human Services tells us that 60 percent of Americans turning sixty-five years old can expect to need some sort of long-term care. If both spouses live to age sixty-five, then there is a 50 percent chance that one will live to age ninety or longer.

Long-term care insurance has traditionally cost more than many middle-class buyers are comfortable paying, so insurance companies have started restructuring the way it's offered. Some insurers now offer customized plans with different levels of coverage to attract a greater cross-section of buyers.

The American Association for Long-Term Care Insurance (AALTCI) recommends that you buy long-term care insurance when you are in your mid-fifties. If that gives you pause, understand the reason: the younger and healthier you are, the lower the premium. According to the AALTCI, nearly a quarter of applicants in their sixties are turned down for coverage, compared to only 14 percent of those in their fifties.

Traditional Long-Term Care Insurance

Traditional long-term care insurance has been on the market for more than forty years. Generally, it reimburses the cost of care for someone who needs help with specified daily tasks of living. These activities of daily living, or ADLs, are formally defined in the insurance world as bathing, toileting, getting in and out of bed, walking, continence, and eating. To make a claim against your long-term care insurance policy, you must be unable to perform two of the six ADLs.

NOTE

A key exception to the two-out-of-six ADL standard is cognitive impairment. If you are deemed to have a cognitive impairment, you can make a claim against your policy.

The amount of benefits received depends on the plan, but policy limits are usually between $1,500 and $12,000 a month. Depending on your plan, you can receive benefits for two to six years. When looking for a long-term care insurance policy, be sure to ask about the elimination policy, which is the amount of time you would have to wait for benefits to kick in. And ask what optional coverage is available, as sometimes it is worth paying a little more for. An example might be an inflation protection rider, which would increase benefits to keep up with inflation.

NOTE

You can find a Long-Term Care Needs calculator on my website at snowfinancialgroup.com/resource-center/calculators.

It is important to realize that a person does not have to be in a nursing care facility to have access to long-term care insurance. The insurance can be used to pay for in-home care, assisted living, adult day care, or respite services.

CAUTION

Be careful about *when* you make your claim against your long-term care insurance policy. Most policies offer a specific number of years' worth of coverage, and once those years elapse, benefits cease. In many cases your best option is to try to foot the bill out of pocket during the initial stages of in-home care or assisted living, when activity is only moderately limited. When your loved one needs more in-depth, persistent, specialized (and expensive) care, then it may be time to make your claim.

Hybrid Long-Term Care Insurance

A newer and popular alternative to traditional long-term care insurance is hybrid coverage, also known as combo or linked-benefit insurance. Hybrid plans are newer product designs, and they have an advantage over traditional plans. Basically, a hybrid long-term care policy combines the benefits of life insurance with long-term care insurance.

A hybrid policy can be purchased with a one-time, lump sum payment or paid for over time, usually up to ten years. Typical costs associated with this type of policy range from $70,000 to $120,000 per person when paid as a lump sum, depending on the company and the age of the policyholder. When paid in annual installments, the cumulative cost is about 15 to 20 percent higher. If it turns out that a long-term care benefit is not needed, a death benefit is paid to a beneficiary when the insured person dies. If long-term care is needed, the policy pays benefits toward those expenses. As with traditional long-term care insurance, the insured person chooses the amount of benefits and the time for which they will be paid.

These hybrid plans have become popular for good reason. Standard long-term care insurance operates much like your typical auto insurance policy: you still pay premiums even if you never have a claim, so all the money you pay in is essentially lost. Hybrid plans, like whole life policies, have a cash value component. Your lump sum payment or series of premiums create a cash value in the policy, which will be returned to you or your family members, one way or another, and often with leverage. If you need long-term care, then the policy will pay you approximately three times its cash value. If you use the hybrid plan as life insurance upon the policyholder's death, beneficiaries will receive approximately one and a half to two times the cash value. Finally, if you cancel your insurance and surrender your policy, you will be given back the current cash value.

Policies are usually required to be held for six years before a 100 percent refund will be given upon cancellation. There is some variance depending on the insurance company.

To fund a hybrid long-term care policy, consider reallocating assets you've invested elsewhere that are earmarked for this type of care. For example, Bob and Jane have $350,000 earmarked for long-term care expenses. They use $200,000 to purchase policies for each of them. The policies provide leverage. If both policies are exercised to provide long-term care, benefits may approximate three times the policy cost, or $600,000. If both policies are exercised to provide a death benefit, then benefits may approximate one and a half times the policy cost, or $300,000. With the newfound security attained through the insurance policy, Bob and Jane no longer must scrupulously manage their remaining earmarked funds. With their remaining $150,000, they are free to consider new and more fun ways to spend their savings or free it up for more opportunistic investing.

MY TAKE

Just as disability insurance is important to your financial plan while you are working, long-term care insurance is equally important after you retire and are living on your savings.

Property and Casualty Insurance

Everyone should conduct an annual review of their property and casualty insurance policy. If it has been a while since you have done so, review it now with your CFP® practitioner. As circumstances change, it may be prudent to adjust the amount of coverage you have. If you have put on an addition and completely remodeled your home, for instance, you may need to increase your homeowners policy.

Property and casualty insurance, also known as P&C insurance, protects you and assets you own. Although you can buy separate policies for property and casualty, they usually come bundled in one policy. Property insurance protects property such as your home and your car. Casualty insurance is liability coverage to protect you in the event someone sues you after falling down your porch steps or being injured in a car accident that you caused.

Having the proper insurance is important at any stage of life, whether you are just starting your career or getting ready to finish it. If there are policies you think you should have but do not, consult your CFP® practitioner for counsel, and then talk to your agent about buying the policy. Be aware, however, that you can end up paying more than necessary by overestimating the value of items you are insuring.

Homeowners Insurance

Most homeowner policies include liability insurance, which means they protect your home, its contents, and you. Your home and belongings are protected against events like fire and theft, and you are protected if someone is injured at your home.

On a standard policy, hazard insurance typically covers disasters such as lightning strikes, hail, hurricanes, or tornados, but normally does not cover events like floods or earthquakes. If you live in an area where those types of events occur frequently or are beginning to occur more frequently, investigate the possibility of adding insurance to protect yourself from those kinds of disasters.

Auto Insurance

Like homeowners insurance, auto insurance protects your vehicle and you. Most states require a minimum amount of liability insurance, which protects you if you are at fault for an accident. Comprehensive and collision coverage pays for damage to your automobile, due to either an accident or another cause. Auto insurance policies vary greatly, so be sure to shop around and get what you need.

Umbrella Insurance

Umbrella insurance provides extra liability coverage, beyond what is included in your home and auto policies. I believe it is underutilized—it can be a lifesaver if someone is injured on your property or another mishap occurs.

If your car skids on the ice and injures a pedestrian, you could be looking at a lawsuit that threatens to wipe out your savings. Umbrella insurance, which normally is relatively inexpensive, can help solve that problem. Umbrella insurance has a reputation for being applicable only to high-wealth individuals and families, but it can be applicable to anyone at any level of wealth.

IN PRACTICE: From what I've seen in my practice, most families who purchase umbrella policies have a household income of $85,000 or higher. One of the reasons people balk at getting umbrella policies is that they typically must have already purchased auto and homeowners policies with maximum allowable liability coverage limits. Umbrella policy holders are often motivated by horror stories of judgments that greatly exceed the limits of standard insurance coverage and are capable of seriously diminishing one's net worth.

A couple with an umbrella policy has a teenage child who is at fault in an auto accident caused by texting while driving. The couple is found liable for $1.9 million, an amount that far exceeds the $500,000 coverage limits on their auto insurance policy. The umbrella policy kicks in and covers an addition $1 million in liabilities, leaving only $400,000 (as opposed to $1.4 million) of the couple's personal assets exposed to the settlement.

I often recommend that my clients opt for the highest limits of liability coverage on their home and auto policies. Doing so can be less expensive than you might think, and it can help protect your personal assets.

With the highest liability limits selected on your home and auto, you can qualify for an umbrella policy, which further protects your personal assets in the event of a claim. The value of the umbrella policy can be quite high. Depending on where you live, you can get $1 million in extra coverage for about $300 in annual premiums.

Professional Liability Insurance

If you own a business, you should seriously consider some form of malpractice or liability insurance. Every year, between 36 and 56 percent of small businesses are involved in some type of litigation, according to statistics.

I would not dream of operating my business without errors and omissions insurance, which protects my clients from unintentional mistakes that I may make. In nearly thirty-four years, I have never had to make a claim on this policy. Hopefully, I never will, but it gives me peace of mind to know that it is in place. I also carry cyber insurance, which I would need if any of my client records were breached or hacked. We know that cybercrime is rampant, and having that insurance covers me in case any client information is affected.

If part of your retirement plan involves running your own business, check that you have the correct liability insurance to create some separation between your professional life and your personal wealth.

You can insure practically anything, but the policies described in this chapter are the ones most families need. You can work with a CFP® practitioner first, to guide you and educate you, then turn to an insurance agent in your community to put in place the policies you need. Do not neglect the issue of insurance in your overall retirement planning, as it is a key component in controlling your risks and protecting your assets.

IN PRACTICE: Strive to view insurance as a vehicle for empowerment. We know that unexpected and expensive events are destined to occur. We don't know what form they will take, only that they loom persistently on the horizon. Insurance is a valuable financial tool for keeping our retirement plans on track as we venture through the unexpected, unknown, and, to some degree, certain financial setbacks that will arise.

Chapter Recap

» Disability insurance is invaluable in the event you cannot work.

» Term life insurance makes sense for many people.

» A lack of long-term care insurance can derail your financial plan.

» Property and casualty insurance protects what you own—and you.

| 4 |
Understanding Your Retirement Needs

> *Always plan ahead. It wasn't raining when Noah built the ark.*
> – CARDINAL RICHARD JAMES CUSHING

While planning when and how you will retire, and well before you do retire, you need to be radically diligent and intrepid in assessing what you have and what you will need. Understanding those two things, the "when" and the "how," is crucial to a successful retirement. If your needs are more than what you have, you may have to keep working or figure out an alternative means of income for when you leave your job. If you have been able to accumulate wealth that is greater than what you will need in retirement, congratulate yourself and plan on using some of that money in a way that benefits others.

No one can predict the future, that's for certain. You can, however, look at historical returns and calculations in order to make your best guesses about how well your investments may perform, how long you will need to live off those investments, and how your needs will change as you age, among other factors—and all this before you retire. Let's start by looking at how you can calculate what your expenses will look like in retirement.

Calculating Expenses

Most experts, including myself, recommend that you plan for retirement income of at least 80 percent of your pre-retirement income. That number will depend on factors such as whether you will need to pay for health insurance, whether you plan to downsize to a smaller home, how extensively you intend to travel, and so forth.

NOTE

The Bureau of Labor Statistics (BLS) reports that the typical retiree spends about $46,000 a year. With an average retirement of eighteen years, that adds up to $828,000. And, according to the Employee Benefit Research Institute, about 33 percent of households spend more money in the first six years after retiring than they did while working, a factor attributed largely to increased costs for health care.

While many of your expenses will remain about the same, some, like health care, could increase. Others, like transportation or your clothing budget, might decrease. Research shows that Americans tend to spend less as they age (figure 16), so if you are typical, you can expect your household budget to decrease over time. There are many worksheets available to help you understand what your retirement expenses will look like.

DIGITAL ASSETS

On the Snow Financial Group website I have several budgeting, tax management, and investing calculators for retirees and those who are working toward their retirement. Find these and more at snowfinancialgroup.com/resource-center/calculators.

AVERAGE ANNUAL HOUSEHOLD INCOME AND EXPENDITURES BY AGE GROUP

fig. 16

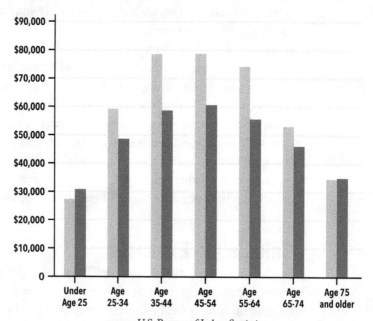

source: U.S. Bureau of Labor Statistics

Average annual household income and expenditures by age group

MY TAKE

It is impossible to predict your retirement expenses with guaranteed accuracy. Do the best you can, and make sure to include a buffer to safeguard against unexpected expenditures.

Once you have figured out your anticipated expenses, you can apply the 4 percent rule. This rule of thumb has been around for a long time; it assumes that you can safely withdraw 4 percent of your retirement nest egg each year without ever running out of money. Take whatever income you will get in retirement, such as Social Security or a pension, and couple it with 4 percent of your retirement savings. If this amount will not cover your expenses, you will need to get creative about how to spend less.

NOTE

IN PRACTICE: I advise my clients to be conservative with the 4 percent rule and lean toward spending down only 2.5 or 3 percent per year. With inflation and recent investment trends, I consider those numbers to be more prudent than 4 percent. This more conservative approach may require you to save more throughout your working years.

Expenses to consider in retirement include housing, transportation (including the cost of owning a vehicle), utilities, health care (including the cost of prescriptions), communication (including phone, cable, and internet), food, and leisure. As you calculate your expenses in each of these areas, do some thinking about how you might reduce the amount you spend. Let's look at a few spending categories and how you might save some money.

Housing Costs

If you have a mortgage, I strongly recommend paying it off before you retire, if possible. Going into retirement mortgage-free is a real asset that will lighten your financial load, as that cost is about 30 percent of the average worker's take-home pay.

Another way to cut housing costs is to downsize. Do you really need the four-bedroom house now that the kids are out? Sure, an extra bedroom for grandkids or out-of-town friends would be nice, but many retirees have much more house than they need. A smaller place could save you maintenance and utility costs, lower your property taxes, and give you less to care for.

In 2008 and 2012, my wife and I had a chance to spend some time in China for a ministry we created to share our faith abroad. It turned out to be a game-changer for us. As we visited with people in their homes, we were astonished at the basic minimalism and simplicity with which they lived. Small homes with tiny kitchens and few possessions were the rule, and yet everyone seemed content and happy.

That experience caused us to rethink our own situation, and we ended up transitioning from our home to a 900-square-foot apartment, giving away many of our possessions in the process. I know a move like that is not for everyone, but for us, it has been completely liberating. I never realized what a burden possessions can become, and I do not miss any of the things we gave away. When I tell this story, many look at me like I'm a cyclops with a unicorn horn. Not being tied down to "things" has made a way for us to give of ourselves and our money more generously. As a result of our decision, my wife, Mary, and I are happier than we've ever been in our twenty-one years of marriage. There are more facets to this story, so if you want to know more, I welcome you to visit with me about it.

Transportation

Another form of downsizing to consider is getting rid of a vehicle. I know a lot of retired couples who keep two cars, even though there are very few times when they are both in use. With a little planning you could get away with having one vehicle, which would result in considerable savings.

According to AAA, it costs an average of $725 per month to own a car, when you figure in registration, insurance, maintenance, fuel, and other costs. Do the math and you could save almost $9,000 a year by reducing your fleet from two vehicles to one.

Health Care

Paying for health care is a problem for many retirees, despite the availability of *Medicare*, the national health insurance program that is available to you when you turn sixty-five. Medicare does not cover all health care costs, so you will need to buy *supplemental insurance plans* to take care of services like dental, vision, and prescription drugs.

Medicare coverage consists of four parts (Part A, Part B, Part C, and Part D), so be sure you understand the various components and what is covered and what is not when you enroll.

Communications

I am sometimes astounded at how much money we spend to communicate and stay in touch with the world. Expensive smartphones that need to be periodically updated, pricey cable bills, smart speakers to tell us what the weather is like and to turn the lights on and off, internet connections—these costs can add up to thousands of dollars a year. But there are ways to minimize these costs if you are willing to give up some television channels and downgrade your data plan.

Building a Retirement Budget

Once you have a good idea of what your expenses in retirement will look like, you will be able to plan a budget that makes sense for you. As you know, expenses are just one side of a household budget; you will also want to consider sources of income. The next section of this book takes a deep dive into possible sources of income, including Social Security, pensions, portfolio withdrawals, annuities, part-time work, and others.

As I said before, getting a budget in place well before you leave your job is important, because if you cannot figure out a workable plan that clearly shows you will have enough money to live on, you should continue working and saving as much as you can.

NOTE

Americans love their pets, but keeping them can be expensive. The American Society for the Prevention of Cruelty to Animals (ASPCA) estimates that the first year of dog ownership, which includes expenses like spaying/neutering, medical fees, a crate, and training, can cost between $1,300 and $1,843. If you add in pet sitting, dental care, emergency vet visits, and other expenses, the cost of owning a dog can top out at almost $3,000 a year, according to Rover.com.

Let's have a look at how the average monthly spending breaks down for a household headed by a person of retirement age, according to MarketWatch, a website that provides financial information and news.

» **Housing: $1,322**
Housing is the largest expenditure for all age groups, including retirees. This average monthly housing cost for a retirement-age household includes taxes, insurance, maintenance, repairs, utilities, and supplies.

» **Transportation: $567**
The monthly cost for transportation is about one-third lower than the average cost for households of other ages, but it's still considerable. It includes the costs of gas, insurance, repairs, and maintenance.

» **Health Care: $499**
Health care is a spending category you can expect to increase as you age.

» **Food: $483**
Food is another big budget item for all age categories. For retirees, it is about 20 percent less than for younger age groups.

» **Cash Contributions: $202**
This monthly amount, which includes charitable contributions, adds up to $2,424 a year, about $350 more than for households of younger people.

» **Entertainment: $197**
This is less than the spending in other-age households, which averages $243 a month.

Building a budget is not difficult, and, as with expense calculators, you can find a variety of templates to use. Your retirement budget will include most of the same expense categories as the budget you employed prior to stopping work, but the income side will probably look different. Use your past financial records to get a realistic idea of your spending patterns. Study your credit card statements and bank statements to understand how much you have spent and what the money was used for.

NOTE

Be sure to consider money you spend on gifts and events when planning your retirement budget. Is there a wedding in the future for which you will be paying or helping to pay? Are you hoping to establish college savings plans for your grandchildren? Might you be buying some appliances for an adult child who is purchasing a home? Any of these expenses would need to be factored into your budget.

Add up all your monthly expenses—those that are the same every month and those that vary—and then think about any one-time expenses you might encounter during the year, such as a vacation or a new car. You can also add to this category occasional expenses like birthday and holiday gifts. Once you have a handle on expenses, consider your retirement income. Compare your expenses to your income and then, if necessary, start to tweak the numbers, considering how you can cut expenses or increase income, if necessary.

Calculating Your Life Expectancy

You read a little bit in chapter 2 about the risks of outliving your money, something that has become more common as life expectancy rates have increased over the past few decades. Fifty years ago, the average life expectancy in the United States was 70.78 years. In 2020, not considering deaths from the COVID-19 virus, the average life expectancy was 78.93, an increase of more than eight years (figure 17).

INCREASING (AND PROJECTED INCREASES TO) LIFE EXPECTANCY

fig. 17

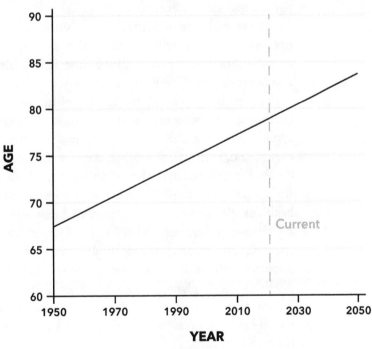

source: Macrotrends.net

If you expect to live to be one hundred, you will need to have a different plan than if you think your life expectancy is more like seventy-five. That's a big difference in the number of years you will need to make your money last. To help with planning, use a life expectancy calculator that you can find online. Just google one or more of the following:

» Living to 100
» Blue Zones Vitality Compass
» Blueprint Income
» Snow Financial Group (snowfinancialgroup.com/resource-center/calculators)

You can somewhat gauge your lifespan by looking at the health of your parents or, if your parents are deceased, looking at how long they lived. Studies indicate that people whose parents had longer lives tend to have longer lives themselves. A report published in 2016 in the *Journal of the American College of Cardiology* stated that a person's risk of death drops 17 percent for each decade that at least one parent lived beyond the age of seventy. And children of parents who lived beyond seventy experience less heart disease, stroke, high cholesterol, high blood pressure, and atrial fibrillation than those whose parents had shorter lives.

However, if one or both of your parents died at a relatively young age, do not assume that you will too. Medical technologies continue to improve, and scientists are learning more all the time about serious conditions like cancer and heart disease. There are also steps you can take to improve your health, such as reaching and maintaining a healthy weight; getting regular medical checkups; exercising on a daily or almost-daily basis; quitting smoking, if applicable; eating well; participating in self-checks, such as skin and breast exams; and, if you drink alcohol, doing so in moderation.

As I mentioned in the introduction to this book, I've personally recovered from a period of negligent self-care. By losing fifty pounds and adopting a healthier diet and an active lifestyle, I knew I was doing right by my wife, my clients, and myself. What kind of hypocritical fiduciary would I be if I spent my career urging people to plan responsibly for their retirement, while I concurrently neglected to care for myself, barely got any exercise, and ate poorly? I wasn't planning for retirement. I was planning for an early grave. All the saving, 401(k) matching, asset allocation, and portfolio rebalancing would have been completely in vain had I not taken the time to look out for my own health.

In addition to attending to your physical wellness, nurturing your social health is also especially important. A study by the American Psychological Association found that low social interaction is as detrimental to longevity as smoking, alcoholism, lack of exercise, and obesity.

No one can predict with accuracy how long they will live. However, you can make an educated guess and increase your chances by practicing a healthy lifestyle. When it comes to retirement, it is best to plan conservatively, assuming you will live longer than you might think.

Life After Work

When planning for retirement, many people focus solely on their financial situation. They worry about whether they will have enough to maintain a comfortable lifestyle, whether the value of their portfolio will continue to increase, and whether there will be any money left for their children or grandchildren after their death. To be sure, all of those are valid concerns and an important part of being prepared for retirement.

But there are other things to consider. What will you do with the extra time you'll have when you stop working? What activities might give you the sense of purpose and fulfillment that previously came from your job? How will you replace the social interactions you had at your workplace? How can you keep your mind active and stimulated? Working in a traditional job with others provides a built-in routine and ready-made relationships with coworkers. Finding success in a job you enjoy is a source of satisfaction. When the job goes away, those benefits can disappear as well.

Most people I have encountered who were preparing to retire were both anticipatory and nervous. That is understandable because you cannot really know what retirement will look like and feel like until you are in it. It's like jumping off a dock into a lake—you can never be quite sure what the water will feel like until you take the plunge. It is important to acknowledge that not everyone does well with retirement, especially at first. Research has shown that more than half of all new retirees do not enjoy their first year off work. And, if you live with someone else, retirement does not affect only you. Couples who are now both at home need to establish new routines. If your spouse is still working, you might be expected to take on more responsibility with housework, laundry, and cooking. Data from the National Center for Health Statistics and the US Census Bureau reveal that the divorce rate for people sixty-five and over has tripled in the past thirty years, and that the fastest growing divorce rate is among couples who are fifty-five and older.

Researchers at Harvard Medical School warn that both overactivity and underactivity can result in symptoms such as depression, anxiety, memory impairment, loss of appetite, and insomnia. A study by the London-based Institute of Economic Affairs found that someone is 44 percent more likely to experience depression after retiring. Considering that, it is important to find activities that you enjoy and that are meaningful to you.

I passionately believe that you should retire *to* something rather than merely retiring *from* something. As soon as a client so much as hints at being uncertain about their post-retirement life, I encourage them to talk to me about what they might want to do in retirement that will fill their life with purpose and meaning. For those who have not made any plans and are having trouble envisioning their post-retirement life, I encourage them to pick one or two meaningful activities and start doing them now, before they retire. If you begin to actualize your post-retirement identity sooner rather than later, then this important and often difficult transition may be a lot easier.

We will take a closer look at retirement lifestyles in chapter 11, but for now, suffice it to say that assessing your goals and aspirations in areas other than your finances is vitally important. You could have a $20 million retirement fund, but if you have no plan for how to use it for yourself and others, it really is of little value.

Chapter Recap

» When planning for retirement, it is imperative to fully understand your financial situation, especially what you have and what you will need.

» Be realistic about the expenses you will have in retirement and whether you will be able to cover them by using just a small percentage of your retirement savings each year.

» Be prepared to consider how you can cut back on expenses if you need to.

» Having an idea of your life expectancy is a valuable tool in figuring out how much money you will need to retire.

» Retirement planning goes beyond being prepared financially.

| 5 |

Accelerating Your Retirement Timeline

Chapter Overview
» FIRE: A Growing Movement
» Claiming Control of Your Finances
» How FIRE Began
» Who Is Joining the Movement?
» Lessons from FIRE

Achieving *financial independence*, which simply means saving enough money to support your lifestyle for the rest of your life, is a goal most people strive to attain by the time they retire, usually at some point between the ages of sixty and seventy. Three-quarters of Americans work until they are at least sixty, with more than half retiring between the ages of sixty-one and sixty-five. The information presented so far in this book was written with the assumption that you too are probably planning to work until you reach age sixty or older.

A growing number of people, however, have resolved that working into their seventh decade is not in the cards for them, and they are readjusting both their attitudes and their lifestyles to achieve financial independence at a much earlier age.

These folks, members of the popular "Financial Independence, Retire Early" movement, or FIRE, make the very conscious decision to save a large portion of their earnings (usually between 50 and 70 percent), live extremely frugally, and claim their lives as financially independent retirees long before the average retirement age. This movement is certainly not feasible or right for everyone, but it's interesting and I thought you might like to learn a little more about it.

Live like no one else now, so later you can live and give like no one else.

– DAVE RAMSEY

The extent to which individuals participate in the movement varies. While some live in a rented room and eat boxed macaroni and cheese while saving 85 percent of their income, others are more moderate and live a more traditional lifestyle while still saving more than the average investor who, according to the US Bureau of Labor Statistics, saves less than 10 percent of their annual income.

The FIRE movement, in my opinion, has brought to light the fact that many people have more control over when they retire than we normally assume—perhaps not everyone, as for some life is difficult and just getting by is a struggle, but many people can choose to adjust their lifestyles and, therefore, how long they will need to work before achieving financial independence.

The Origins of the FIRE Movement

The FIRE movement got its start almost thirty years ago, when Vicki Robin and Joe Dominguez wrote a best-seller called *Your Money or Your Life: 9 Steps to Transforming Your Relationship with Money and Achieving Financial Independence*. The book inspired readers to examine their relationship with their work and their money by asking questions such as these:

- » Do you have enough money?
- » Do you spend enough time with family and friends?
- » Do you have time to participate in things you believe are worthwhile?
- » Are you at peace with money?
- » Are you satisfied with the contributions you have made to the world?
- » Does your job reflect your values?
- » Do you have enough savings to see you through six months of normal living expenses?
- » Do you come home from your job feeling full of life?

Basically, the book charged readers with putting a time value on every expense. So, if an individual earned $30,000 a year and paid $10,000 a year in rent, she spent one-third of every weekday working to pay her rent. If someone earned $40,000 a year, or about $770 a week, and bought a car for $15,000, he would need to work more than nineteen weeks to pay for the car. A $50 pair of shoes would cost a little more than two and a half hours of work. Then readers were challenged to examine whether the cost was worth the time they spent working to pay it. Was that pair of shoes worth two and a half hours of time you could have spent playing with your child, taking care of an elderly parent, or relaxing on the beach?

The questions and ideas presented in the book got people thinking and talking, and the movement gained more traction when the internet brought forth a variety of financial sites and discussion platforms in the early 2000s. In 2007, a Danish astrophysicist named Jacob Lund Fisker began writing a blog about the benefits of frugal living and saving as much as possible. Called *Early Retirement Extreme*, the blog attracted a large audience and Fisker wrote a book with the same title. True to his advice, Fisker saved 80 percent of his income and retired from his astrophysics career in 2009 at age thirty-three. He did go back to work for several years at a financial firm in Chicago, citing personal interest, not a need for money.

Other blogs and websites devoted to FIRE have been developed and are attracting more followers than ever. Some popular ones include *Mr. Money Mustache*, *Financial Samurai*, *Mad Fientist*, *Chief Mom Officer*, and *Our Next Life*.

Who Are the FIRE Proponents?

Followers of the FIRE movement come from different backgrounds and life experiences, but many have some common characteristics. To be able to save enough to retire when you are thirty-five, forty, or forty-five, you need to have significant income. Many FIRE proponents tend to hold positions such as software engineer, financial analyst, or software developer, which pay high salaries and allow them to save and invest and grow a lot of money. Achieving that type of job requires higher education, which is not attainable for everyone. That leads to criticism of the FIRE movement, which some say is weighted toward individuals who are already more well-off than some of their peers.

Pete Adeney, who runs the *Mr. Money Mustache* blog, was an engineer and his wife a computer scientist; they retired before they were thirty to begin a family. They lived frugally, invested all they could, and bought a couple of rental properties for income. Adeney is all about living without what you don't absolutely need; for example, opening windows instead of paying for air conditioning. He gauges his lifestyle to be about 50 percent less expensive than those of most of his peers, and this gave him the ability to save a lot early in his life.

WORKING YEARS UNTIL RETIREMENT

GRAPHIC

fig. 18

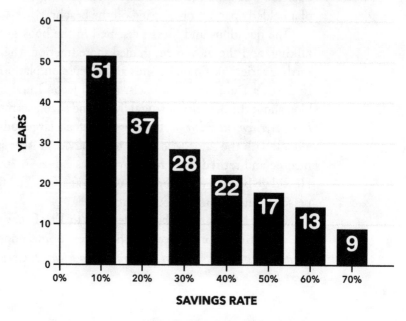

source: www.mrmoneymustache.com.

The number of years it will take to achieve financial independence, based on the percentage of income you save. These numbers assume a 5 percent return on saved money after inflation, a 4 percent annual withdrawal rate after retirement, and a large enough portfolio to sustain withdrawals over a lifetime.

Some proponents of the FIRE movement did not get off to smooth starts, financially speaking. The blogger who writes *Traveling Wallet*, Melissa Neacato, is the US-born daughter of immigrant parents. A year and a half away from earning a degree in mechanical engineering, she discovered she was pregnant. Despite being told by a counselor at her university that her chances of graduating were slim, she remained determined to finish her education.

She did, relying on student loans and public assistance to support herself and her baby. Neacato found a job after graduating and was able to support herself, her baby, and her mother while working to pay off the debt she had accumulated in student loans and credit cards. She was inspired by the idea of the FIRE movement when she listened to a podcast featuring Pete Adeney, aka "Mr. Money Mustache." She put herself on a five year plan to wipe out her more than $100,000 of debt while working and supporting her family, reaching her goal in three and a half years. She hopes her blog is an inspiration to others struggling with their finances.

"Even if you think you're starting off at a disadvantage, you still have a lot of power to create the life that you want to create," she said during an interview with *Forbes*. "It's going to be more difficult, but it's possible."

MY TAKE

I applaud anyone who lives below, and even well below, their means and doesn't give in to the pressure to buy the latest gadgets, have the big house, and drive the luxury cars, just to keep up with their friends. It not only enables them to save and invest, but to have assets to use to help others, as well.

Downsides of the FIRE Lifestyle

Some people who follow the FIRE lifestyle claim it's the only way to go, the best decision they've ever made. Others are less enthusiastic. A lot of people write about the FIRE movement online, so it's easy to find opinions on both sides of the issue.

Some downsides of the FIRE movement mentioned in various blogs include the difficulty of constantly denying yourself things or experiences you would like to have, and the need to work as much as you possibly can during your FIRE years of earning and saving. Let's break those down a bit.

Most people seek reward from hard work, and most people do not like to defer that reward for a decade or more to obtain the eventual prize of early retirement. Say you work sixty or seventy hours a week; it might be nice to go out for dinner on a Saturday night. However, if you adhere strictly to FIRE standards, you may be reluctant to do that. You might experience guilt for wanting to enjoy something most people would take for granted.

Some FIRE skeptics mention that putting so much focus on work resulted in strained relationships and kept them from doing things such as spending time with their parents, other relatives, or friends. Another criticism I've observed comes from individuals who claim the FIRE lifestyle made them way too obsessed with money. One writer noted that he had spent years constantly comparing himself to other FIRE proponents to see who was working and saving more.

You can also read online posts from people who joined the FIRE movement, retired early, and soon went back to work because they missed the camaraderie of the workplace or other aspects of employment. One software developer said he began looking for work six months after he retired early, not realizing that the burnout he had experienced could have been addressed with a six-month sabbatical instead of retirement.

Still, despite the drawbacks, there are plenty of people who note that saving aggressively early on provided options like being able to work part time or start a home-based business rather than being tied down to a forty-hour work week.

Lessons from the FIRE Movement

The FIRE movement is not for everyone, but perhaps everyone can take some lessons from it. Scaling back on what we buy and spend, and saving, investing, and giving more, can lead to a more satisfying life.

The number of people willing to live with fewer material possessions seems to be on the rise, as indicated by the popularity of Marie Kondo's book, *The Life-Changing Magic of Tidying Up: The Japanese Art of Decluttering and Organizing*, and the rise of the minimalism movement, led by Ryan Nicodemus and Joshua Fields Millburn, childhood friends who left high-paying careers, branded themselves "the Minimalists," and in 2016 released *Minimalism: A Documentary About Important Things*.

You read earlier about my own experience with downsizing and moving toward minimalism. My wife, Mary, and I sold our home, parted with many of our possessions, and now live more happily than ever in an apartment. We feel freed up of both clutter and the responsibilities that go along with owning a home.

If you are not yet retired, maybe you'll be inspired to accelerate the pace of your saving to reach that goal earlier. In addition to living below your means to generate savings, how and where you invest those savings can also affect your financial independence. Every individual and family has their own goals and strategies, but remember that when planning your retirement, taking advantage of an employer match on your 401(k) plan, using IRAs—especially Roth IRAs—for tax advantages, and building a portfolio that is geared toward growth are key steps in achieving financial independence.

IN PRACTICE: Over many years, my best clients have been people who attain financial independence by possessing three essential attributes. They are disciplined and consistent savers, they exhibit good investment behavior by avoiding pitfalls such as market timing, and they adhere to a budget that controls their spending.

If you are already retired, perhaps you'll reevaluate your spending level and be inclined to do with less, so you are able to give more and minimize worry about outliving your savings. Maybe it's time to downsize from the big family home, letting go of some possessions but holding on to all your memories. If you are a two-car household, maybe one vehicle would be enough. There are many ways to save, and often people find that the adage "less is more" is true.

MY TAKE

I find that most people fall somewhere between the "all-in with FIRE" and the "can't save a dollar" categories. My recommendation is to position yourself in a way that provides you and your family a unified understanding of what you use your money for and why, and continue to reinforce that goal. If you can save 70 percent of your salary, good for you! If you can't save that much, find a level at which you experience peace and contentment, knowing it may take a little longer to realize your retirement goal.

Achieving financial independence is a worthy goal, and necessary if you are to live comfortably and securely in retirement. But another important goal should be to find happiness and satisfaction as you work toward that independence.

Chapter Recap

» "Financial Independence, Retire Early," or FIRE, is a growing movement of people determined not to keep working until they are sixty, sixty-five, or seventy.

» The FIRE movement got its start almost thirty years ago with the publication of a book called *Your Money or Your Life: 9 Steps to Transforming Your Relationship with Money and Achieving Financial Independence.*

» FIRE calls for participants to save a larger-than-average percentage of their incomes and decrease their spending.

» While FIRE works for some people, it is not a lifestyle that is manageable for everyone.

» Many people find that scaling back on spending, and then saving, giving, and investing more, is a satisfying way to live.

PART II

TRANSITIONING TO RETIREMENT

| 6 |

Social Security and Pensions
Are Nice, But Not the Whole Picture

Chapter Overview
- » Social Security and Pensions
- » When to Start Taking Social Security
- » Lump Sum or Monthly Pension Benefits

The system is not intended as a substitute for private savings, pension plans, and insurance protection. It is, rather, intended as the foundation upon which these other forms of protection can be soundly built.

— DWIGHT D. EISENHOWER

speaking on the value of Social Security

The first part of this book was all about choosing accounts and getting strategies in place to help secure your retirement plan and move forward with confidence. Hopefully, it got you thinking about your retirement expenses and how much money you'll need to live comfortably, be able to enjoy life, and perhaps have something left to pass along to heirs.

Ideally, picturing the retirement you would like to have and planning how to fund it is something you are doing at a reasonably young age. If you are not yet forty and have a retirement plan in place, you're probably in good shape for the future. Hopefully, by the time you reach your fifties and sixties, you will have been able to save a substantial amount of money that is invested and will continue to grow. As you get closer to retirement age, you will begin to transition—or at least think about transitioning—from full-time work to something different.

You might plan to stop working altogether and begin the travel you've been putting off. Maybe you plan to work part time or offer your expertise on a consulting basis. Perhaps you have always dreamed of starting your own small business, putting your skills and experience to good use. Or maybe you've invested in some real estate and plan to generate some income as an investment property owner.

MY TAKE

Thinking about and planning for retirement is exciting if you are prepared. If you are not, it can seem downright frightening. If you are not absolutely clear regarding your finances and your financial health (you would be surprised how many people do not have a handle on that), then I highly recommend that before you announce a retirement date to your boss, you seek the advice of a financial professional, preferably one who specializes in disciplines including investment management and retirement, taxation, estate, and insurance planning to help coordinate these areas and determine whether it is feasible for you to stop working.

Whether you continue with some form of employment or not, you will require income during retirement. You are counting on Social Security, and maybe you are fortunate enough to have a pension, which, as you read earlier, has become much less common over the years, especially for employees in the private sector. Perhaps you have invested in annuities, a financial product that offers a guaranteed income stream during retirement (more about annuities in the next chapter).

If you have one or more of these income streams, be thankful; not everyone does. Do not, however, assume that any of them, and perhaps not even all of them, will provide you with enough money to fund the retirement you envision. These funding sources can be reliable, and they certainly are helpful. But if you think Social Security or a small pension will comfortably suffice as your sole source of income, you may need to rethink your financial situation.

Social Security—Its History and (Not So Certain) Future

A 2019 Gallup poll revealed that 36 percent of respondents who had not yet retired were counting on Social Security as a major source of income in retirement. Among respondents who had already retired, 58 percent said Social Security was a major source of their income. But, despite their dependence on this federal money, 41 percent of those polled reported worrying a great deal about the future of the system, and another 26 percent reported worrying a fair amount.

While many Americans count on their Social Security benefits, either as a primary income source or a secondary one, there is uncertainty about how long the Social Security system will be able to continue operating in its current structure without modifications to shore up the trust fund. Let's take a quick look at how Social Security got started and where it could be headed.

President Franklin D. Roosevelt signed the Social Security Act into law on August 14, 1935. To put that in historical perspective, 1935 was just about smack in the middle of the Great Depression, which dragged on from 1929 until 1939. The new law called for workers to make payroll tax contributions over the course of their working lives and receive benefits when they retired at age sixty-five. Though the act was signed into law in 1935, the first Social Security benefits were not paid until 1940.

> *We can never insure 100 percent of the population against 100 percent of the hazards and vicissitudes of life, but we have tried to frame a law which will give some measure of protection to the average citizen and to his family against the loss of a job and against poverty-ridden old age.*
>
> – PRESIDENT FRANKLIN D. ROOSEVELT
> upon signing the Social Security Act

I was surprised when I read that in 1935 the average life expectancy in the United States was just sixty-one years. But that number needs to be put into context. The infant mortality rate in the 1930s was quite high, significantly reducing the average life expectancy. More than half of people who lived into adulthood could expect to live to sixty-five. According to the Social Security Administration, a man who retired at sixty-five could expect to collect Social Security for almost thirteen years, and a woman almost fifteen years.

Social Security was a need for many workers who had been negatively impacted by the depression, some losing their life's savings. Through the years, the Social Security program has evolved, and the makeup of American society has changed tremendously, creating a situation that causes many people to believe the system is not sustainable.

In 1940, less than 1 percent of the population received Social Security benefits. In 2017, about 65 million Americans were collecting benefits each month, accounting for about 20 percent of the population. One or more family members in every four families receives a Social Security benefit. While most of that money—about 80 percent—goes to elderly Americans, the system also benefits those who receive Social Security Disability Insurance (SSDI) and children of workers who have died.

All those benefits amount to more than $1 trillion a year, and the fact that the percentage of elderly Americans continues to grow and life expectancy is increasing has some economists worried. About 56 million Americans were sixty-five or older in 2020. By 2035, that number is expected to increase to about 78 million. The percentage of people working and contributing to Social Security will be lower, decreasing from 2.8 workers for each Social Security beneficiary in 2020 to 2.3 workers for each beneficiary in 2035. That is due to a substantial decline in the birth rate between the baby boom period following World War II and the late 1960s. During the baby boom, the birth rate per woman over a lifetime was 3.3 children. That dropped to two children per woman in the latter part of the 1960s, resulting in fewer workers to support more beneficiaries.

It is projected that without meaningful and successful reform, the **Social Security Trust Fund**, which is the surplus of funds resulting from more money being paid into Social Security than is paid out, is expected to be depleted by 2034, a year shy of a century from when the Social Security Act was signed into law. That does not mean that the program will completely disappear, but benefits would need to be reduced by an estimated 25 percent. Someone expecting to receive $2,000 a month in benefits would instead receive only $1,500. When you throw in rising costs of living and the risk of inflation, that does not bode well for those who will be retiring, and the prospect creates a fair amount of anxiety.

MY TAKE

If there was one piece of advice I would give to every young person starting to earn money, it is to sacrifice today for the benefit of tomorrow. Sure, it's fun to buy the latest gadgets and head to the beach on spring break, but spending more now means there will be less to spend when you retire. Saving when you are young is key to ensuring an enjoyable and financially secure retirement.

GRAPHIC

fig. 19

SOCIAL SECURITY

PENSIONS

RETIREMENT SAVINGS

Having read those concerns about the future of Social Security, I hope you understand the danger of relying too much on it for retirement income. Social Security is intended to be one leg of a three-legged stool, the other two legs being a pension and your retirement savings (figure 19). You may not get a pension, and the future of Social Security is not all that secure; this points to your own savings as being essential.

When and How to File for Social Security

Explaining how to file for Social Security benefits is easy. Advising about when to file is more complicated.

If you are closing in on retirement, it's likely you have been paying into Social Security for a long time. If you worked for someone else, that employer has been contributing into the system on your behalf through taxes paid under the Federal Insurance Contributions Act (FICA). If you are self-employed, you have had to pay the combined employer and employee amounts of FICA taxes.

With some exceptions, individuals need to make contributions of at least $1,410 to the Social Security fund over a minimum of forty quarters to be eligible for retirement benefits.

The FICA tax is a combination of taxes to support Social Security and Medicare. In 2020, both employer and employee contributed 6.2 percent of the employee's earnings to Social Security and 1.45 percent to Medicare. Self-employed folks paid the combined amount: 12.4 percent to Social Security and 2.9 percent to Medicare. If you have high earnings, you do not have to pay FICA taxes on all of it. In 2020, employers and employees each paid taxes on up to $137,700 of earnings. A self-employed person paid the employer and employee portions of the tax on earnings up to the same amount.

The Social Security benefits you receive are calculated based on your year of birth, your lifetime earnings, and the age at which you start taking benefits. The amount of benefits you receive is based on your income during the thirty-five years in which your earnings were highest, with adjustments made for increases in the average wage level of workers. Since workers with higher earnings paid more into the system, they generally get more out in benefits. There is a limit on what you can get, though. The maximum amount in 2020 was $3,790 a month.

You can find out what your Social Security benefits will by using the SSA's benefits calculator. Find it at ssa.gov/benefits/calculators. And you can get a record of your contributions at ssa.gov/myaccount.

NOTE

Higher-wage earners invest more into the Social Security system over the course of their careers and will get higher monthly benefits than those who earned lower wages over the course of their careers. The lower-wage worker, however, will receive a higher-percentage benefit than someone who earned more. Someone who earned only 45 percent of the average wage of all workers will receive Social Security benefits upon retiring that will replace about half of their prior income. Someone who earned 160 percent of the average wage of all workers will get benefits replacing only about one-quarter of their prior earnings. Sure, the high-wage earner will still get a bigger payment than the low-wage earner, but the progressive benefits are designed to protect people who worked in low-paying jobs.

The earliest age at which you can collect Social Security is sixty-two. And that is the age at which most people start collecting. According to data from the Social Security Administration, 34.3 percent of Americans jump onto the Social Security bandwagon at age sixty-two—by far the largest cohort of any age between sixty-two and seventy. And more than half of all Americans start collecting before they reach their full retirement age, which varies between sixty-six and sixty-seven, depending on your birth year (figure 20). This comes from a "bird in the hand" mentality, and, while I can understand that sentiment, it is not always the most prudent strategy, because you can only get your full benefit if you wait until your full retirement age. If your full retirement age is sixty-six and you start taking benefits at sixty-two, you will get only three-quarters of your full benefit. Let's look at some pros and cons of turning on Social Security before you reach your full retirement age.

EXAMPLE

If your full retirement age is sixty-six and you start receiving Social Security benefits when you're sixty-two, your full retirement benefit of $1,000 would be reduced to $750 a month—or 25 percent less. If you are married and your spouse is entitled to a spousal benefit, which is a benefit a spouse receives based on their spouse's work history, the *spousal benefit* would be reduced from 50 percent to 35 percent of your benefit.

WHEN PEOPLE CLAIM SOCIAL SECURITY

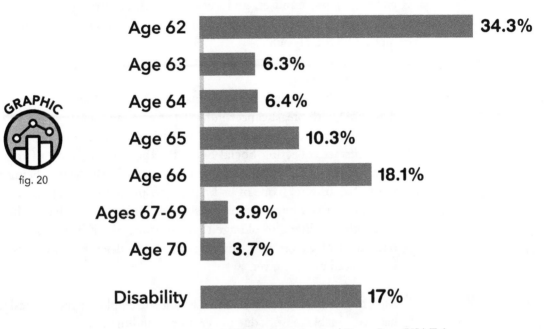

Age 62	34.3%
Age 63	6.3%
Age 64	6.4%
Age 65	10.3%
Age 66	18.1%
Ages 67-69	3.9%
Age 70	3.7%
Disability	17%

fig. 20

source: Social Security Administration | George Petras/USA Today

Reasons to Collect Before Your Full Retirement Age

I am one of many Americans who was lucky to benefit from Social Security early in life, and it set the stage for me to be able to advance my education and, eventually, my career. My parents were older when I was born, and both started collecting Social Security when they were sixty-two. At the time my dad started receiving the benefit I was only seventeen, which meant I also received a monthly benefit. I was able to use that money to pay for classes at the local community college during my senior year of high school, giving me a head start on college. The benefits also meant I didn't have to work during the college academic year, which enabled me to concentrate on my coursework.

While there are many reasons to wait until you reach your full retirement age or longer to begin collecting Social Security, there also are some compelling reasons for certain individuals to start collecting when they turn sixty-two. Maybe you are in poor health and don't expect to reach your full retirement age. Or, if you are looking to start a small business and don't want to dip into your IRA or 401(k) account, it might make sense to start your benefits early.

When to begin taking Social Security depends on personal circumstances, mindset, and outlook for the future. Waiting to start collecting will give you a bigger monthly check but doesn't guarantee the highest lifetime benefits.

Reason #1: Health

Consider this example of a woman I will call Kay, who was first diagnosed with breast cancer in her late forties and underwent a second case in her fifties. She is about to turn sixty-two and has already filed to start collecting Social Security. There are a couple of reasons why collecting early makes sense for her, her health status being the most obvious one. None of us knows how many years we have on this earth, but if you have a family history of longevity, you have a higher probability of living to old age than someone like Kay, whose parents both died of cancer at a fairly young age and whose sister has also experienced breast cancer.

Also, there have been periods when Kay, a self-employed graphic designer, has been unable to work due to her illness, and there is no guarantee that she will stay well and be able to continue earning until her full retirement age of sixty-six and six months. If Kay were my client and asked for my advice, I would consider this a strong argument for her to start collecting when she turns sixty-two.

Reason #2: Loss of Income

A reason other than health to collect at sixty-two is if you lose your job and do not have a steady source of income. Ideally, you have an emergency fund that could carry you through until you find other employment but, unfortunately, finding a comparable job when you are in your sixties is not always easy to do.

If you turn on your Social Security benefits, you could still work and earn up to $18,240 per year (the limit for 2020) without it affecting your benefits. If you earn more than that amount, you will have one dollar withheld from your benefit for every two dollars you earn, effectively cutting the additional earnings in half. If you need Social Security to pay your bills and buy groceries, this may be a compelling reason to begin collecting early.

Reason #3: Capital Opportunity

A third reason it could make sense to take your benefits early is if you will not be relying on Social Security as your primary source of retirement income. Consider this example of a man who started collecting Social Security when he turned sixty-two because he wanted extra income to start a small business and was reluctant to withdraw funds from his IRA or 401(k), both of which were doing well. Taking Social Security early made sense for him because he was able to use it early in his retirement to help fund a business that he was confident would be successful.

When someone needs to start collecting Social Security depends largely on circumstances, and there are plenty of people who have no choice but to take it early. If you are able, however, there are some compelling reasons to wait until you reach at least your full retirement age.

GRAPHIC

fig. 21

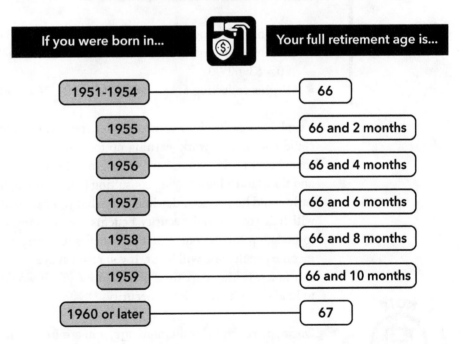

RETIREMENT AGES FOR FULL SOCIAL SECURITY BENEFITS

If you were born in...	Your full retirement age is...
1951-1954	66
1955	66 and 2 months
1956	66 and 4 months
1957	66 and 6 months
1958	66 and 8 months
1959	66 and 10 months
1960 or later	67

Arguments for Waiting Until Full Retirement Age or Later

If it's possible to wait until you reach full retirement age before starting to collect Social Security, you can benefit in several ways. This topic is complex, and we cannot fully explore it in the space allotted in this book.

But it is worth exploring further, and I recommend that you investigate the work of Mary Beth Franklin, a CERTIFIED FINANCIAL PLANNER™ practitioner who speaks and has written extensively about many aspects of Social Security. You can find her books online and watch some videos she has on YouTube.

An important factor to keep in mind is that if you start collecting Social Security before your full retirement age, there is no practical way of going back. Your benefit will be permanently reduced. You will get cost-of-living adjustments (COLAs), but you will not receive your full benefit, even when you reach your full retirement age. And because your benefit is lower, your COLAs, which are a percentage of your benefit, will also be lower.

Robert lives to be eighty-six years old. The age at which he starts taking Social Security benefits will make a big difference in the total amount he will collect. To figure it out, we'll multiply the monthly benefit amount times twelve months times the number of years over which he collects.

» Begins collecting at age 62: $1,200 x 12 x 24 = $345,600
» Begins collecting at age 66 (his full retirement age): $1,650 x 12 x 20 = $396,000
» Begins collecting at age 70: $2,100 x 12 x 16 = $403,200

I explained earlier how someone who starts collecting at age sixty-two could continue to work, earning up to $18,240 a year without affecting their benefits. However, say you begin collecting Social Security early and then land a high-paying consulting job; having opted to take benefits early could be a serious detriment to what you can earn. The government will halt your Social Security benefits for as many months as it takes to make up for the one dollar in benefits for every two dollars of work income penalty you will incur. If you retire at age sixty-two but expect to continue working part-time in a lucrative job, it would be better for you to hold off on taking Social Security.

Once you reach full retirement age, you are free to earn any amount of salary without having your benefits reduced.

Many, but not all, who receive Social Security pay federal income taxes on their benefits. A formula calculated by the Social Security Administration and based on income determines the percentage of Social Security benefits that are considered taxable income. If your income is under a certain amount your benefits will not be taxed, but if you exceed that amount, you will have to pay taxes on 50 to 85 percent of your benefits. The Social Security Administration lists the income amounts at which your benefits will be taxed at www.ssa.gov/benefits/retirement/planner/taxes.html.

Waiting until full retirement age to start Social Security not only assures you of higher benefits, it may also increase the amount of benefits your spouse will receive in the event of your death. If you are married and your benefits are more than what your spouse gets, your benefit rate will replace your spouse's rate if you die.

Another option is to defer benefits until you're past full retirement age; you can choose to receive *delayed retirement credits* until you are seventy. For each year you hold off on taking benefits after your full retirement age, you earn 8 percent of your *primary insurance amount*, which is the amount of your full retirement age benefit.

Barbara and her husband, Jon, are the same age and both retire when they are sixty-six and a half—their full retirement age. Barbara's primary insurance amount of $2,200 a month is slightly higher than Jon's, and she begins receiving benefits when she retires. Barbara and Jon both get relatively high-paying part-time jobs and determine they can live well on that income and Barbara's benefits. Jon delays his benefits and receives delayed retirement credits, meaning he accrues 8 percent a year on his primary insurance amount until he is seventy. Therefore, when Jon turns seventy and starts receiving benefits, he will earn nearly a third more than he would have at age sixty-six.

Again, deciding when to turn on your Social Security benefits is a personal decision, with arguments to be made for taking benefits early and for deferring them as long as you can. Do your homework, assess your personal situation, and seek advice from a professional if you need to. With Social Security an essential part of retirement income for many, when and how you take it is important.

How to File for Social Security

Filing for Social Security, believe it or not, is simple, something that cannot be said for many tasks involving a federal agency. You can access and complete an application online at ssa.gov. The online application is available seven days a week, but not twenty-four hours a day. You can access it from 5:00 a.m. until 1:00 a.m. (eastern time) Monday through Friday, from 5:00 a.m. until 11:00 p.m. on Saturday, and from 8:00 a.m. until 11:30 p.m. on Sunday.

You must be at least sixty-one and nine months old to apply for benefits, and you can request your benefits to start no more than four months in the future. You can also apply for spousal benefits online. If for some reason you do not wish to file an online application, you can call the Social Security Administration at 1-800-772-1213 or visit your local SSA office.

IN PRACTICE: While it's possible to apply for Social Security benefits in person or over the phone, I believe it's probably better to enroll online. Employees in the Social Security office are not your fiduciaries and may not always advocate for your best interests regarding the benefits you receive. Applying online ensures that you can choose the strategy that benefits you the most.

Now let's have a look at another leg of the three-legged stool: pensions.

Pensions

Even after many years, it is difficult for me to talk about pensions. My father made a terrible mistake when claiming his pension, and it still pains me. Acting on advice from a friend with no financial education, my dad took the pension in his name only, with no survivorship benefits. He did this because it paid out more each month than a plan that came with survivorship benefits, but it resulted in a terrible loss for my mother. My dad died only thirteen years after activating his pension, leaving my mother with no income from it for the rest of her life, which was another twenty-five years. Clearly, he acted on some advice that was good for his friend's situation, but not for his own, and his decision negatively affected my mom for years. That action played a large part in why I decided to become a CFP® practitioner—so I could help hardworking people, like my dad and mom, to build a more secure financial future. Base your financial decisions on what is best for your family's needs rather than someone else's.

In chapter 1, I mentioned that pensions used to be a common source of retirement income for workers in a wide range of businesses and industries. Everybody from bankers to factory workers looked forward to retiring and getting a nice pension that, along with Social Security, would provide a stable financial situation. But companies started moving away from pensions, for reasons including costs, financial risks for employers, high mandatory funding requirements, a decline in the influence that unions once had, and the rise of other types of retirement savings plans, such as 401(k)s.

According to the Department of Labor's Employee Benefits Security Administration, the number of pension plans offering defined benefits (which guarantee the benefits) decreased 73 percent between 1986 and 2016, and you can bet the number has dropped even more since then. According to Mercer's 2020 Defined Benefit Outlook, more than half of companies still offering defined benefit pension plans are considering terminating them within the next five years.

A lot of pension funds have suffered due to low interest rates and for other reasons, and many funds are no longer viable enough to meet their obligations over time. General Electric, in late 2019, offered lump sum pension buyouts to about 100,000 former employees who had not yet started collecting their pensions, and other large companies are following suit. If you are getting a pension, consider yourself fortunate. If you are working for a company that offers pensions, be wary. And if you are just starting out in your career, do not necessarily expect to land a job that comes with a pension plan.

It is a different story, however, if you are a public employee and work for a federal, state, county, or municipal government. Workers at state colleges and universities, law enforcement officers, firefighters, judges, public health workers, city and county planners, social workers, and other public workers are still likely to qualify for pensions. In fact, according to the Pension Rights Center, an organization founded in 1976 that works to ensure that Americans will have enough money to live on in retirement, three-quarters of all state and local government workers participate in a pension plan, and even more are eligible for pensions but do not participate.

All of the US government's civilian employees are covered by the *Federal Employees Retirement System* (FERS), under which employees receive retirement benefits from a pension, Social Security, and the *Thrift Savings Plan*, which is similar to a 401(k) plan. If that sounds like a good deal to you, it should. The FERS is considered one of the best retirement plans available.

10 JOBS
Likely To Offer Traditional Pensions

GRAPHIC

fig. 22

 Teacher

 State and Local Government

 Utilities

Protective Services

Insurance

 Pharmaceuticals

 Nurse

 Transportation

 Military

 Union Jobs

source: U.S. News

Although workers covered by the Federal Employees Retirement System pay into and receive Social Security benefits, not all public workers participate. In some states, public employees, including teachers, do not contribute to Social Security and will not get benefits from it when they retire. These employees fall under the *public sector exemption from Social Security*. If they remain in the same state retirement system, they will qualify for state pensions when they retire. However, many teachers don't remain in the system long enough to qualify for a pension, and others, depending on the type of plan, end up with pensions that are worth less than the contributions they've made. States in which public employees do not pay into Social Security are Alaska, California, Colorado, Connecticut, Illinois, Louisiana, Maine, Massachusetts, Missouri, Nevada, Ohio, and Texas. Three other states—Georgia, Kentucky, and Rhode Island—have different levels of coverage for public employees, meaning that some participate in Social Security and others do not.

Like many private pension funds, some public pension funds have fallen on hard times. As government agencies at every level are looking for ways to cut costs, many are considering alternative, less costly forms of retirement plans when hiring new employees.

If you have a pension, there are some considerations to keep in mind. A plus for pensions is that, because they are defined benefit plans, you know how much you will be paid in retirement. That is helpful for planning purposes.

Unlike 401(k)s or IRAs, pensions are usually managed by a division of the company or government entity that offers them. Sometimes a third party, like an insurance company, manages them. Having a pension means that your employer contributes money on your behalf, for your future benefit.

Q: How is pension money invested and who is in charge?

Investing pension money involves an investment team that formulates an investment policy statement. That team typically includes the following:

» An actuary who makes sure the money is invested in a sustainable manner and determines how much money needs to be put into the fund each year
» A third-party administrator (TPA) who performs tax filing and compliance testing for the plan
» An investment management team that provides access to the securities market so that the fund can grow based on the assumptions of the actuary and the TPA
» The employer that sponsors the defined benefit pension plan

If you have a pension through a private employer, you should get a notice every year telling you how well-funded the plan is. You can also find the funding status of your plan on the website of the Securities and Exchange Commission (SEC) at www.sec.gov. Ideally, the fund is *fully funded*, which means it has enough assets to cover both the benefits it currently pays and those it will need to pay in the future. An *underfunded pension* is one that does not have enough assets to fund its obligations, and an *unfunded plan* is one that uses company income to make pension payments as it becomes necessary to do so. Unfunded plans also are known as pay-as-you-go plans, as there are no assets set aside.

While some pensions are fully funded, most are not, and some are woefully underfunded. The Teachers Retirement System pension in Texas is considered a sound plan, and it is funded at only 77 percent.

Public pensions are not overseen by the SEC, but those enrolled in public pensions can keep an eye on them by accessing a report by the Pew Charitable Trusts, a nonprofit that works to inform the public and improve public policy. The organization analyzes and reports on many public pensions. You can find their latest reports at pewtrusts.org/topics/retirement.

A big decision for pensioned employees who are preparing to retire is whether to go the traditional route and elect to receive a monthly pension payment, or to take a lump sum. Let's look at some of the benefits and risks of each of those options.

Taking a Monthly Pension Benefit

A monthly pension benefit is a beautiful thing. You know how much the payment will be and you can count on it coming every month for the rest of your life. Depending on the plan, benefits might even continue for your spouse after your death. Some pensions come with COLAs (cost-of-living adjustments), but not all do, so that is something you would want to know before deciding between a monthly benefit and a lump sum (figure 23).

Another factor to consider is the financial health of your company. It would be quite stressful to be counting on a monthly pension check amid rumors or news that the company offering the benefit is in serious financial trouble. Fortunately, even if the company's pension plan fails, pensioners have a small safety net in the Pension Benefit Guaranty Corporation (PBGC), a federal agency that will step in to pay at least some of the benefits. Employers who offer a defined benefit plan are obligated to pay premiums to the PBGC, which would be used to benefit employees in the event the pension plan failed. There's no guarantee of getting your full pension, but you may receive some payment. In 2020, the maximum monthly benefit guaranteed by the PBGC was $5,812 for most people who retire at age sixty-five. That amount is adjusted downward for those retiring earlier than sixty-five and upward for those retiring later. If your monthly pension payments were higher than the maximum guaranteed by the PBGC, you would stand to see reductions to your benefit in the event your company's pension failed.

If you are a government employee, the government can act as a sovereign power and elect to lower the amount of your benefits. That happened to Detroit's municipal workers in 2013 when the city filed for bankruptcy protection and thousands of workers had their pensions cut by 4.5 percent. To add insult to injury, cost-of-living adjustments were also cut, and health care benefits were reduced.

If you like the idea of having monthly benefits you can count on and plan around, the traditional benefit option makes sense, especially if your family has a strong history of longevity. Some retirees, however, take a different view.

Taking a Lump Sum

If you decide to take your pension as a lump sum, it is yours to spend in the manner you see fit. You could take the trip of a lifetime, traveling around the world and seeing sights you had only dreamed of. You could put the money in a savings account, ensuring its safety, or you could invest it with the intent that its value would increase over time.

One option is to put the money in an IRA and invest it in stocks, bonds, or mutual funds. Or you could build your own pension by investing in an annuity, a financial product that provides an income stream. (You will read more about annuities in the next chapter.) Using the pension money to buy an annuity ensures that you would be able to leave the unused amount to a non-spouse beneficiary, something you cannot always do with a corporate pension.

IN PRACTICE: I educate all my retiring clients on the lump sum option for pensions. I believe that taking the lump sum gives them greater flexibility and control over their money because it is in their hands. Many clients value control over a slightly higher monthly payment.

Some of my clients have told me they prefer the lump sum option because it puts them in control of their money, and they can invest it and have assets to pass along to children and grandchildren when they die. That's fine if you are a seasoned investor, but if not, I strongly recommend you get some advice from a CFP® practitioner before taking that step, as a pension payout may be the largest amount of money ever to come your way, and it is likely that you will need to depend on it as retirement income.

If a retiree takes a company pension benefit, it is critically important to understand the options, as they can be confusing. Choosing the wrong option may create a major unintended consequence: disinheriting your spouse and children.

Because income from pensions is usually subject to federal taxes, it might make sense to roll over the lump sum into an IRA. That way, you can control when you withdraw money you will need to pay taxes on. You must start taking required minimum distributions from your IRA when you turn seventy-two, but your money can remain tax-deferred in the IRA until then.

REASONS FOR PREFERRING GUARANTEED LIFETIME INCOME

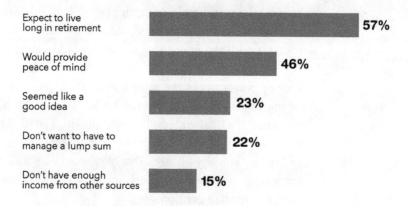

Expect to live long in retirement	57%
Would provide peace of mind	46%
Seemed like a good idea	23%
Don't want to have to manage a lump sum	22%
Don't have enough income from other sources	15%

fig. 23

REASONS FOR PREFERRING A LUMP SUM

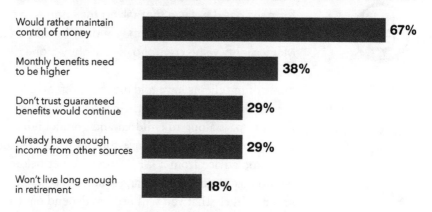

Would rather maintain control of money	67%
Monthly benefits need to be higher	38%
Don't trust guaranteed benefits would continue	29%
Already have enough income from other sources	29%
Won't live long enough in retirement	18%

source: LIMRA Secure Retirement Income (2018)

Reasons consumers choose either guaranteed lifetime income or a lump sum

Some states tax pension income and others do not. You are in luck if you live in Alaska, Florida, Illinois, Mississippi, Nevada, New Hampshire, Pennsylvania, South Dakota, Tennessee, Texas, Washington, or Wyoming—all states that do not tax pensions. Some other states decline to tax certain types of pension income, but not all.

Another option is to roll over the lump sum payment into an IRA and then use some of the money in the IRA to buy an *immediate annuity* from an insurance company. An immediate annuity will give you guaranteed and ongoing benefits for an agreed-upon period.

"Guarantees" are based on the claim-paying ability of the issuer.

Immediate annuity payouts, which typically are turned on within a year of when you buy the annuity and often much sooner than that, can continue over as little as five years or be drawn out over your lifetime. This option ensures that you have an income stream but also have money invested in an IRA that, hopefully, can keep pace with inflation and cover unexpected expenses.

Deciding what to do with a large sum of money should involve careful thought and planning. The primary concern is ensuring you will have enough money to live on throughout your retirement, regardless of how many years that might be. For most people, Social Security and a pension are important pieces of retirement income but do not provide the entire picture.

Retirement income is a three-legged stool: Social Security, pension, and income from your retirement accounts.

Chapter Recap

» While many Americans rely on Social Security as a major part of their retirement income, other sources of income also are necessary.

» It may make sense to start collecting Social Security at age sixty-two if you experience many health problems, if you lose your job and need the income, or if you want the benefits at an early age to fund a venture from which you will benefit later.

» Consider waiting until you are at least sixty-seven to start taking Social Security if you want to collect your full amount, be able to work and earn money without penalty, or have a strong family history of longevity.

» Pensions are still common for public employees, but most private companies have eliminated or reduced pension plans.

» Consider benefits and risks when deciding whether to take monthly pension benefits or accept a lump sum.

| 7 |
Annuities

Chapter Overview
- » An Annuity Provides an Income Stream
- » Types of Annuities
- » Immediate or Deferred Payouts
- » Fees and Value

Just about every expert who has studied annuities believes they are the most effective safeguard against "longevity risk," or the possibility of outliving your wealth.

– MOSHE MILEVSKY

Annuities are a financial product that people seem to either love or hate. Moshe Milevsky, a respected professor of finance at the Schulich School of Business at York University in Toronto, has gone on record as saying everyone should have some annuities as part of their financial and investment plans. Then there are other advisors who steer clients away from anything resembling an annuity.

IN PRACTICE: Personally, I wouldn't say I love annuities, but I do think they make sense for the right situation. Whether you should purchase annuities depends on circumstances such as other sources of income, the size of your portfolio, and your tolerance for or aversion to risk. A good financial advisor can help you determine whether an annuity would fit into your financial plan and be beneficial for your personal situation.

Information pertaining to annuities can be confusing. Critics warn of the expenses associated with these financial products, while advocates tout the advantages of the guaranteed income they provide. Many people who do not receive pensions buy annuities because they don't want Social Security to be their only source of lifelong fixed income.

An *annuity* is a financial product that provides an income stream over a specified amount of time or for life. It is a contract between you and an insurance company. You can buy annuities from virtually any insurance company. Just remember that when dealing with one company you will probably get to see only that company's product. A better way to go may be to buy your annuity through a CFP® practitioner who can shop the market for you to find the best options for your situation. Once you've decided on the annuity you want, you agree to pay either a lump sum or a series of contributions to the company that sells it, and the company agrees to return that money to you in the form of regular benefits later.

In addition to the consistent cash flow, all annuities carry the advantages of tax deferral and inheritance, meaning you can designate one or more beneficiaries to inherit the annuity money. Assets in an annuity grow tax deferred until you begin to withdraw them. Annuities are often appropriate for people who have contributed the maximum amounts to 401(k) plans and IRAs, because some of the same tax advantages are available with annuities as with those types of accounts.

Recall from the previous chapter that I discussed the strategy of opting to take a pension payment in a lump sum and using some of that money to purchase an annuity. If you roll the lump sum pension over into an IRA, then withdraw some of the money to buy an annuity, you are leaving some funds in an account with growth potential while using other funds to guarantee income in the future.

The period during which you pay money to the insurance company is called the *accumulation phase*, and the period during which you get money back is the *annuitization phase*.

There are other methods for taking money out of an annuity besides annuitization, but they are beyond the scope of this book. Thus, for purposes of our discussion, we will assume annuitization is the principal way by which annuity owners withdraw funds.

Annuities are an insurance product because they transfer risk from you, the owner of the annuity, to the insurance company. The risk you are covering is longevity risk, the risk that you will outlive your money.

If you are getting tired of reading about longevity as a risk, I understand. We are so conditioned to think about longevity as a good thing that referring to it as a risk seems counterintuitive. The fact is, though, many people outlive their money and end up struggling with small, fixed incomes from Social Security or another source. An annuity transfers the risk for potential longevity from you to the insurance company by guaranteeing an income over your lifetime.

NOTE

While some people are critical of annuities, there are a whole lot of folks who like them because they provide peace of mind. Total sales of annuities reached $241.7 billion in 2019, the highest yearly total since 2008, according to the Secure Retirement Institute Fourth Quarter U.S. Annuity Sales Survey and reported in *Financial Advisor* magazine.

All annuities serve the purpose of providing income, but not all annuities are the same. I will start by breaking them down into the broad categories of fixed, indexed, and variable annuities. Then we'll discuss the differences between annuities that are "immediate" and those that are "deferred." The key distinctions, simply put, are expressed in figure 24.

fig. 24

ANNUITY TYPES

FIXED ANNUITY	INDEXED ANNUITY	VARIABLE ANNUITY	IMMEDIATE ANNUITY	DEFERRED ANNUITY
· Guaranteed payment at future date · Can be immediate or deferred · Surrender period varies in length · Low risk	· Can provide a return with a rise of a market index, such as the S&P 500 · Contains features of both fixed and variable annuities · If index is negative, annuity is credited with 0% interest	· You invest your money from a range of subaccounts · Carries more risk but also increases possibility for profit · Value of the annuity dependent on performance of subaccounts	· Begins payments shortly after it is purchased · Can be either fixed or variable · Also known as income annuity	· Payments begin at a future date, selected by annuity owner · Can be fixed, indexed, or variable · Money grows on a tax-deferred basis

Fixed, Indexed, and Variable Annuities

A *fixed annuity* can be compared to a certificate of deposit you would get at a bank. You hand over a certain amount of money and the bank agrees to pay a specified interest rate over a given period. With an annuity, you hand your money over to an insurance company rather than a bank, and the insurance company pays you interest. You sign a contract that states how much interest you will receive, and the length of the *surrender period* of the annuity. The surrender period, sometimes called the surrender charge period, is the period during which you cannot withdraw money from your annuity without incurring a penalty. Surrender periods vary in length. Normally, the penalty you pay for withdrawing money before the end of the surrender period decreases over time. For instance, if your surrender period is seven years and you take out money after two years, you might incur a 5 percent penalty. If you wait six years before withdrawing funds, you may only be charged 1 percent.

A criticism of annuities is that the interest you earn is low compared to average stock market returns. At the time of this writing, interest rates on a fixed annuity with a three-year surrender period ranged from about 1.75 percent to 2.25 percent. Rates on a ten-year-surrender-period annuity ranged between 1.80 percent and 3.25 percent. When you compare that to an average annual return of 9 percent in the stock market, the rates are low.

The upside, of course, is that with guaranteed interest rates you don't have to worry about losing your money, as is a possibility with the stock market. You perhaps should be concerned, though, that inflation can take its toll on the purchasing power of a low-interest annuity. Another benefit of an annuity is that you know ahead of time how much income you will get when the annuitization phase starts, which can be helpful for budgeting and planning.

An *indexed annuity* provides some features of a fixed annuity but also offers the possibility that your money can grow if the financial markets perform well. They are often referred to as hybrids, as they contain features of both a fixed annuity and a *variable annuity*, which is a type of annuity that gains or loses value depending on the performance of the subaccounts on which it is based. In the event the index is negative in any given year, an indexed annuity will be credited with 0 percent interest for that same time, meaning that you incur no downside risk. If there is a rise in the performance of a market index, such as the S&P 500, to which the annuity is tied, you can get a return. Even though indexed annuity owners are not directly invested in an index, they can benefit if the financial markets perform well. However, most contracts call for a cap on gains, so your earnings will not be as high as the actual gain in the index. Generally, indexed annuities are considered riskier than fixed annuities but do not carry as much risk as variable annuities.

NOTE

Fixed annuities credit interest each year, indexed annuities may not credit any interest if the index they are tied to is negative, and variable annuities can lose value just like a 401(k) in a year when financial markets are down, if there are no other guarantee riders purchased on the annuity. Indexed annuities have become popular in recent years, with sales reaching $73.5 billion in 2019, up 6 percent from 2018, according to the LIMRA Secure Retirement Institute, a trade association.

With a variable annuity you choose where to invest your money from a range of subaccounts, and the value of the annuity will vary depending on the performance of the investments within the subaccounts. There is no guaranteed rate of return as there is with a fixed or indexed annuity.

NOTE

Before purchasing any annuity, investors should obtain and read a copy of the prospectus from the company.

As with any investment, the increased risk associated with a variable annuity also means an increased possibility for profit. Though fixed and indexed annuities offer a higher degree of safety, the returns will likely not be as high as with a variable annuity. In fact, with a fixed or indexed annuity, you need to make sure you are earning enough interest to at least keep up with a historical average 3 percent inflation rate, or you will risk losing purchasing power.

NOTE

Some fixed and variable annuity contracts allow you to add cost-of-living adjustment riders for an extra fee.

On the other side of the risk/benefit equation, however, is the possibility that a variable annuity could lose value while your money is invested. If you are experienced with subaccount investing and understand the risks involved, or you are looking at a long investment period before you will start taking regular payouts, a variable annuity may make sense. If you are not comfortable choosing investments, you may be better off with a fixed or indexed annuity.

Immediate and Deferred Annuities

As explained in chapter 6, an immediate annuity is one where benefits begin shortly after it is purchased. A **deferred annuity**, on the other hand, does not begin payouts until a future date, selected by the annuity owner.

Many people who are retired or close to retiring buy immediate annuities, also known as single-premium immediate annuities (SPIAs) or income annuities. Immediate annuities appeal to this cohort because there is no accumulation phase and payouts can begin quickly. You hand over a lump sum and choose how often you want benefits to be paid to you—usually monthly, quarterly, semiannually, or annually.

Immediate annuities can provide income for the rest of your life, or for a specific period such as ten or twenty years. Most immediate annuities come with fixed payouts for the period of the contract, but some companies offer immediate variable annuities. Some immediate annuities contain inflation protection, meaning that your benefit may increase to keep up with inflation, like COLAs.

NOTE

If you are thinking about buying an annuity, it's fun to plug in some hypothetical numbers and see what your monthly payouts would be. You can find an annuity calculator that's easy to use and provides a lot of options at calculator.net/annuity-calculator.html.

If not structured properly, benefits with an immediate annuity may end with the death of the owner, with the insurance company keeping any balance. That would be a disastrous mistake that would negatively impact the surviving spouse's financial future, so be sure you understand exactly how the annuity operates. If you buy an immediate annuity with no survivorship benefits when you are sixty-five and die when you are seventy, the insurance company benefits because you have only received five annual payouts. If you live to be ninety-five, on the other hand, you are likely to end up getting benefits greater than what you put in.

A deferred annuity can be fixed, indexed, or variable. Regardless of which type, they grow on a tax-deferred basis, meaning your money won't be taxed until you start receiving your payouts. At that point, the withdrawals are taxed as ordinary income. If you buy the annuity with money from an IRA or other tax-advantaged retirement plan, you might be able to deduct the cost of the annuity from your taxable income.

A potential downside of deferred annuities is their lack of liquidity. Most contracts limit the amount of money you can take out each year, depending on the contract, and if you are under age fifty-nine and a half, you may pay a 10 percent penalty on withdrawals in addition to income tax if the contract is not structured properly.

Choosing the Right Annuity

Annuities are complex financial products. They come in many flavors, have tax and estate planning implications, and can keep your money tied up for a long period of time. They also come with a lot of add-ons and optional plans, some of which I mentioned earlier. The more protections and riders you add, the lower your regular benefit will be. Still, some of those protections may be worth considering. For instance, ***premium protection*** guarantees you will get at least as much money back in benefits as you originally invested. If you die before that occurs, your heirs will receive the rest of what you would have gotten in benefits.

Expenses associated with annuities turn some people off from the idea of buying them. It's important, when thinking about an annuity, to thoroughly understand the terms of the contract before signing, because some policies carry much higher expenses than others. Different types of annuities are associated with different expenses, and, generally, the more complicated the annuity, the higher the expenses will be. However, if you add the right features to your contract, the expense could be well worth the benefit you receive. Fixed annuities come with lower expenses than the variable and indexed varieties. That is because they are relatively simple, not linked to investment portfolios or indexes, and pay at a fixed rate.

More complicated annuities charge higher ***commissions***, which are a portion of the expense of the annuity given to the agent or broker who sold it. Commission costs are normally built into the price of the annuity and may not be specifically mentioned in the contract. Commissions can vary widely, ranging from 1 and 10 percent of the total value of the contract. However, if you purchase the annuity through a CFP® practitioner or an RIA, both of which have fiduciary responsibility to the buyer, there may be no commission involved. By contrast, some insurance agents who sell annuities may have access to a limited product variety, may be captive to sell only one company's annuity, or may try to promote an annuity that carries a high commission.

There are expenses associated with most financial products, including 401(k)s and IRAs. It is always a good idea to be sure you understand the expenses you will incur with any type of investment, and to weigh the value against the expenses.

Annuities might not be for everyone, despite Milevsky's assertion, but I think many retirees can benefit from them. One of the best features of annuities is the peace of mind that comes with knowing you will have a guaranteed stream of income. According to a recent Gallup poll, more than half of American adults are worried about not having enough money for retirement. Maybe the security of annuity income can be what helps you sleep at night. If the benefits of annuities hold great value for you, the fees you incur may be well worth it.

As stated previously, indexed and variable annuities are complex products. The intricacies of annuity contracts are not easy to understand. Ensure that the advisor you work with knows the product well. If he or she doesn't, neither might you. This could result in your being stuck in the contract until the surrender charge expires, upwards of seven to ten years, or more on some contracts.

Annuity Fun Facts

Who said annuities can't be fun? Here are a few fun facts about annuities:

» **Fact 1: You can use annuities to support your favorite charities.**
You can set up a charitable gift annuity that enables you to continue contributing to a charity that's important to you after you die, or use annuity money to support a family member who has financial needs.

» **Fact 2: Dissatisfied? You can swap one annuity for another—but beware.**
There is a clause in the IRS tax code called the "1035 exchange option." The 1035 lets you exchange one annuity for another while avoiding some IRS penalties that could apply. However, be aware that employing the 1035 option may still result in surrender charges on your current contract, which would decrease the value of your annuity. Using the 1035 exchange option may be possible but is not always a smart move.

Be aware that exchanging one annuity for another could mean the surrender period begins anew, sometimes for ten years or even longer. If you plan to start taking money from the annuity before the surrender period ends, you could incur penalties of several percentage points on each withdrawl.

» **Fact 3: You can take a tax-deductible loss on your annuity.**
Many people assume that since an annuity is a tax-deferred vehicle, they won't be able to deduct any losses from their taxes. What they don't know is that there is a little-known IRS rule, Rule 16-201, that provides the opportunity to take a tax-deductible loss on an annuity contract.

A.M. BEST		S&P		MOODY'S		FITCH RATINGS	
A++	SUPERIOR	AAA	EXTREMELY STRONG	Aaa	EXCEPTIONAL	AAA	EXCEPTIONALLY STRONG
A+	SUPERIOR	AA+	VERY STRONG	Aa1	EXCELLENT	AA+	VERY STRONG
A	EXCELLENT	AA	VERY STRONG	Aa2	EXCELLENT	AA	VERY STRONG
A-	EXCELLENT	AA-	VERY STRONG	Aa3	EXCELLENT	AA-	VERY STRONG
B++	GOOD	A+	STRONG	A1	GOOD	A+	STRONG
B+	GOOD	A	STRONG	A2	GOOD	A	STRONG
B	FAIR	A-	STRONG	A3	GOOD	A-	STRONG
B-	FAIR	BBB+	GOOD	Baa1	ADEQUATE	BBB+	GOOD
C++	MARGINAL	BBB	GOOD	Baa2	ADEQUATE	BBB	GOOD
C+	MARGINAL	BBB-	GOOD	Baa3	ADEQUATE	BBB-	GOOD
C	WEAK	BB+	MARGINAL	Ba1	QUESTIONABLE	BB+	MARGINAL
C-	WEAK	BB	MARGINAL	Ba2	QUESTIONABLE	BB	MARGINAL
D	POOR	BB-	MARGINAL	Ba3	QUESTIONABLE	BB-	MARGINAL
E	UNDER REGULATORY SUPERVISION	B+	WEAK	B1	POOR	B+	WEAK
F	IN LIQUIDATION	B	WEAK	B2	POOR	B	WEAK
		B-	WEAK	B3	POOR	B-	WEAK
		CCC+	VERY WEAK	Caa1	VERY POOR	CCC+	VERY WEAK
		CCC	VERY WEAK	Caa2	VERY POOR	CCC	VERY WEAK
		CCC-	VERY WEAK	Caa3	VERY POOR	CCC-	VERY WEAK
		CC	EXTREMELY WEAK	Ca	EXTREMELY POOR	CC	EXTREMELY WEAK
				C	LOWEST	C	DISTRESSED

GRAPHIC

fig. 25

source: AnnuityAdvantage

Scales used by rating agencies to indicate the financial strength of insurance companies

> » **Fact 4: You can (and should) check the rating of your prospective annuity company.**
> Insurance companies that offer annuities are graded by rating agencies on their ability to pay the benefits they promise to customers. A.M. Best is a rating agency that focuses only on the insurance industry, so you will often see A.M. Best ratings when you compare annuities. Different rating agencies use different lettering systems in their ratings. An insurance company rated A++ or A+ by A.M. Best is considered "superior," and companies rated A or A- are considered "excellent" (figure 25).

There is a lot to unpack when it comes to annuities, and it is probably best to consult with a CFP® practitioner whom you trust before purchasing.

As noted in chapter 1, working with a CFP® practitioner or registered investment advisor can provide peace of mind and confidence that a professional is working in your best interests.

Chapter Recap

> » An annuity provides income over a specific period or for the rest of your life.

> » Different types of annuities carry varying degrees of risk.

> » Some annuity benefits begin shortly after purchase, while others are deferred.

> » Annuities carry fees and costs but can provide highly valued peace of mind and security.

| 8 |

Reaping the Rewards
of Sound Retirement Planning

Chapter Overview
» Generating Income through Portfolio Withdrawals
» How to Minimize Your Taxes
» Claiming Dividend Income
» Starting a Business
» Real Estate Income

Wealth is not his that has it, but his that enjoys it.

– BENJAMIN FRANKLIN

I'm thinking about a television commercial that ran a few years ago. A retirement-aged father, his son, and their spouses have finished eating dinner in a nice restaurant and a waiter brings the check to their table. The father and son reach for it at the same time, with the father eventually allowing the son to take it. All the while, the father and son are looking at one another and worrying about the other's financial situation—the father hoping his son is saving enough for retirement and the son concerned about whether his father has already saved enough.

The planning and saving you did during the design phase of your retirement has, hopefully, resulted in a respectable portfolio that will enable you to retire and maintain a comfortable standard of living. The point of all that planning and saving, after all, is to be able to reap the benefits and enjoy your retirement.

IN PRACTICE: I am most often hired by couples planning a joint retirement. I make clear that in order to do the best job I can for them, they should hire me not only to manage their investments, but also to coordinate multiple aspects of their financial planning, covering all the content found in this book. Two important facets are helping them to know, based on collaborative assumptions, how much money they need to have accumulated by retirement, and the sustainability of distributions over their joint lifetime based on those assumptions. Many of my clients come to me not knowing these projections. You need to know these numbers.

Chapter 4 dealt with the calculation of post-retirement expenses, finding an answer to that all-important question, How much will I need during retirement? But people still find themselves wondering whether they have enough saved, even after making these calculations and projections. As a result, they often ask about supplementing their retirement income, either with a part-time job, withdrawals from their portfolio, rental income, or other means.

Finding ways to supplement your income makes sense on several levels. First, it can shore up your financial situation, so you don't need to worry if the refrigerator breaks down or your car needs a major repair. We know that unexpected health care costs can strain a budget. Knowing you have some extra cash on hand to pay for those expenses can be reassuring. And, if inflation becomes an issue, you might find that additional earnings can help make up for income that is not keeping pace with rising rates of inflation.

An obvious way to supplement your retirement income is by getting a job. Surveys reveal that the number of retirees who are working has increased, along with the number of soon-to-be-retirees planning to work after retirement. The LIMRA Secure Retirement Institute reported in 2019 that nearly one in five retirees is working part time, and 27 percent say they plan to work part time in retirement.

According to the American Association of Retired Persons (AARP), the ten most common part-time jobs held by workers who are fifty-five and older are full-charge bookkeeper, bookkeeper, dental hygienist, school bus driver, office manager, registered nurse, administrative assistant, secretary, licensed practical nurse, and paralegal.

Ideally, you would find a job that not only generates extra income but provides fulfillment and a sense of purpose. Think about what you most enjoy doing and what you do well. If you love golfing, you might get a part-time job at a golf course that comes with the perk of free rounds. If you enjoy crafting jewelry, perhaps there's a shop in your community that would be happy to offer what you make to its customers. Perhaps you're an excellent pianist and would enjoy teaching children to play.

There are many organizations dedicated to doing good work in the interest of bettering society. If you are thinking of finding a job, consider working for a nonprofit that addresses desperate situations such as poverty, food insecurity, suicide prevention, or human trafficking. You would not only experience the financial benefits of a job, but the satisfaction of knowing you are working to help improve lives.

Looking forward to doing a job you enjoy provides benefits that go far beyond extra income. Having a job can help you maintain social connections, keep you physically active, and provide a feeling of satisfaction. As mentioned earlier, however, a job is not the only way to generate income during retirement. Let's start by looking at the possibilities and implications of withdrawing money from your portfolio.

Making Portfolio Withdrawals

When you were designing your retirement, you established retirement accounts like IRAs and 401(k)s. The next rung of the investment ladder may be investing in stocks, bonds, and perhaps some real estate, either through REITs or buying an investment property to rent out. If you started investing early enough and were diligent about it, chances are those accounts are well "stocked," so to speak, and will see you through what hopefully will be a long and successful retirement, with you reaping the rewards of your hard work and investing discipline. However, many people who have retirement and brokerage accounts are uncertain about when and how to withdraw money from them.

If you have a 401(k) or a traditional IRA, you will need to start taking *required minimum distributions* at age seventy-two. The amount you will need to take is calculated by dividing the prior year-end balance of your account by a life expectancy factor determined by the IRS. You can find a required minimum distribution calculator on Investor.gov, the US Securities and Exchange Commission's website:

For an required minimum distribution calculator and other free Digital Assets for this title, visit go.quickstartguides.com/retirement

You do not have to take required minimum distributions from a 401(k) account if you are still working after you turn seventy-two and do not own at least 5 percent of the company. But you must take required minimum distributions from a traditional IRA at that age.

IMPORTANT

It is imperative that you be aware of how much you are required to take in minimum distributions. The penalty for not taking a required minimum distribution is 50 percent of the difference between what you should have taken and what you have taken for that calendar year. Be sure to take at least your minimum distribution each year.

EXAMPLE

Mark's account balance was $200,000 at the end of 2019. When 2020 ended, Mark was seventy-four years old. His required distribution was $8,403.36. Unfortunately, Mark did not understand the requirement and withdrew only $4,000 from his account. The IRS levied a penalty of 50 percent of the difference between what he should have withdrawn and what he did withdraw. Mark ended up making a $2,201.68 mistake because he misunderstood the requirement and took a smaller distribution than he should have.

If you need extra money before age seventy-two, you can start taking *qualified distributions* when you reach age fifty-nine and a half. Taking qualified distributions from a tax-deferred plan like a 401(k) or a traditional IRA means that although you will need to pay income tax on the money you withdraw, you will avoid the early withdrawal penalty you would be charged if you were younger than fifty-nine and a half. If you retire and don't yet need your 401(k) money, then you can leave it, although you will no longer be able to contribute. If you want to continue to make contributions, then you'll need to roll the 401(k) over into an IRA.

NOTE

The SECURE Act, passed into law on December 20, 2019, raised the age (from 70½ to 72) at which you must start taking required minimum contributions from your traditional IRA, 401(k), 403(b), and other plan types. SECURE, in case you are wondering, is an acronym for Setting Every Community Up for Retirement Enhancement.

If you have a Roth IRA, you have already paid income tax on your contributions. In addition, any growth withdrawn over what you contributed will not be taxed if you are over fifty-nine and a half. All contributions can be withdrawn prior to age fifty-nine and a half if you have held the Roth IRA for at least five years, because it is considered a return of your (already taxed) principal.

If you decide to withdraw money from a brokerage account, you will first need to sell some of your investments, such as stocks, bonds, mutual funds, index funds, or ETFs. Getting money from your brokerage account is a bit more complicated than withdrawing from a bank account. Choosing which assets to sell at a given time can be tricky, as you want to stick to the principle of buying low and selling high, despite the temptation to unload investments whose value has fallen. A better way to choose what to sell is to select investments that allow you to maintain a balanced portfolio, a topic you will learn more about in chapter 10, "Managing Your Portfolio."

Once you have selected the investments you want to sell, you'll need to notify your advisor or brokerage. They will help you take care of the sale, after which you must wait for the trade to settle, which can take a couple of days. Once the money from the sale is in your account, you can request that it be transferred to a bank account or that a check be mailed to you.

IN PRACTICE: I encourage my clients to link their bank account to their brokerage account. If they need money, we can securely transfer money to their bank account electronically rather than sending a paper check to their mailbox, which is much less secure.

Regardless of whether you withdraw money from an IRA, a 401(k), or a brokerage account, it's important to consider the tax consequences.

Minimizing Tax Consequences

One thing we know is that the government is always looking for its share of our money, paid through taxes. As I've said before, however, the need to pay taxes implies that you have money, so taxes are a good problem. But no one wants to pay more than their fair share. The first thing to understand is that different types of accounts are taxed differently.

As the chart in figure 26 illustrates, sales of securities at a gain in taxable accounts such as brokerage accounts are subject to capital gains taxes. Money you withdraw from a traditional IRA or 401(k) account is taxed at your regular income tax rate, and distributions from Roth IRAs are not taxed.

Moving money from being taxable to being tax free is a powerful thing. Once you pay taxes on the money you put into an account, the distributions you take in the future will be forevermore tax-free, regardless of the balance of the account.

GRAPHIC

fig. 26

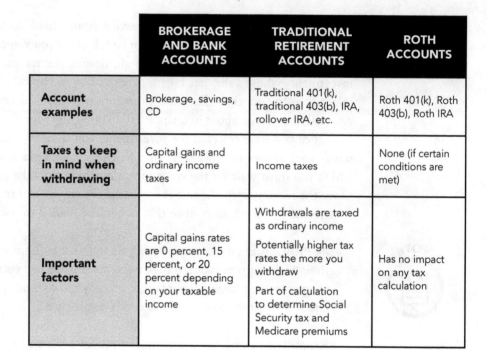

	BROKERAGE AND BANK ACCOUNTS	TRADITIONAL RETIREMENT ACCOUNTS	ROTH ACCOUNTS
Account examples	Brokerage, savings, CD	Traditional 401(k), traditional 403(b), IRA, rollover IRA, etc.	Roth 401(k), Roth 403(b), Roth IRA
Taxes to keep in mind when withdrawing	Capital gains and ordinary income taxes	Income taxes	None (if certain conditions are met)
Important factors	Capital gains rates are 0 percent, 15 percent, or 20 percent depending on your taxable income	Withdrawals are taxed as ordinary income Potentially higher tax rates the more you withdraw Part of calculation to determine Social Security tax and Medicare premiums	Has no impact on any tax calculation

How different types of accounts are taxed

NOTE

IN PRACTICE: If you need to withdraw money from your accounts to supplement your retirement income, I recommend you turn first to traditional IRAs and your 401(k), then to taxable brokerage accounts, and finally to your Roth IRA (figure 27). To many, this may sound counterintuitive. However, there are several reasons for it, mostly related to how those accounts are taxed. Some advisors might take a slightly different approach, but this is how I order the distributions for my clients.

ORDER OF ACCOUNTS FROM WHICH TO WITHDRAW MONEY

GRAPHIC

fig. 27

Withdrawal strategy hierarchy

If you need money from an account in your portfolio before you turn seventy-two, withdrawing money first from traditional IRAs and 401(k) accounts will reduce the value of those accounts and make it less likely you will have to take large required minimum distributions that could push you into a higher tax bracket when you turn seventy-two. Until you are seventy-two, you can control the amount of money you withdraw, keeping it to a figure that may not change your tax bracket. When you turn seventy-two, the IRS will determine for you the amount you need to take.

Selling brokerage investments can result in *capital gains taxes*, which are taxes you must pay when you sell an asset for more than you paid for it. *Capital gains* apply to most investments, like real estate, stocks, bonds, and other capital assets that have appreciated in value. If you sell an investment you have held for a year or less, you will have to pay short-term capital gains. If you've had the investment for more than a year, you pay long-term capital gains, which are more favorable than short-term. Capital gains rates vary depending on your income and how you file your taxes. They can be quite high, though, making it worthwhile to look for strategies to reduce them.

One way is to wait until you've held an investment for more than a year before selling it. Another is to offset capital gains with *capital losses*, which occur when you sell an investment for less than you paid for it. That practice is known as *tax-loss harvesting*. Capital losses can only offset capital gains on investments that are sold within the same year. Reducing your taxable income by incurring capital losses can also result in lower capital gains taxes, so be sure to maximize your tax-loss harvesting strategy. We'll walk you through an example of tax-loss harvesting in chapter 10.

Roth IRAs do not come with required minimum distributions, meaning that while you spend down your traditional retirement accounts and/or brokerage accounts, your Roth can remain undisturbed and continue to grow in value, tax-free. If you eventually need your Roth money, the withdrawals you take will not increase your tax bracket or cause your Social Security benefits to be taxed, and your distribution will have no taxes due.

NOTE

IN PRACTICE: Roth IRAs are sometimes referred to as "legacy investments," because when they are passed on to heirs, the distributions remain tax-free. That rule does not apply to a traditional IRA. With the passage of the SECURE Act, non-spouse beneficiaries must take distributions of all monies from inherited IRAs within ten years of receipt. You can take a lump sum, spread out the distributions, or take them all at the end of the ten years. Taxes will be due on all distributions from traditional IRAs, but no taxes will be due on Roth IRAs.

Entire books have been written about tax strategies, so obviously there is much more to consider than what you've read here. Find a professional to walk you through the finer points of minimizing taxes when withdrawing funds from your portfolio.

Generating Cash Flow with Real Estate

Owning one or more rental properties can generate an income stream and can be a good resource for supplementing your retirement funds. Rental properties provide some nice tax benefits, and if your properties are in desirable locations you may be able to generate a sizable monthly income. The US Census Bureau reports that nearly one-third of all occupied housing in the United States is inhabited by renters, so there clearly is a market. Physical real estate has historically been more stable than equities; this could benefit your portfolio if you are nearing or at retirement age.

If you are considering purchasing an investment property, there are (of course) some decisions to make. Will you purchase residential or commercial property? If residential, are you interested in a single or multifamily home, condominium, or townhome? If commercial, would you consider a retail strip center, office building, warehouse, or some other type of structure? Regardless of what you buy, your first consideration should be whether you can turn a profit. Will you have enough positive cash flow to pay for the maintenance of the property?

Some costs to consider:
»   Mortgage payment and interest rate
»   Property taxes, which can be quite high, depending on where you live
»   Insurance
»   Repairs and maintenance
»   Tenant improvements

Having an idea of these costs will help you decide what type of property to buy and what rent to charge to help ensure profit and generate a positive cash flow. You should also get an idea of the cost of comparable rentals in your area. A general rule of thumb for setting a rental fee is that it should be around 1 percent of the purchase price of the property. If you buy a house for $200,000, you should charge at least $2,000 a month in rent.

The 1 percent rule, however, does not apply in every market. If the property is in a high-property-tax state like New Jersey or Connecticut or is in an area that requires flood or hurricane insurance, 1 percent of the purchase price might not be enough. The same could apply if the property needs a lot of repairs or has high maintenance costs.

NOTE

Before purchasing rental property, find out what nearby property values have been doing. If they are on the rise and the area is stable, then it's likely that the value of your property will increase. If the area is unstable and property values have declined, you might end up paying more for the property than you would be able to sell if for. Remember, though, if the value of the property increases, you'll face capital gains taxes when you sell. A great location is essential. People in the real estate industry say that your main profit is made on the purchase, so buy right.

If the home you live in is larger than what you need, you could employ the strategy of downsizing to a smaller home while maintaining ownership of your larger home as a rental property. If the school district in which your home is located is well regarded, the home could be a particularly attractive rental for a family.

As with every investment, real estate comes with risks. Commercial properties can become difficult to rent during tough economic times, meaning you could end up paying for and maintaining an empty building. And not every tenant is pleasant and pays their rent on time. Renting property entails responsibility and has legal implications, so getting some professional advice is always a good idea.

If you have more than one or two rental properties, you might consider hiring a property manager. You might also consider setting up a ***limited liability company*** (LLC), which is a business structure designed to limit liability to the asset(s) in the LLC and protect your personal assets in the event that you are sued. A ***simple LLC*** is fine if you have only one rental property. If you own several properties, consider a ***series LLC***, which covers a series of assets and keeps them siloed off from one another's potential liabilities. Not all states offer series LLCs, so you will have to check to see if this business entity is allowable in your state.

You can learn more about setting up LLCs to protect property and personal assets in the *Real Estate Investing QuickStart Guide*, written by Symon He.

IN PRACTICE: I advise my clients with investment real estate to take the steps necessary to run it like a business, protecting themselves, their properties, and their personal assets.

Claiming Dividends

Stocks that pay dividends can provide another source of income in retirement. Dividends, as you read in chapter 2, "Investment Strategies," are payments a company makes to its shareholders when it has excess earnings. The amount of the dividends varies, but they are normally paid quarterly. Preferred stock usually carries a fixed dividend, which tends to be higher than dividends paid on common stock. Preferred stockholders are paid before common shareholders. Mutual funds often offer aggregate dividends from dividend-paying stocks held within the fund.

Dividends can be paid as a check or in additional shares of stock. Paying dividends by issuing additional stock is called ***dividend reinvestment*** and is normally accomplished through use of a ***dividend reinvestment plan***, or DRIP. The beauty of dividend reinvestment is that it increases the number of shares you own, which increases the amount of dividend payments. If you are looking for an additional income source and have been reinvesting dividends through a DRIP, consider taking dividend payments instead.

While many retirees count on dividends, they are not always a reliable source of income. Many companies reduced or cut dividends during the Great Recession of 2008, and many more followed suit during the COVID-19 pandemic of 2020. By the end of the second quarter of 2020, more than fifty S&P 500 companies had cut or suspended dividend payments, including Wells Fargo, Gap, Dick's Sporting Goods, Estée Lauder, Carnival, and AMC Entertainment. Many REITs also cut or suspended dividend payments.

Dividends are taxable income, but different types of dividends are taxed differently (figure 28). ***Qualified dividends*** are taxed at the capital gains rate, and ***unqualified dividends*** are taxed at the standard income tax rate, which is higher than the capital gains rate. Dividends taxed at the lower rate must be paid by a US company or a foreign company that meets certain qualifications, and they can only be paid on stock that meets holding period requirements. Most dividends paid by US companies are qualified dividends.

MY TAKE

The accumulation of shares is the catalyst for your wealth. Reinvesting your dividends is a great way to accumulate more shares that will distribute more income to you when you need it in retirement.

Unqualified dividends, sometimes called ordinary dividends, include those paid by REITs, the real estate investment trusts that you read about in chapter 2. Dividends from tax-exempt corporations and those from capital gains distributions are other examples of unqualified dividends. How much tax someone pays on either type of dividend depends on their tax bracket after deductions, exemptions, and any other credits tallied on their tax return.

GRAPHIC

fig. 28

TAX RATES FOR 2021

REGULAR INCOME		QUALIFIED DIVIDENDS & CAPITAL GAINS	
INCOME BRACKET	**TAX RATE**	**INCOME BRACKET**	**TAX RATE**
up to $9,950	10%	up to $40,400	0%
$9,951 to $40,525	12%		
$40,526 to $86,375	22%	$40,401 to $445,850	15%
$86,376 to $164,925	24%		
$164,926 to $209,425	32%		
$209,426 to $523,600	35%	$445,851 or more	20%
$523,601 or more	37%		

Dividend tax rate, based on income for single tax payers

Despite carrying the higher tax rate, dividends paid by REITs tend to be higher than those paid on many stocks, making REITs popular investments among people looking for regular income. Many REITs that meet specific requirements enjoy special tax benefits that exempt them from paying taxes on the corporate level. For a REIT to maintain tax-free status with the IRS, it must pay at least 90 percent of its yearly earnings in dividends to investors. While most REITs pay out quarterly, others offer monthly dividends.

A REIT has similarities to a mutual fund or ETF in that it pools funds from investors. Funds are used to buy real estate assets. Income collected from leasing the real estate is distributed to shareholders as dividends.

While stocks that pay dividends are generally considered safer investments than growth stocks or other types of non-dividend stocks, they still carry risk. It is not unheard-of for a company to return too much of its profit to shareholders as dividends, thereby limiting funds available to put back into the business. And some companies have used dividends to keep investors happy even when the value of the stock is just holding steady or falling. If you are tempted to swap growth stocks in your portfolio for those that pay dividends, do some homework; learn how the dividend stock is performing currently and has performed over time.

Is It Too Late to Start My Own Small Business?

Retirement requires planning on many levels. Financial planning is certainly important, but you'll also need to consider factors such as how you'll spend your time, how you will remain involved and interested in life, and how you can best care for your physical, emotional, and spiritual health. For some retirees, starting a small business is the answer to all those questions.

Like finding a job that brings you satisfaction, starting a business doing something you enjoy can benefit you in various ways. It most likely would involve contact with other people, which is important on many of life's levels. Depression is not uncommon among older Americans, and there are many proven connections between depression and loneliness. Having your own business can also keep you up and moving about, which is good for your health.

Operating a small business that has low start-up and operating costs can generate extra income for travel and other activities you enjoy, or simply help with day-to-day expenses. And many people of retirement age are well suited to opening their own business. They are generally loaded with expertise and knowledge acquired over the years, have fewer family responsibilities than before, and have more time and resources to get a business up and operating. The Small Business Administration (SBA) has a name for these older business owners: encore entrepreneurs.

Amanda, who is sixty-six, retired twice before eventually starting a management consulting firm with two partners in Tampa. She retired for the first time from a job in investment banking when she was in her forties. After eighteen months of leisure, she got a job in banking and private equity sales. In 2014 she retired again. Three years later, at age sixty-four, Amanda and two partners, also of retirement age, started a firm that advises senior business leaders in sales, talent management, finance, and corporate government.

Having said all that, starting a business in retirement is not something to be done on a whim. It only makes financial sense to start a business if you are relatively confident it will succeed. Nothing, of course, is guaranteed, but if you are going to start a business it should be based on something in which you have a good degree of expertise. It wouldn't make sense to start a construction business if you didn't know the difference between a drill and a chisel and had never so much as hung pictures on the wall. When the entrepreneur cited in the previous example started a management consulting firm, she was building on prior experience, relationships, and knowledge acquired over decades. For that reason, her new venture had an excellent chance of succeeding.

When it comes to financing a startup, I urge extreme caution. Some people bet their 401(k)s on a successful business venture, but if the business eats up your cash and ultimately does not survive, then you're left with a failed business and, potentially, no retirement funds. Be especially careful about starting a business that requires a physical location, like a coffee shop or specialty store. Purchasing or leasing a storefront can be expensive, and if the business fails you could be stuck with continued lease payments.

My advice if you are considering starting a business is to identify one that has low start-up costs, so you can avoid going into debt. Many jobs can be done from home, something we learned from the COVID-19 pandemic that forced many businesses to have employees work remotely. A home-based business generally requires much lower start-up and overhead costs. Start small; choose a business that matches your skills, talents, and interests; have a plan for building the business; and take advantage of your contacts and social networks.

I have a friend, Raymond Harris, who, nearly thirty-six years ago, founded a small architecture firm in Dallas. Wanting to avoid going into debt, he started out on a shoestring, doing all the work himself at first. Later he hired several employees, and within ten years the firm was established as a regional leader. Over its lifetime, RHA Architects produced more than eight thousand projects across the country. In the first quarter of 2020, RHA Architects merged with BRR Architecture. Harris started small, built up slowly, and became a huge success without ever incurring debt.

It took ten years to be an overnight success.

– RAYMOND HARRIS
founder and principal, RHA Architects

If you're thinking about starting a business, you may come across information about a type of transaction called Rollovers as Business Startups (ROBS). This financing option allows you to roll over money from a qualified 401(k) or IRA to invest in a business without incurring penalties or tax consequences. It might seem like a solution to funding a business, but it still means you are putting your retirement money at risk.

IN PRACTICE: It is my humble and professional opinion that, though using a ROBS strategy may be a legitimate way to finance a business, it is one that I would not recommend to my clients.

If you do start a business, be sure to find out what types of insurance you will need. As you read in chapter 3, you will need malpractice, cybercrime, errors and omissions, or some other form of liability insurance. I highly recommend that you consult with your team of professionals, including a CFP® practitioner, an attorney, and a CPA, before committing to starting a business.

Chapter Recap

» You can withdraw money from your retirement funds, but there will be tax consequences.

» Dividend-paying stocks can generate income during retirement.

» Rental property can be a passive way to generate income, but be sure to protect your personal assets with an LLC.

» If you choose to start a business, try to find one with low start-up and overhead costs.

19 | Fraud

Chapter Overview

» The Prevalence of Fraud
» Cybercrime Includes Phishing and Identity Theft
» Not All Fraud Is Computer-Generated
» Protecting Yourself from Fraud and Scams

QUOTE

Honestly, we're all at risk. Whether you're talking about a large enterprise or an individual.

–HEATHER RICCIUTO
global leader of IBM Security's academic outreach program

GRAPHIC
fig. 29

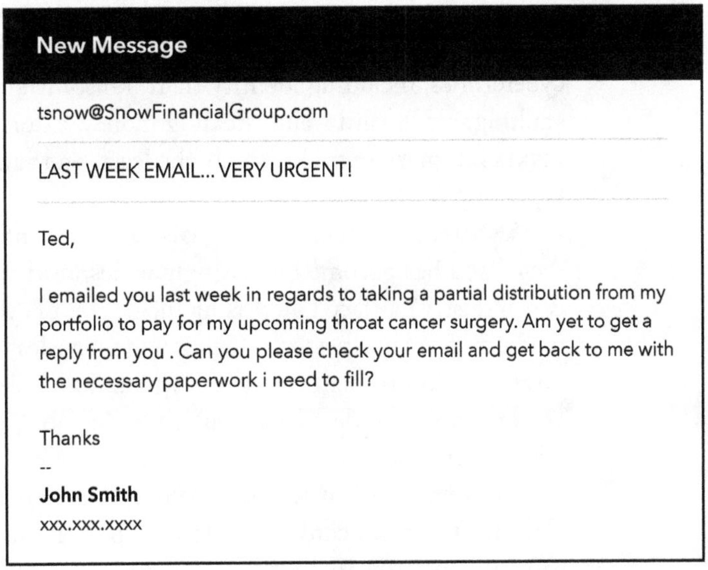
New Message

tsnow@SnowFinancialGroup.com

LAST WEEK EMAIL... VERY URGENT!

Ted,

I emailed you last week in regards to taking a partial distribution from my portfolio to pay for my upcoming throat cancer surgery. Am yet to get a reply from you . Can you please check your email and get back to me with the necessary paperwork i need to fill?

Thanks
--
John Smith
xxx.xxx.xxxx

A fraudulent email containing awkward language and errors, such as a space between the word "you" and the period that follows and the personal pronoun "I" that is not capitalized. Errors like these are common in many fraudulent emails and should be a warning sign to recipients.

As I was working on this chapter, I received the email shown in figure 29, supposedly from an elderly woman who had been my client for many years. She is no longer a client, so I was surprised to get this email, which stated that she needed to take a partial distribution from her portfolio to pay for cancer surgery. The email requested that I reply by sending the necessary paperwork for her to get the money. Alarm bells rang all over the place, since the email contained errors and language that did not sound like that of the woman with whom I'd worked over a long period of time. I called my former client to discuss, and sure enough, she had not sent any such email—it was fraudulent. There was no chance I would have replied to the email with anyone's personal information, but I can imagine scenarios where that could have occurred.

This is just one example of a growing problem with the potential to affect everyone. For most of us, technology is a vital tool in our lives. We use our computers or other devices to bank, shop, pay bills, keep up with friends, and the list goes on. While technology enables us to accomplish a variety of tasks, as well as work and conduct business with others, it is an area that is fraught with risk. You have worked hard to plan for retirement—saving, investing, making sure you have the right insurance products—and as you read in the previous chapter, you should be looking forward to reaping the rewards of your sound planning. The truth is, however, fraud poses a threat to everyone's finances and it's beneficial to be aware of what you can do to avoid it.

There are some very smart people out there who, instead of using their expertise and knowledge for good, employ it to conduct a wide range of cybercrimes, including identity theft, ransomware, password theft, phishing, stalking, credit card fraud, stealing money, extortion, and many others. This makes internet use tricky, to say the least, and can leave you vulnerable to all types of risks.

Cybercrime affects individuals, governments, and businesses in every sector and has become increasingly widespread and problematic. The health care industry has faced increasing incidences of cybercrime, as have small and medium-sized businesses, which tend to have less sophisticated cybersecurity systems. Government agencies, which have plenty of information about citizens, are considered particularly vulnerable, as are the energy industry and higher education.

In July of 2019 it was discovered that more than one hundred million Capital One credit card accounts and applications had been compromised. A software engineer in Seattle was arrested and charged with hacking into a Capital One server and stealing personal data from more than one hundred million people. Target, Home Depot, Anthem, Marriott International, and many other corporations also have been targets of cybercrime.

The FBI reported that in 2019 it dealt with more than 467,000 cybercrime complaints that resulted in about $3.5 billion in losses. The amount of losses more than tripled in just five years, according to the agency.

 The United States government as well as consumer advocacy groups offer various resources that will help you stay vigilant, savvy, and up to date when it comes to fraud. We've prepared a "Fraud Prevention Catalog" for you as part of your Digital Assets, which can be found at go.quickstartguides.com/retirement.

Not all fraud occurs electronically. It is not unheard of for a "contractor" to show up at someone's home to discuss an obvious problem such as a roof that needs repair; they request payment up front, then disappear with the money without doing any work. Another scheme is when an elderly person gets a phone call from someone claiming to be their granddaughter who was just in a car accident and needs money so she can have her car towed.

All this information is not meant to scare you, just to make you aware of the huge scope of this problem. Because, while some cybercriminals and con artists target credit card companies and other large-scale organizations, others target individuals like you and me. And statistics show that older adults are more likely to be victims of cybercrime and other forms of fraud than those who are younger. The Federal Trade Commission estimates that eight out of ten scam victims are sixty-five or older. Reasons include the fact that seniors may be less technology-savvy, many have savings, and they tend to be more trusting than younger people. The good news is that there are steps you can take to protect yourself from becoming a victim of cybercrime.

Cybersecurity

We hear a lot of talk about *cybersecurity*, but what exactly is it? According to Digital Guardian, a data loss prevention software company based in Massachusetts, cybersecurity is all the systems, processes, and technologies in place to protect computer networks, data, devices, and programs from attack or damage.

An important part of cybersecurity, and one that every individual can employ, is awareness. If you use technology for any purpose, it is imperative that you be aware of common ploys and know how to avoid them. Criminals prey on the unaware and those who do not take steps to protect themselves. It's far more likely that a thief will enter an unlocked car to steal a cell phone left on the seat than to smash a window to get it. Why? It's easier, and less likely to attract attention. The same is true with cybercrime.

Being vigilant and aware of how cybercriminals operate will go a long way toward protecting yourself online. As many people have growing numbers of connected devices such as thermostats, cameras, smart TVs, garage door openers, voice-activated speakers, baby monitors, and refrigerators, all of which can be hacked, it's important to understand your risks.

Phishing is a method of trying to obtain personal information, such as your Social Security number, a password, or a credit card or bank account number. It's an extremely common form of cybercrime. Phishing occurs in several ways, but all are designed to trick you. A phishing email or text message might look like it's from your bank, an online store, or another organization you recognize, but it's not. The message will try to trick you into clicking a link or opening an attachment using tactics like telling you that you've won a prize, claiming there's a problem with your account, asking you to click on a link to make a payment, or saying you need to confirm some information (figure 30). If you do, harmful software could be installed onto your computer, your computer system could be frozen, or sensitive information could be revealed.

The best way to avoid these scams is to consider carefully before opening an email or text message. If an email claiming to be from UPS tells you to click on a link to locate your package, and you did not order anything that would be shipped by UPS, do not fall for a possible scam. If you get an email that looks like it's from your bank alerting you to a problem with your account, call the bank to request more information instead of opening the email.

fig. 30

From: Office 365 Security Admin [mailto:security-noreply@office365.net]
Sent: Tuesday, June 19, 2018 10:37 AM
To: USER
Subject: Suspicious Activity Detected on Your Account

Office365 Security

Hello USER

Please complete your account verification and re-validate account ownership security.

To help keep you safe, upgrade to a more secured outlook account platform.

Note: Outlook will help you take corrective actions on mail malfunction after this process.

To review your recent account activity CLICK HERE

Thanks.

Microsoft Head Office
2018 Windows Corporation. All rights reserved. | Acceptable Use Policy | Privacy Notice.

source: Center for Internet Security

An example of a phishing email

NOTE

A good rule of thumb is to simply not open any emails or text messages that are from an unknown source or are urging you to take immediate action. Phishing scams rely on evoking an emotional response to cause you to act quickly.

Unfortunately, it is not all that difficult for someone to gain access to your personal information and use it to steal your identity. Identity theft can be accomplished through phishing, a phone call, stealing your mail or other documents like a driver's license or credit card, or using information that you share online. Someone who gets your personal information can commit crimes like opening new credit accounts, opening bank accounts in your name, making withdrawals from your bank accounts, and even committing other crimes and identifying themselves as you when they're caught.

Vigilance may be your best defense against identity theft and fraud. Consider enabling two-factor authentication, which adds an extra layer of security to your accounts. Two-factor authentication simply means that your account provider will rely on at least one other security mechanism other than your password to authenticate your identity. They might, for instance, send a specific numeric code to your mobile phone and ask you to provide it prior to logging in. Be extremely careful when using a credit card online. Know whom you are paying and the exact amount. Keep an eye on your bank, credit card, and any other accounts you have, and contact the bank or credit card company immediately if you notice any unusual activity. Give your Social Security number only when necessary. Don't leave mail sitting once it's been delivered.

CAUTION

One reason you are advised to file your taxes early is that it's become increasingly common for scammers to steal your personal information and use it to file a return in your name, claiming the refund to which you are entitled; then when you file your taxes, you are notified that the refund has already been claimed.

There are many other types of scams and tricks that cybercriminals use to steal your information, take your money, or otherwise make life very unpleasant. Here are a few other forms of cybercrime:

» **Bank loan scam.** A common scam is a fake offer from a supposed bank that wants to loan you a large sum of money at an incredibly low interest rate. To take advantage of the offer, you need to pay processing fees, which, of course, the scammers keep. If you get such an offer, always call the bank to verify.

» **The IRS scam.** The IRS does not contact you by email, phone, or text message to ask for private information. If you get something through email or text that appears to be from the IRS, do not open it.

» **Romance scam.** An online "admirer" cultivates a relationship that eventually leads to asking you for money or personal financial information.

» **Greeting card scam.** What looks like a greeting card in your email could be a tool to download malicious software onto your computer. That can cause problems ranging from annoying pop-ups to theft of sensitive information.

» **Home title fraud.** Someone who steals your identity can obtain the title of your property and change the ownership from your name to theirs, then use the equity in the home as collateral for other loans. You could be completely unaware that this has happened until you get a letter saying your home will be foreclosed upon.

» **Theft of a child's Social Security number.** This is an increasing area of concern to authorities, who warn about thieves who obtain a child's Social Security number and use it to apply for government benefits, open bank accounts, apply for credit cards, or rent a place to live. This can occur when the child's information is given to someone at their school or other organization, and it can have long-reaching effects on the child's future.

» **Social security fraud.** This happens when someone has your Social Security number and they go to www.ssa.gov and establish an account, which locks you out of being able to create a legitimate account for yourself. This is one of the most difficult frauds to reverse. So go to www.ssa.gov and establish accounts for each one of your family members.

Your best defense against computer-generated fraud and scams is vigilance and common sense. If you get an email with an offer that seems too good to be true, it probably is. Any email requesting personal information, account numbers, or a payment should raise alarm bells. If you shop online, it's a good idea to purchase only from established sites with which you have done business in the past.

NOTE

You can report online scams or attempted fraud at the FBI's Internet Crime Complaint Center at www.ic3.gov.

Also be aware that some websites are secure—which means they generally use encryption and authentication to protect the confidentiality of web transactions—and others are not. You can tell if a website is secure by the URL, which will begin with "https" instead of the unsecured "http."

Don't be tempted to use the same password for all your accounts, no matter how much easier it seems to be. Having a single password gives a cybercriminal access to all your online accounts. Use unique passwords with nine to thirteen characters or longer, including symbols, numbers, and capital and lowercase letters. You can easily generate strong, random passwords by going to Norton or Avast and using their random password generator tools.

Consider purchasing an identity theft protection program such as IdentityForce, LifeLock, or IDShield. These types of programs provide credit monitoring and other services designed to make identity theft more difficult. If your identity is stolen, they usually provide complete identity restoration as part of your subscription. Also available are antivirus programs that protect your computer from malware, which is any software designed to gain access to your personal information or to damage your computer. Examples of antivirus programs include McAfee and Norton. You can buy these services and download them onto your computer.

Other Forms of Fraud

Computer-generated fraud gets a lot of attention because it's so prevalent and potentially damaging, but it's also important to be on the lookout for more old-fashioned techniques.

Mail fraud occurs in the form of someone stealing mail or using the mail to try to extort money or personal information from you. Health care fraud occurs when someone gains access to your insurance information and uses it to pay for their own medical care. Someone can simply steal your purse and gain access to credit card numbers and other information.

Fraud attempts over the telephone also are common. Don't ever agree to purchase something over the phone and then supply a credit card number. Be alert to phone calls asking for donations to worthy causes such as a fund for veterans or families of police officers who were killed while on duty. I strongly encourage donating to worthy causes, but you certainly have the right to refuse to make payment over the phone.

Be wary if someone who claims to know you calls and asks you for money, either for themselves or on behalf of someone else. If you get a call from someone claiming to represent a bank, medical office, store, or business who claims to need your bank account number or other personal information for any reason, do not provide it.

A woman got a phone call one night from someone claiming to be her grandson. The caller told her he had decided to enroll in culinary school, and he needed money to hold a spot open. The woman did have a grandson, but he was a professional firefighter who had never expressed interest in any type of culinary activity, let alone cooking school. She thought the caller had said it was Jonathan, which was her grandson's name, but she couldn't be sure. Fortunately, she said she could not give him any money, and the caller hung up.

It may be impossible to detect and avoid every type of fraud, particularly that which is computer-generated. Unfortunately, criminals and cybercriminals are always working one step ahead, and it is extremely difficult to predict what they will do next. Being aware of what you are looking at and with whom you are communicating are probably your best defenses against cybercrime and other forms of fraud. If you are concerned that you've been a victim of fraud, don't be afraid to ask for help, either from a family member, a trusted friend, or an agency that addresses issues of fraud.

Even if you are working with a financial advisor, your financial accounts are still online, and account activities are conducted via the internet. Therefore, it is imperative that you are aware of online tactics designed to steal your information. Thieves are particularly interested in your bank account numbers, credit card accounts, passwords, and other information that can be used to rob you, so beware when discussing or making changes to financial information with anyone other than a professional whom you know and trust. Check your accounts frequently—credit cards, checking accounts, brokerage accounts, etc.—for irregular activity.

Chapter Recap

» Fraud and scams have increased dramatically in the past five years, with cybercriminals responsible for many of them.

» Understanding how cybercrime is conducted is an important step in being able to recognize it.

» Fraud can also occur over the phone, via mail, or by someone who shows up at your door.

» There are tools available to help you avoid fraud and scams.

| 10 |
Managing Your Portfolio

There's one robust new idea in finance that has investment implications maybe every 10 or 15 years, but there is a marketing idea every week.

– NOBEL LAUREATE EUGENE FAMA

Managing a portfolio is an ongoing, lifelong task. Any time you experience a change in life circumstances, there is a great opportunity to assess your portfolio and contemplate any adjustments that might be needed. If managed correctly, your portfolio will look different when you are thirty than it will when you are seventy.

Getting married, buying a home, starting a family, raising kids, and sending kids to college are all events that can alter the allocation of funds in your portfolio. So are getting divorced, losing a job, starting a business, retiring, experiencing medical issues, and losing a spouse. Life happens, and your portfolio must reflect changes that inevitably occur over time. I recently heard someone compare managing a portfolio to tending a garden. Both require ongoing care and attention in order to thrive. I think that is a sound analogy.

Times of dramatic market changes, as we saw during the COVID-19 crisis, are also opportune times to ask if your portfolio needs a tune-up. It's not a time to panic and start selling off your assets (you'll read more about handling market downturns a little later in the chapter), but it may be time to think about a little rebalancing or possibly buying additional securities when prices drop.

Keeping watch over your portfolio becomes increasingly important as you near and enter retirement and begin to reassess your risk tolerance and shift toward less risky investments. The goal is to keep your investments growing, but in a manner that balances that growth with an appropriate risk tolerance.

Asset Allocation

Though asset allocation is a key component of portfolio management, it does not ensure profits or protect losses. Nevertheless, it is an important part of an overall strategy.

As you read in chapter 2, "Investment Strategies," asset allocation is a method used to balance the assets held in your portfolio. Basically, asset allocation divides your money between stocks, bonds, cash, and cash equivalents, which include assets like money market mutual funds and short-term bond funds (figure 31). As with most things, asset allocation changes over time.

IMPORTANCE OF ASSET ALLOCATION

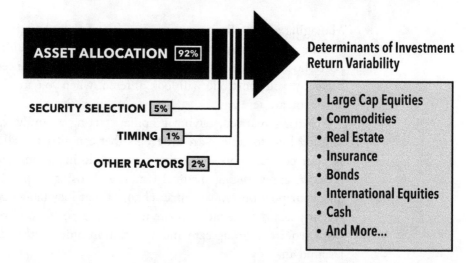

fig. 31

Asset allocation is a huge determinant in investment return variability.

Asset allocation largely depends on two things: how long your money will remain invested and your tolerance for risk. When there are decades between you and retirement, you may want to be primarily invested in stocks or growth mutual funds. That's because you have plenty of time to make up for any setbacks, and you can afford to assume more risk with the goal of the higher returns that stocks typically produce over time. As you get closer to retirement there's less time remaining before you will need your savings to live on, so you want to allocate them by moving to an asset mix with lower risk, typically one that is more weighted toward bonds. However, assets should not be tailored to be overly conservative, even as you approach and enter retirement.

In my experience, investing too conservatively is one of the most common mistakes made by people throughout their working years and into their retirement.

Just because you are retiring doesn't mean your investment portfolio should quit working hard too. Many people now live twenty or thirty years past retirement age, which means portfolios need to be allocated to perform throughout that time frame. It is a mistake to retreat into overly conservative positions as soon as you reach retirement age.

Cash and cash equivalents provide even more security. One of the most commonly used cash equivalent instruments is the ***money market mutual fund***. Shares of money market mutual funds are designed to remain equal to one dollar. Historically, interest returns earned on money market mutual funds are higher than those earned on savings accounts. Relative to stocks and other higher-risk investments, however, money market mutual funds do not produce high returns. Instead they are used to buffer investors from the ups and downs of the markets. Having access to cash and cash equivalents also allows you to buy investments on sale when prices go down, and who doesn't like a sale? If you liked something before it went on sale, you'll love it now that it is selling for less.

I will tell you how to become rich. Close the doors. Be fearful when others are greedy. Be greedy when others are fearful.

— WARREN BUFFETT

It's important throughout your financial life to have cash available for a crisis, but it becomes increasingly important as you get older and more likely to encounter high costs for health care and other unanticipated expenses.

There are no real rules about how much cash should be in your portfolio. Some advisors recommend keeping between 3 and 5 percent of your assets in cash, and others urge you to go as high as 20 or even 30 percent. Again, it has a lot to do with your attitudes about risk. Just remember that if the inflation rate is higher than the return you are earning on your cash, you have a negative return and are losing money every day you hold a cash position.

Regarding asset allocation between stocks and bonds, as you read in chapter 2, the rule of thumb used to be that you should hold a percentage of stocks that when added to your age equals one hundred, and keep the rest of your non-cash money in bonds. That thinking has changed, and for good reason. Life expectancy has increased dramatically, rising more than eight years during the last half-decade. That means you're likely to need more money in retirement, and we know that stocks have historically given higher returns than bonds. Yes, there is greater risk, but if your stock portfolio includes a good mixture of stock sectors and different categories of stocks, the risk may be reduced.

NOTE

IN PRACTICE: "Safe" is not always safe. Safe is safe in the short term, but it becomes risky in the long term because of the effects of inflation. Risky may be risky in the short term, but in the long term it becomes safe because of the potential for appreciation.

That brings us to another aspect of asset allocation, which is the allocation of funds between various types and categories of a particular asset, such as a stock. You can buy ready-made asset allocation mutual funds that contain a mix of stocks, bonds, and cash. Or you can pick individual stocks. If you prefer to pick your own, you'll want to include some from a variety of sectors, such as health care, energy, technology, and financial. You also should have stocks spread across the major stock categories, which are growth, value, large-cap, mid-cap, and small-cap. You may want to consider a handful of international stocks as well.

The same goes for bonds. You never want all your eggs in the same basket, so you should not, for instance, buy only corporate bonds; mix them with treasury bonds and municipal bonds. You can also get some good bond-based mutual funds or ETFs that give you the diversity you want.

Diversifying across a wide range of asset classes is a good idea because asset classes vary in their performance from year to year. In 2012, emerging market stocks resulted in 18.63 percent earnings, according to Morningstar. In 2013 they fell into negative territory and stayed there for three years, dropping all the way to negative 14.60 percent in 2015. They rebounded in 2016, returning 11.60 percent, and then—get this—in 2017 they saw a 37.75 percent return. Emerging market stock owners didn't need to get overly excited, though, because in 2018 emerging stocks dropped again to a negative 14.25 percent return, only to rebound and yield 18.90 percent in 2019.

GRAPHIC

fig. 32

2012	2013	2014	2015	2016	2017	2018	2019
Emerging Market Equities 18.23%	Small-Cap Equities 38.82%	Large-Cap Equities 13.69%	Large-Cap Equities 1.38%	Small-Cap Equities 21.31%	Emerging Market Equities 37.28%	US Fixed Income (Bonds) 0.01%	Large-Cap Equities 31.49%
Small-Cap Equities 16.35%	Large-Cap Equities 32.39%	US Fixed Income (Bonds) 5.97%	US Fixed Income (Bonds) 0.55%	Large-Cap Equities 11.96%	Large-Cap Equities 21.83%	Large-Cap Equities -4.38%	Small-Cap Equities 25.52%
Large-Cap Equities 16.00%	US Fixed Income (Bonds) -2.02%	Small-Cap Equities 4.89%	Small-Cap Equities -4.41%	Emerging Market Equities 11.19%	Small-Cap Equities 14.65%	Small-Cap Equities -11.01%	Emerging Market Equities -14.57%
US Fixed Income (Bonds) 4.21%	Emerging Market Equities -2.60%	Emerging Market Equities -2.19%	Emerging Market Equities -14.92%	US Fixed Income (Bonds) 2.65%	US Fixed Income (Bonds) 3.54%	Emerging Market Equities -14.57%	US Fixed Income (Bonds) 8.72%

source: Callan.com

A simplified rendition of a Callan Table showing the performance of various asset classes over time

I hope that example convinces you of the need to have a mix of stocks and bonds. It also points out the difficulty of *market timing*, a technique in which investors buy and sell securities in anticipation of their performance. The performance of stocks is dependent on many factors and can change quickly. Past performance does not always predict future performance.

QUOTE

It's extremely rare to hear of anyone winning at market timing over a period of years. Indeed, I've never heard of such a genius.

–JACK BRENNAN

CAUTION

Do not chase returns. Buying what was "hot" last year could turn out to be disastrous for you. Make an investment plan and stick to it.

Thoughts and theories regarding asset allocation are all over the place because investors have varying degrees of risk tolerance and their own ideas about how their money should be invested. You can find a variety of asset allocation calculators online that divide up your money for you based on factors such as your age, how much you save each year, your tax rate, your risk tolerance, your outlook regarding the economic forecast, and how much income you need from your investments.

If you work with a CFP® practitioner or an RIA, he or she will, with your input, attend to the asset allocation of your portfolio and provide you with online access to view it. When your asset allocation shifts due to varying returns among different stocks and asset classes, it may be time to rebalance your portfolio.

Rebalancing Your Portfolio

The weight of your investments changes due to the varying performance of each type. If you have equal amounts of stocks and bonds and the value of your stocks increases dramatically but the bonds only gain a minimal return, you no longer have equal amounts of stocks and bonds. Let's look at a simplified example.

Mary Jo is sixty-three and has $10,000 she wants to invest. Not wanting to incur too much risk, she invests 50 percent of the money in stocks and the other 50 percent in a bond fund. Over five years, the value of her stock doubles, but the value of the bond fund increases by only 20 percent. The value of her portfolio has increased, which is a good thing. However, the balance of her portfolio has shifted and is overly dependent on the performance of the stocks, which now represent 60 percent of her portfolio. The shifting of the value of the stocks and bonds has put Mary Jo, who is now sixty-eight, at greater investment risk, which is what she wanted to avoid in the first place.

To resolve the problem, Mary Jo needs to rebalance her portfolio. She can easily do that by selling some of the stock she owns and buying more bonds to restore the 50 percent to 50 percent ratio. If necessary, she can also rebalance her assets based on stock sector and category.

Your advisor can help you rebalance your portfolio. If you are rebalancing within a retirement plan such as a 401(k), it's likely that there is an automatic rebalancing feature. Some retirement accounts can be set up to automatically rebalance at a time interval of your choice.

Some investors rebalance their portfolios at regular time intervals, and others do so when an asset allocation changes by a certain amount, usually 5 percent.

IN PRACTICE: Rebalancing stocks, growth mutual funds, or growth ETFs can be done in two ways. One is to take profit off the table when the stocks are seen at a high point. Another way is to buy more when stocks have reached a low point. Personally, I like to buy more when the markets are down, rather than selling at high points. The reason is because accumulation of shares (not decumulation of shares) is the catalyst for wealth.

Dealing with Market Downturns

In the early part of 2020, just as I was just starting to map out an outline for this book, we started hearing about a novel coronavirus that was spreading in China. In January, the Centers for Disease Control (CDC) reported the first case of COVID-19 in the United States in a patient who had recently returned from China. Investors quickly became jittery, and by late March stocks had fallen from record highs to *bear market territory*, which generally refers to a stock market that loses 20 percent or more of its value, resulting in investor fear and widespread sale of investments. In June, a group of economists determined that the US economy had entered a recession in February, with more than 40 million jobs lost between the middle of March and the end of May.

Most economists agree that the economy is in recession when the country's gross domestic product (GDP) experiences a negative growth rate for two or more consecutive quarters.

The market came back up in the following months, signaling to many a quick economic recovery. But with the coronavirus on the upswing again in August, economists were predicting there could be more economic trouble ahead. A problem during a down market is trying to gauge whether the ups and downs are just dips and bounces or real indicators of either an upswing or a further downturn. Basically, it's a wait-and-see position, and unsettling for some investors. As we strove to get a handle on the situation, I reached out to my clients with some advice that I will also share with you.

Downturns happen, and, historically, they are followed by upturns. Including the 2020 recession caused by the COVID-19 crisis, the US economy has gone into recession fourteen times since the end of the Great Depression in 1933. The good news is that most recessions are fairly short and tend not to last as long as bull markets. The average recession since 1900 has lasted about fifteen months. Contrast that with periods of economic prosperity and expansion, which last about sixty to seventy-two months, on average. There were no recessions between 2010 and the end of 2019, the first time in US history that we've experienced an entire decade without one (figure 33).

 BEAR AND BULL MARKETS

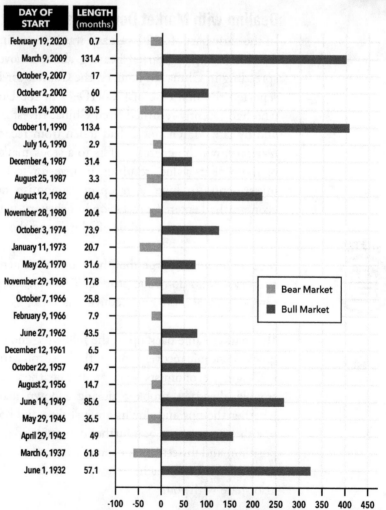

DAY OF START	LENGTH (months)
February 19, 2020	0.7
March 9, 2009	131.4
October 9, 2007	17
October 2, 2002	60
March 24, 2000	30.5
October 11, 1990	113.4
July 16, 1990	2.9
December 4, 1987	31.4
August 25, 1987	3.3
August 12, 1982	60.4
November 28, 1980	20.4
October 3, 1974	73.9
January 11, 1973	20.7
May 26, 1970	31.6
November 29, 1968	17.8
October 7, 1966	25.8
February 9, 1966	7.9
June 27, 1962	43.5
December 12, 1961	6.5
October 22, 1957	49.7
August 2, 1956	14.7
June 14, 1949	85.6
May 29, 1946	36.5
April 29, 1942	49
March 6, 1937	61.8
June 1, 1932	57.1

Legend: Bear Market, Bull Market

X-axis: MARKET GROWTH (%) — -100, -50, 0, 50, 100, 150, 200, 250, 300, 350, 400, 450

GRAPHIC

fig. 33

source: S&P Dow Jones Indices

The key to surviving a recession is to avoid making panic decisions, especially regarding the sale of stock. You know the rule. Buy when prices are low and sell when prices are high. In fact, if you have some cash on the sidelines, a bear market is a great time to buy some securities, because prices are lower than they would be during a **bull market**, or a market that is gaining in value in a stable economy.

Still, many investors race to sell off stock when a bear market strikes. That's because they panic and react. Instead, try to remain patient and wait for markets to recover. It is not easy to watch the value of your portfolio fall, especially when you are preparing to retire or are in retirement. But trust me when I tell you that pulling out of the market is not the answer to surviving a recession.

Bill and Ann were in their early fifties and hoping to retire in their early sixties when the Great Recession of 2007–2009 hit. The value of their IRAs and 401(k)s, which were heavily weighted toward individual stock holdings, dropped by more than 50 percent. Panicked and working against the advice of their broker, Bill and Ann started employing various trading strategies, such as timing the market, to try to make up some of their losses. In doing so, they got into even deeper trouble and missed out on the market rebound that started in March of 2009. Bill and Ann lost confidence in their ability to manage their portfolio and late in 2011 shifted their assets almost entirely into cash and cash equivalents, where they remained for several years. Ten years after the start of the Great Recession, they still had not recovered their losses. If they had stayed the course, their portfolios would have recovered and grown, enabling them to follow through with their retirement plans. Because they veered off course, they expect to have to work until they are at least sixty-five.

The blow to the US economy caused by the COVID crisis was lessened due to the government's response of propping up the economy. By the end of July 2020, the federal government had committed $2.4 trillion—a nearly unimaginable amount—to relief for American businesses and individuals. That response may result in another set of problems down the road, but many economists predict the market will be stronger in 2021 (figure 34).

HISTORY OF MARKET CRASHES

GRAPHIC

fig. 34

EVENT	DATE	16-DAY CHANGE
Wall Street Crash of 1929	October 29, 1929	-33.6%
Black Monday	October 19, 1987	-31.3%
End of Gold Standard	October 5, 1931	-26.7%
Lehman Crisis	November 20, 2008	-25.2%
World War II	May 21, 1940	-24.6%
COVID-19 Outbreak	March 12, 2020	-20.7%
Dot-com Bubble	Jult 23, 2002	-19.3%
Post-WWII Demand Stock	September 10, 1946	-16.9%
US Debt Downgrade	August 8, 2011	-16.7%
Great Financial Crisis	March 4, 2009	-13.8%
LTCM	August 5, 1998	-8.7%

source: BofA Global Investment Strategy, Bloomberg

Having an appropriate asset allocation that includes stocks, bonds, and cash should help assure you that downturns pass, and keep you looking forward to economic recovery. A market downturn is a good time to reexamine your investment goals, risk tolerance, and financial situation to assess whether your asset allocation is on track or needs to be rebalanced.

QUOTE

There will always be someone predicting disaster and someone predicting great fortune. At one time or another, each will be closer to correct than the other. But it won't matter to you if you understand this and have invested properly. You have a long-term plan: Stick with it.

– PETER LYNCH

Reinvesting

You read about reinvesting dividends in chapter 8, "Reaping the Rewards of Sound Retirement Planning." Many people like the idea of dividend reinvestment because it results in additional shares of stock, which yields higher dividends. Reinvesting dividends and other assets like capital gains can also help you maintain your portfolio.

If you have dividend-paying stocks such as Chevron Corp. or Disney, you are not obligated to reinvest the dividend payments into Chevron or Disney stock. You can place dividend money or capital gains into a cash account, then use those funds to buy another type of stock or a different investment entirely.

This helps you to keep your portfolio diversified and to take advantage of investments that in time may add value to your portfolio. You could use the dividends paid on a US stock to buy international stock that was performing well and was less expensive than the US stock. That would increase the diversity of your holdings and give you value potential for the future.

You can set up a *periodic investment plan* with your broker that draws a certain dollar amount from your cash account at regular intervals to reinvest in designated securities. Such a plan lets you take advantage of compounding and achieve further gains down the road. This can add substantial value to your portfolio.

Tax Planning

Tax planning is an important part of managing your portfolio. Taxes take a big bite out of our incomes, but there are ways for investors to minimize taxes and realize better after-tax returns. Some of these methods include asset location, a strategy that considers what types of securities should be held in tax-deferred accounts and which in taxable accounts, in order to minimize taxes; tax-loss harvesting, which was covered briefly in chapter 8; and consideration of the types of taxes that are levied on different types of investments. State-issued municipal bonds, for instance, may not be subject to state income tax.

You can also see if you might be able to move into a lower tax bracket by delaying Social Security or a pension or annuity payment and setting up a *systematic withdrawal plan* that allows you to automatically take money out of an account (or accounts) on a regular basis; this helps you avoid tax issues.

While there will always be taxes, there are some strategies you can use to increase your tax advantage.

» Let's start by exploring the concept of asset location. As you read in chapter 8, different types of accounts are subject to different tax treatments. There are taxable accounts; tax-deferred accounts, such as traditional IRAs and 401(k)s; and tax-exempt accounts, such as Roth IRAs and Roth 401(k)s.

For instance, if you own Zoom stock, listed on the Nasdaq as ZM, a Roth IRA would be the perfect place to have it because of its rapidly appreciating stock price. You'd pay no tax on it, regardless of how much its value increased. Stocks that aren't as growth oriented but pay out regular dividends might be better in a taxable account, even though you'd be taxed at ordinary income rates. You would still have easy access to the cash flow, which could be supplemental income.

» Tax-loss harvesting allows you to offset a capital gains tax by selling an investment at a loss. The loss you incur is deducted from the gain and lowers, or offsets, the tax you owe. After selling an investment, you'd want to purchase a similar type of security to retain a proper asset allocation.

If you had $10,000 in losses, you could offset them with $10,000 in gains. The result would be $0 in taxes.

If you want to buy back shares you sold at a loss, you'll need to wait thirty days to harvest the loss. This is called the "wash sale" rule. However, you can always buy back an investment you sold at a gain at any time without being affected by the wash sale rule, because the rule only pertains to the sale of a security at a loss.

» Different types of bonds are impacted differently by federal and state taxes, and, as you read in chapter 2, some are tax-exempt. Most municipal bonds are not subject to federal or state taxes, and some are also exempt from local taxes. Comparing the after-tax rates of return on different types of bonds may enable you to pay less in taxes.

» Holding a stock that has increased in value for at least a year before selling it can give you a tax advantage, in that you will be taxed at the long-term capital gains rate, which is lower than the short-term capital gains rate that applies if you sell the security before a year has passed. The maximum short-term gain tax is nearly twice as much as the maximum long-term rate (39.6 percent versus 20 percent), so holding on to that appreciated stock can result in significant tax savings, depending on your tax bracket.

» Delaying Social Security, pension, or annuity payments can lower your taxable income and therefore your taxes owed. Many people don't have this option, but it could be something to consider. If your income is over a certain amount, you'll have to pay federal and, in some states, state taxes on your Social Security. Pension income is taxable in some states but not in others. It could make sense to think about taking IRA withdrawals before signing up for Social Security or pension payments, as you might be able to lower your taxable income while increasing the value of the Social Security or pension payments by taking them at a later date (figure 35).

fig. 35

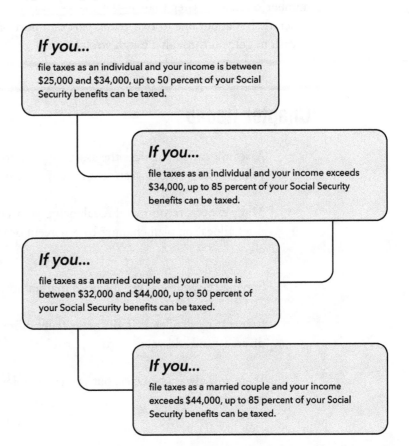

If you...

file taxes as an individual and your income is between $25,000 and $34,000, up to 50 percent of your Social Security benefits can be taxed.

If you...

file taxes as an individual and your income exceeds $34,000, up to 85 percent of your Social Security benefits can be taxed.

If you...

file taxes as a married couple and your income is between $32,000 and $44,000, up to 50 percent of your Social Security benefits can be taxed.

If you...

file taxes as a married couple and your income exceeds $44,000, up to 85 percent of your Social Security benefits can be taxed.

Rates at which Social Security benefits are taxed

» A systematic withdrawal plan, which is a strategy that enables you to set up regular withdrawals from a mutual fund or other account, can result in some tax advantages, in that the withdrawals are made from capital and the long-term gains are taxed at a lower rate, if structured correctly. These plans are popular with many retirees who rely on their investments for income. In addition to mutual funds, systematic withdrawal plans can be applied to IRAs, 401(k) accounts, brokerage accounts, annuities, and other investment vehicles, but no tax advantage is gained by using this strategy with IRAs or 401(k)s. The reason is that everything taken out of IRAs and 401(k)s is going to be taxed as ordinary income.

A disadvantage of a systematic withdrawal plan is that when the value of your investment drops, you need to sell more shares to continue receiving a predetermined amount of income. If the value of your investment remains lowered, as it may during a bear market, the withdrawals can decrease the number of shares faster than if the market was growing. Since recessions generally last about one to two years, part of a portfolio should be allocated to cash to get you through a tough stretch.

Chapter Recap

» Asset allocation balances the assets in your portfolio according to your risk tolerance, investment time frame, and long-term goals.

» Many experts recommend rebalancing your portfolio when your asset allocation plan changes by 5 percent or more in any one asset class.

» Staying the course is key during a market downturn.

» Reinvesting dividends in different types of investments can help diversify and add value to your portfolio.

» There will always be taxes, but you can employ strategies to minimize them.

PART III

LIFE AFTER RETIREMENT

| 11 |
Retiring from Work and Into Life

Retirement is a blank sheet of paper. It is a chance to redesign your life into something new and different.

– PATRICK FOLEY

We've been focusing mainly on financial aspects of retirement, but it's also important to think about the psychological implications of leaving work. This is a relatively new area of study, but doctors and psychologists have been giving increasing attention to what can happen emotionally as someone shifts away from the workplace.

Life is a series of transitions. Typically, one transitions from a childhood home to college, or maybe to a job and an apartment. Moving into a full-time job is another transition, as is getting married, having children, losing parents, and so on. Not the least of all life's transitions is retirement, and experts advise that retirement is best thought of as a process, not an event.

Most retirements begin with a honeymoon period, during which life is good. Not having to go to work every day is a relief. You can sleep late, visit with friends and relatives you haven't seen for a while, play some golf, tend to the garden, do some traveling, sit, and read a book in the middle of the day—you get the picture.

When that stage ends, usually after a year or so, a disenchantment stage may set in. This is the period of disorientation. Time starts to drag, and those things you had so enjoyed doing start to seem a little tiresome. You might be bored with reading and golfing and feel like you should be doing something more relevant or important. It seems silly to complain—after all, you're retired!—but you feel unfulfilled and fear your life may lack meaning. You may miss the respect and responsibility you encountered while working or being part of a team striving toward a shared goal. It's not uncommon for depression to occur during this retirement stage.

NOTE

This phase of disenchantment and disorientation, if handled well, can be a time of reflection and growth. With help, if needed, you can work toward freeing yourself from overreliance on your workplace identity and embracing who you are on a more holistic basis.

During the next stage, reorientation and stability, the retiree moves from choppy waters back to dry land. Ideas develop, plans are put into place, and a new sense of confidence and satisfaction begins. You might by this point be established in volunteer work that gives you fulfillment, or a post-retirement job that you enjoy. Maybe you care for grandkids on a regular basis or have fallen into a routine of helping your aging neighbor with some of her yardwork. When reorientation occurs, you become as secure in retirement as you were in your job, experiencing a sense of purpose and reasons to get up in the morning (figure 36).

MY TAKE

Practice makes perfect, as the saying goes, and I believe that pertains to retirement. Staying active during retirement can be easier if you were already used to engaging in various activities prior to leaving work. For instance, you may be more likely to continue taking a morning walk if you have become accustomed to doing so, rather than beginning to walk after you have retired. Also, you're likely to spend a lot more time with your spouse once you retire, so it's important to find some activities you both enjoy doing. Another idea is to think practically about the hours in a day and assess whether you engage in enough interesting activities to fill those hours. Practicing these strategies may help you ease into retirement with less stress.

Everyone, of course, experiences retirement differently. Some workers retire and never look back, settling immediately into a lifestyle that suits them, while others struggle for years before they finally settle in to being retired. Your retirement will be a personal journey, and I wish you well. In this chapter we will look at some issues and opportunities you may face in retirement. We'll delve a little more deeply into the need for purpose and identity and look at some different ways retirees have achieved those things. We'll discuss the value of lifelong learning, travel, and staying open to new experiences and adventures. And we'll have another look at the possibility of starting a new career or getting a job, but this time more from the angle of personal satisfaction than financial reward.

THE 3 STAGES OF RETIREMENT

GRAPHIC

fig. 36

The Honeymoon Stage

The Disenchantment

The Reorientation

Purpose, Passions, and Plans

A lot about life depends on your attitude. We know that attitude affects physical health. Harvard University researchers have found that possessing a sense of optimism and purpose is related to better health outcomes. Doctors there found that *emotional vitality*, a trait that encompasses enthusiasm, hopefulness, engagement in life, and the ability to face life's stresses with emotional balance, may substantially reduce risk for heart attack and stroke.

Attitude also affects your emotional health. A positive attitude can reduce stress and enhance how you feel about yourself and others, according to a report from Duke University. And, while a positive outlook may be largely inborn, you can train yourself to change your thinking patterns in a way that changes negative thoughts to more positive ones. Remember that old book by Norman Vincent Peale, *The Power of Positive Thinking*? It was written in 1952, but it's still plenty relevant today.

Maintaining a positive attitude when you are retired is not always easy. You might experience loneliness or second-guess yourself on whether retiring was the right thing to do. Perhaps you're a little anxious about your financial situation, worried about grown children or grandchildren, or uncertain about what the future holds for you regarding your health or that of a loved one.

While it's normal to experience some misgivings and concerns, it's important not to let them overwhelm you. If you're struggling with being retired, remind yourself that you may be in the stage of disorientation, which eventually will give way to the stage of reorientation and stability.

Discovering what you are passionate about can provide purpose and go a long way toward making retirement an exciting and rewarding period of your life. Preferably before you retire, assess what it is that makes you feel happy and fulfilled. Take notice of times when you feel most alive and, in those moments, note what you're doing. Maybe you lose yourself in watercolor painting or feel most authentic when organizing and helping with a food and clothing drive in your community. Perhaps it's traveling, exploring other cultures, and getting to know new places that brings you fully to life.

Identifying and acting on your passions can make a big difference during retirement and can serve as a fine replacement for a job that for many years consumed most of your time and probably provided a significant amount of meaning in your life. Victor Frankl was a famous psychologist who wrote *Man's Search for Meaning*. He believed that pursuing happiness does not result in happiness; indeed, the pursuit is the very thing that keeps you from finding it. What does bring happiness, asserted Frankl, is meaning. And meaning can be achieved through the pursuit of those activities about which you are passionate.

> *Happiness cannot be pursued, it must ensue. One must have a reason to be happy.*
>
> – VICTOR FRANKL

Research suggests that people who use their time and resources to help others report higher levels of health and happiness than those who do not. A study in the journal *Social Science & Medicine* reported that people who volunteer more than once a month but less than once a week are 12 percent more likely to say they are "very happy" than someone who does not volunteer or who does so infrequently. Those who volunteer weekly are 16 percent more likely to report being "very happy."

One thing is certain: there are no shortages of opportunities to help, either in your community, another area of the United States, or the world. I have personally volunteered both at home and abroad and have found it tremendously rewarding.

NOTE

According to Independent Sector, a national organization that works with nonprofits, foundations, and corporations to facilitate charitable efforts, about 63 million Americans did some type of volunteer service in 2018, giving about 8 billion hours of their time, valued at $203.4 billion. Do you want to get out of your comfort zone? Volunteer World, an organization that matches volunteers with opportunities that suit their interests, may be able to match you with a youth mentoring program in Chicago, a stint as a wolf caretaker at an off-the-grid center in California run by US veterans, or a program in which you teach English to children in Vietnam.

Regardless of what your passion is, trust that identifying and putting it into action will result in a sense of purpose and help you plan your retirement life.

Adopting a New Identity

When you meet someone new, there's a good chance that one of the first three questions you'll be asked is "What is it that you do?" and that you'll reply, "I'm an accountant," or "I'm a hair stylist," or "I'm a psychologist," or "I own a furniture refinishing shop." It's natural to identify ourselves based on our work. After all, in many cases, work is where we spend much, even most, of our time and energy. For some people, work is what brings meaning to their lives. Their work becomes their identity, and they believe they are what they do.

And then retirement begins, and suddenly that person's identity crumbles and their sense of purpose and self-worth is lost. They're no longer a banker or an electrician or a surveyor. Without the identity of their career, they don't know who they are. This dilemma is often referred to as the "retirement syndrome."

DETOUR

ART IMITATES LIFE: The challenges brought on by "retirement syndrome" are aptly portrayed by actor Jack Nicholson in a 2002 movie called *About Schmidt*. Nicholson stars as Warren Schmidt, a 67-year-old insurance executive in Omaha, Nebraska, who has been pushed into retiring and is not at all happy about it, particularly because he doesn't like or respect the person who was chosen to replace him.

Totally adrift and without any apparent nonwork interests, Schmidt examines his life, wondering how he came to be in this situation. He and his wife have grown apart and he is alienated from his daughter, who lives in Denver. Desperate to find some meaning in his life, he begins contributing money each month to support Ndugu, a six-year-old African child. He also starts writing letters to Ndugu, establishing what seems to be his only meaningful connection to another person.

Circumstances get worse for Schmidt after his wife dies unexpectedly. Struggling to care for himself, his appearance deteriorates, and he is unable to keep up with the housework. With his daughter's wedding coming up, Schmidt, on a whim, decides to voyage out in the Winnebago his wife had persuaded him to buy. His plan is to take his time and make a few stops on the way to Denver, where his daughter is to be married. Along the way he decides to see what it would be like to connect with other people. His attempts to do so fail miserably, as does the visit with his daughter and her new husband's family.

At the end of the movie we are left with a man filled with regret at what his life has become—a prime example of someone who could not find an identity that wasn't employment-related. The movie can be viewed as a cautionary tale that validates the wise old advice not to put all your eggs in one basket.

Adopting a new identity can take some work, but it's a vital part of retirement. If you have not yet retired, the identity question is something you should address before you do, understanding that being devoted only to work will not serve you well when it's time to leave it. If you are retired and are struggling with this issue, it might be good to address it with the help of a counselor or coach. Meanwhile, you can work on reinventing yourself by engaging in activities you enjoy; working through any past regrets; finding meaningful, fulfilling ways to spend your time; and continuing to move forward with your life.

Your Retirement Does Not Affect Only You

Your retirement will affect not only you, but family members as well, particularly your spouse if you have one. Before you retire, you and your spouse should carefully consider how a retirement, or two retirements if you're leaving work at the same time, will affect you financially and emotionally.

If you retire when you are sixty-five and can get Medicare, but your spouse is only sixty-two and does not have insurance through work, then you'll need to purchase health insurance, which can be pricey. According to eHealth, an organization that partners with more than 180 insurers to help individuals, families, and businesses find health insurance, the average monthly premium in 2019 for someone between fifty-five and sixty-four was $790. This price assumes that the individual is not benefiting from a subsidized reduction to their premium due to having low income. On top of the steep premium expense, there are likely to be deductibles and other out-of-pocket costs.

Depending on your household income, you might qualify for a tax credit, often called a subsidy, if you buy a health plan that's available through the Affordable Care Act (ACA) marketplace. To qualify, you must have income that is no more than four times the *federal poverty level*. That amount is $49,960 a year for an individual, $67,640 for you and a spouse, and $103,000 for a family of four. You would still have to pay for your plan, but you might get some help.

The age at which you decide to start taking Social Security can also affect your spouse if you should die first. If you start taking benefits before your full retirement age (currently pegged at sixty-six or sixty-seven depending on your birthdate), your benefit amount will be lower than if you waited. If your spouse is entitled to survivor benefits, those will be reduced as well.

Also consider that you'll have less income without your salary, even if your spouse continues to work, and you will likely have to make some lifestyle changes to accommodate the reduced amount of earnings. It is important that you and your spouse discuss and agree on what those changes might look like.

If one of you has children from another marriage, be sure you agree about any support you will be providing them. Helping someone else with college or other living expenses can make it difficult to manage your own expenses in retirement, so make sure everyone is on the same page.

IN PRACTICE: I advise clients preparing for retirement to draft a budget outlining what their income needs will be when they are no longer working. They are sometimes surprised to realize they will need to significantly cut back on expenses to be able to accommodate their changed financial situation.

If only one spouse is retiring, consider how it will it affect your relationship and the way you live together. If your spouse will continue to work, will you be expected to pitch in more with chores, perhaps taking over laundry and grocery shopping duty? How will your social life be affected with one of you now at home and the other still going to work? Might you feel resentful because your spouse is engaged with others at work while you are at home alone? Is it possible you will feel neglected because your spouse goes to bed early to get up for work and you prefer to be a night owl?

The Pew Research Center reports that the US divorce rate for adults fifty and over doubled between the 1990s and 2020, and the divorce rate for those sixty-five and over tripled during that same period. This phenomenon, called "gray divorce," can have devastating emotional, physical, and financial consequences.

If you and your spouse retire together, or you retire and your spouse doesn't work outside the home, be prepared for much more "together" time. That can put stress on a marriage, even a healthy one. It's been found that any major life event, even a happy one like marriage or the birth of a child, comes with a degree of stress. Retirement, certainly a major life event, is no exception, and you should expect to experience a period of transition. Perhaps you will both want to spend all your time together, but chances are that you'll occasionally need some breathing room. Trust that you will adjust to a new normal, and don't be afraid to seek some advice or counseling if you experience difficulties.

Choosing a New Career

If you leave your job at a relatively young age, either voluntarily or not, or you find you don't enjoy being retired as much as you thought you would, you might consider going back to work. Starting a small business or finding a part-time job after you retire was discussed in chapter 8, "Reaping the Rewards of Sound Retirement Planning," but it's an important topic from a psychological viewpoint as well as from a financial one.

Beginning something new is exciting and challenging. Maybe you left a job sooner than anticipated because it was unfulfilling or the work environment was awful. Rather than call it an early retirement, you might consider it the open door to a new career. A new career would keep you earning and prevent you from having to dip into retirement funds early, and it could be an exciting venture. Remember that leaving the workforce at age fifty-five or sixty leaves a lot of years ahead of you in retirement.

Steve retired from a career as a teacher and then a high school athletic director when he was sixty-two, having worked in the same school district for forty years. He soon discovered that his limited interests were not conducive to an easy retirement. He met with friends at the local diner every morning, but he was pressed for activities to keep him busy the rest of the day. He had no interest in traveling, there wasn't much to do around the house and yard, and his wife was busy with many volunteer pursuits and not home much during the day. The situation became miserable; neither Steve nor his wife was happy with their new situation. After about a year, Steve's nephew got laid off from a construction job and Steve started thinking about how he might help him while at the same time giving himself something to do. Steve and his nephew each put up some money to buy a truck and some tools, and the two of them opened Conestoga Construction. Steve worked for six more years, after which his nephew bought him out and became sole owner of the business. Steve found the experience to be both financially and personally rewarding, and I'm happy to say that his second retirement has been far more successful than his first.

Some people parlay the skills and experience they have into a new job or career, while others start from the ground up to learn something new. Joan found herself unemployed at age fifty-three after working for years as a paralegal. After thinking about it for a while, she signed up for a phlebotomy course at her local community college and got training to be a phlebotomist. After taking a test to become certified, she found employment at a hospital lab and is quite happy in her new career. Nan, whose first love is making pottery, is looking forward to retiring from her job with an accounting firm when she turns sixty and starting her own pottery business. When Ed, who ran a graphic design firm, lost his biggest client due to economic troubles, he closed the firm and started a dog grooming business at his home.

According to the US Bureau of Labor Statistics (BLS), in 2024 there will be 13 million people aged sixty-five and older who are still working, becoming the fastest-growing segment of the workforce during the decade between 2014 and 2024. While the total number of workers is expected to increase by 5 percent over those ten years, the number of workers aged sixty-five to seventy-four will increase by 55 percent. For workers seventy-five and older, the total increase is expected to be 86 percent.

Reinventing yourself doesn't always require moving into a completely different field. Dale is an ordained minister who spent thirty-five years as a pastor before taking a job teaching at a seminary. Helen was a public school teacher for twenty-six years in New York but couldn't get the certifications she needed to teach when she moved to Pennsylvania. Now she is the administrative assistant for the superintendent of a large school district. Bill is a lawyer who became disillusioned with the fast pace and cutthroat environment of the large firm where he worked. He moved to the nonprofit sector and is now employed by an organization that works to combat hunger.

Whether you choose to put your skills and experience to use in a consulting job, a small business, or working for someone else, choosing a new job or career can be advantageous financially and psychologically.

Learning

With technology accelerating at such a rapid pace, it has become necessary for many people to learn new skills almost constantly. Someone who used to simply write press releases and work with local journalists must now maintain blogs and coordinate social media as well. An automobile mechanic must understand sophisticated car computers that read sensors and send commands to the car's ignition system, fuel injectors, and transmission. A schoolteacher must know how to design a website, make a PowerPoint presentation, and capture numerical data in a spreadsheet that can be displayed in charts and graphs.

The need for many jobs and events to move from being in person to being online during the COVID-19 pandemic led to technology inserting itself ever deeper into our day-to-day lives. Microsoft Teams, Zoom, FaceTime, Facebook Live, and other video services have become business offices, places of worship, classrooms, social meeting places, and conference rooms. We've learned to hold meetings, host birthday parties, visit with long-lost friends, conduct job interviews, and go to school online.

While some people relish constantly learning new skills, others may find it annoying or difficult. Lifelong learning, however, has been proven beneficial in numerous ways and can be applied to much more than technology. A study conducted by a neuroscientist at the University of Texas revealed that older people who learned a new skill, such as digital photography or quilting, performed significantly better in memory tests than those who did not. Learning a new language can also improve memory, as well as concentration and thinking skills.

Developing and turning out lifelong learners has become a goal of many colleges and universities. It is also helpful for retirees who want to remain engaged, learn about different topics, and stay knowledgeable about what's going on in the world. If you're reading this book to learn about how to build a successful retirement, there's a good chance you are a lifelong learner.

If you decide to move into a new career or work in a field that involves technology, chances are you'll have no choice but to become and remain a lifelong learner. Even a part-time job at your local grocery store may require you to learn to use a computer system that monitors and controls stock and performs sales analysis. Don't let the need to learn new skills stop you from pursuing new opportunities.

University and College

Residents of Texas, where I live, can take up to six credit hours per semester at the University of Texas and other state-funded colleges and universities for free if they are sixty-five or older. They can also audit as many as six hours of courses per semester. Paying students get priority, so if the class is already full, the senior citizens can't get in. And they must pay fees and buy textbooks, if applicable. Many other states also allow seniors to take classes at no cost or offer courses specifically for seniors as a service to the community. This benefits the retiree, but it also benefits the younger students with opportunities to learn from the retiree's life and experience.

NOTE

A sampling of colleges and universities that offer free tuition for seniors includes Penn State University, University of Maryland, University of Kentucky, University of Illinois, Georgia Institute of Technology, University of Delaware, University of Connecticut, Clemson University, University of Arkansas, University of Alaska, University of Oregon, and The University of North Carolina. Many community colleges also offer classes for seniors at no cost.

Taking college courses not only gives you a chance to broaden your mind and learn, which has been found to help keep your mind sharp, but it keeps you in touch with young people, which can be refreshing and fun. Many colleges encourage diverse classrooms with a mix of young and older people.

If you do not have a college degree, earning one when you're retired could be a real accomplishment. If you already have a degree, advancing it or earning a second one might prove satisfying. Some retired people relocate to a college town to take courses and enjoy the social life and cultural activities offered. In State College, Pennsylvania, there is a retirement community located next to Penn State University that offers residents a view of the famed Beaver Stadium. Most of the residents have an affiliation with Penn State and many of them are graduates.

Travel

Travel presents new and different experiences and enables you to engage in environments that are much different than what you are accustomed to. If you feel intimidated by international travel, you could opt for a guided tour, which eliminates a lot of decision making and normally puts you in the hand of a guide who speaks your language. Or discover and explore new places in your own country. The point is to see new things and places, relax, and enjoy yourself.

A key to successful travel is planning. It's helpful to learn about your destination's history and culture before you go because it can help you understand the people and places you will encounter there. Know what accommodations are available and book ahead if it makes you more comfortable. Get an idea of what the weather is like so you know what type of clothing you will need. Before you book a tour, try to find out how much walking and other types of physical activity are involved and decide if it's a match for your abilities.

Frommer's Guide to

10 SENIOR-FRIENDLY

Travel Destinations

GRAPHIC

fig. 37

 US National Parks

 Machu Picchu, Peru

 The Caribbean

 Canadian Rockies

 Alaska

 Thailand

 Central Europe's Rivers

 St. Augustine, Florida

 Santa Fe, New Mexico

 South Africa

It is important to gauge the actual cost of travel, which will include more than the cost of getting there. Try to anticipate as many costs as possible to get an idea of how much you'll spend. If you are traveling on your own, you'll need to factor in costs for lodging, food, side trips, transportation, and incidentals. If you travel with a tour, some of those costs are likely to be included, but possibly not all of them. Stretch your travel budget by traveling in the off season, which for Europe and China is November through March, May through June for Australia, and so on.

If you're going on your own to a country with a different language, it's a really good idea to learn a few basic words and phrases before you go. A travel book about your destination will provide a lot of helpful tips about the people, places to go, the weather, and generally what to expect. Remember that travel should be fun and energizing, not a chore. It can be challenging, especially if you travel to another country, so it may not be for everyone.

Location Independence

No longer being tied to a job gives you the ability to freely choose where you live. Retired people move because they want to be closer to their grown children and grandchildren, or because they wish to be in a state where taxes and costs of living are lower. There are other reasons some choose to move in retirement as well. Perhaps they simply prefer a different location over their current one.

Think carefully before making a move to be near your children and grandchildren, because sometimes this backfires. What happens if the family must relocate for a job or another reason? And remember that grandkids grow up quickly and head off to college or to begin careers. It's smart to consider other factors before relocating, such as weather, geography, or culture. It could be a better idea for you to move to a place that your kids and grandkids will want to visit frequently.

The long-distance moving company United Van Lines conducts a national study that tracks state-to-state moves. Among retirees, the states that saw the most inbound moves in 2018 were New Mexico, Florida, Arizona, South Carolina, Idaho, Maine, Vermont, Nevada, Wyoming, and Montana.

Many retirees, however, remain in place or make a local move, preferring to stay near friends, family, and a familiar setting. Another option for some is to purchase a second home. Maybe you've always wanted a beach house or a place on a lake. Some people rent out the home when they are not using it, hoping to defray ownership costs. There are pros and cons to owning a second property, so consider carefully before deciding to buy.

In the *Personal Finance QuickStart Guide*, also published by ClydeBank Media, the author, Morgen Rochard, does a lovely job of walking readers through the pros and cons of purchasing vacation properties.

Regardless of how you choose to spend your time in retirement, be sure to consider the why of whatever it is you do. The why, as described by author and speaker Simon Sinek, is the purpose that drives you. Life without purpose will never be satisfying, but life lived with purpose, though it won't always be easy, will remain interesting and meaningful.

Chapter Recap

» It's important to consider and plan for the psychological aspects of retiring as well as the financial ones.

» Leaving a job you've had for a long time may create a need to establish a new identity.

» Your retirement will affect others besides you, so be sure to consider your spouse, partner, children, and others.

» Starting a new career can be exciting, rewarding, and helpful from an economic standpoint.

» Many states offer seniors the opportunity to attend college without having to pay tuition.

» Travel can be enriching and rewarding, but it's best to plan for it carefully.

| 12 |

Managing Your Health Plans

Chapter Overview
» Health Care Costs Increase with Age
» The Parts of Medicare
» Understanding Medicaid
» Health Savings Plans to Supplement Medicare
» Finding a Plan on Your Own

Being prepared is the best way to avoid panic. Being ready for anything will help you to stay calm, sum up the situation quickly, and proceed with more efficient, capable action.

– NADINE SAUBERS AND JOHN DREHOBL
authors of *The Everything First Aid Book*

Your spending habits are likely to change in retirement. You might spend less on housing and utility bills if you downsize to a smaller home or an apartment. Maybe you eat at home more than you used to, lowering your dining-out expenses. Perhaps you went from having two cars to one, thereby saving money on car maintenance, insurance, and registration fees.

One area in which your spending is likely to increase, however, is health care. Health care can be a big-budget item at any age but is by far the greatest expense for many elderly people. A recent study by Fidelity Investments estimates that the average couple will need $295,000 for medical expenses in retirement, and some estimates show that figure to be much higher. That cost does not include long-term care, such as in assisted living or a nursing home, for which costs range from $19,500 a year for adult day care services to $102,200 a year for a private room in a nursing home, depending on what part of the country you live in.

The healthier you are as you enter retirement, the better. People who practice a healthy lifestyle, getting plenty of exercise, maintaining a healthy weight, not smoking, getting regular checkups, and so forth, generally end up spending less on health care than those who do not. Even people in good health, however, cannot anticipate a future illness or injury and should be prepared for expenses they may incur. If you are counting on Medicare to cover your health care expenses, be aware that Medicare comes with limitations; you will still incur out-of-pocket expenses.

Hopefully, you are in good health and will remain so, but you will still need some type of health insurance. If you retire before you turn sixty-five, which is the age at which you become eligible for Medicare, you will need to buy your own health insurance, unless you have a working spouse and you qualify for benefits under their plan. Or, though it is not particularly common, sometimes a private employer or government organization will agree to continue providing health insurance for an employee who retires before turning sixty-five.

We'll begin this chapter with a good amount of information about Medicare, which can seem like a complex topic. Medicare is an important part of health care for most older Americans and warrants a robust explanation, but if you are new to the subject you may feel as though you are wading through quicksand while reading about the various parts and what they do or do not cover.

I understand it might not seem like riveting information, but try to hang in there and get through it, as my goal is to give you an overview of how Medicare works and how you may be able to maximize its benefits. It's likely you've been paying into the system through taxes taken out of your paycheck for many years, and now is your time to take advantage of the benefits Medicare provides.

We'll also examine some other health care options and have a look at what you can do to plan for medical expenses in retirement.

Medicare

In 1965, President Lyndon B. Johnson signed into law the bill that led to Medicare and Medicaid, and benefits began in 1966. Former president Harry Truman had called for a national health insurance fund to be created early in his presidency in 1945. He and his wife, Bess, were the first two Americans to be issued Medicare cards, during a ceremony when Johnson signed the bill. Medicare remains a federal program, run by the Centers for Medicare & Medicaid Services.

The original Medicare program provided Part A, which covers hospital services, and Part B, which covers medically necessary services. Those remain and are referred to as "*original Medicare.*" Changes were made over the years and the program was expanded to cover more people, such as individuals under the age of sixty-five who have long-term disabilities and those with end-stage renal disease or amyotrophic lateral sclerosis (ALS). Anyone who is sixty-five or older can get Medicare regardless of income level. Medicare will help you pay for medical costs, but as with most insurances, you will also incur costs in addition to the Medicare premiums.

fig. 38

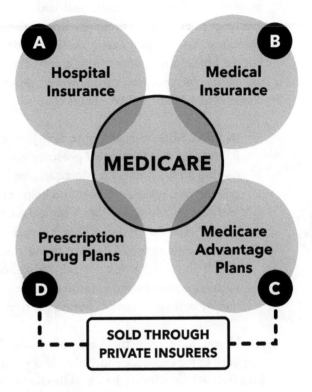

There are four parts to Medicare:

» **Part A,** as stated earlier, is hospital insurance and is part of what is referred to as original Medicare.

» **Part B,** also part of original Medicare, covers a portion of medical costs.

» **Part C,** also called a *Medicare Advantage Plan,* is an alternative to original Medicare that is sold through private insurers who determine premiums. Those insurers must be approved by Medicare to sell Part C plans, and they get money toward your care from Medicare every month. Part C plans cover Part A and Part B, usually Part D, and often benefits beyond those, like vision and dental coverage.

» **Part D** is an optional benefit that helps cover prescription drug costs. It is sold through private insurers approved by Medicare.

In case that information isn't confusing enough, there is another policy type called "Medigap," also known as Medicare Supplement Insurance. It is designed to fill coverage gaps that can occur with Part A and Part B, such as copays, coinsurance costs, and deductibles. Like Medicare Advantage, Medigap policies are purchased from private insurers who determine the premiums. You can purchase a Medicare Advantage Plan or a Medigap policy, but not both, so it's important to know what each includes and decide which works best for you. You can, however, purchase supplemental insurance in addition to a Medicare Advantage Plan or a Medigap policy.

IN PRACTICE: You can opt to take just Medicare Part A and Part B, and add Part D to cover prescription drugs, but I strongly advise getting an Advantage or Medigap plan, which typically limits what you pay out of pocket each year and helps cover deductibles, coinsurance, and copays. Medicare Part A carried a hospital deductible of $1,408 in 2020. The Part B deductible is only $198 per year, but typically you are responsible for 20 percent of the cost of medical services after that. If you suffer a heart attack, stroke, or other serious condition that requires surgeries and extensive medical care, that 20 percent can quickly add up to tens of thousands of dollars.

If you have only the basic Medicare Part A and Part B, you are responsible for copays, deductibles, and partial costs of services. If you are hospitalized or admitted to a skilled nursing facility, Plan A will cover one to sixty days at no cost to you after you have satisfied your deductible. However, you may incur costs if you are hospitalized for longer than sixty days. In 2020, patients were charged a coinsurance rate of $352 a day from day sixty-one to day ninety of hospitalization. After ninety consecutive days of hospitalization, patients were charged $704 daily in coinsurance.

The formula Medicare uses to determine its costs and time limits for hospital care is complicated, but fortunately it does not often come into play, as studies have shown that the average length of a hospital stay covered by Medicare is eight days.

It is important to understand that Medicare and other health plans do not typically cover long-term care. They may pay for a period of care in a nursing home or other facility, but it is usually limited to about one hundred days. Please review the information in chapter 3 regarding long-term care insurance, and consider carefully, as having to pay out of pocket for extended care can wreak financial havoc.

If you have the basic Part B, it typically will pay 80 percent of covered health care services and you will be responsible for the other 20 percent. Part B has a low yearly deductible of $198, but most people pay a $144.60 monthly premium. High-income earners pay more. If you get Social Security or Railroad Retirement Board benefits, your Medicare premium will be deducted from that income. If you don't receive either of those benefits, you will get a monthly bill. There is usually no monthly premium for Part A.

The cost for a Medicare Advantage Plan or a Medigap plan varies depending on who you buy it from and what it includes. The costs for Part D plans also vary, as will the costs for any other type of supplemental plan you purchase.

If you choose original Medicare (Parts A and B), which does not include coverage for prescription drugs, and you do not get Medicare drug coverage (Part D) or Medigap when you are first eligible, you might be charged more if you want to add this coverage later. Since Part A has no premium, it is a practice of mine to advise clients to sign up for Part A at the age of sixty-five. If they are still working, they can keep their current medical coverage and sign up for Part B after they retire. Penalties can be incurred, which will result in higher premiums, if one doesn't get into the system at age sixty-five.

Medicare Advantage and Medigap plans are both supplemental plans, and there are advantages and disadvantages of each. Both types of plan are sold through private insurers, and the companies are licensed by the states to offer Medigap plans. The number of plans offered varies from one state to another, but most states offer about ten different plans. If you buy a Medicare Advantage plan, you're buying a plan that is combined with Part A and Part B.

Choosing a supplemental plan can be confusing because they all have different rules that change from year to year. Some plans might require you to use health care providers who are in the supplemental plan's specific network, while others let you use any provider that is enrolled in Medicare. Some plans require referrals, and others do not. Most supplemental plans, but not all, include prescription drug coverage. Prices for supplemental plans can vary dramatically, so it's important to understand the level of coverage each plan contains. Like other insurances, plans with high deductibles typically cost less than those with low deductibles.

EXAMPLE

The cost of supplemental plans varies, so be sure to shop around. A Wisconsin woman who had just turned sixty-five was shopping for a supplemental plan with an agent, who quoted her a monthly premium of more than $700. Appalled, she told the agent that she was not prepared to pay that high a premium and insisted that he keep exploring available plans. Eventually, the agent found a plan with a $136-per-month premium and deductibles she could work with.

If you are soon to turn sixty-five and wish to get Medicare, then you will need to enroll during a prescribed period called the initial enrollment period, or IEP. The seven-month IEP starts three months before the month of your sixty-fifth birthday, includes your birthday month, and extends three months past your birthday month (figure 39). If your birthday is June 15, for example, your initial enrollment period will begin March 1 and end September 30.

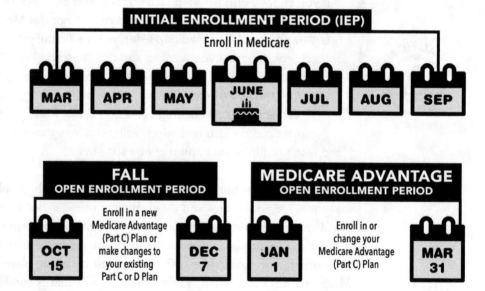

GRAPHIC

fig. 39

If you have already started taking Social Security benefits, the Social Security Administration will automatically sign you up for Medicare Part A and Part B. If you have health insurance through an employer, veteran's benefits, or another source and do not want to pay for Part B, then you will need to opt out. You will find instructions for opting out in a letter the Social Security Administration sends along with your Medicare card. Be sure to meet the deadline for opting out. If you want an enhanced plan (Part C) or prescription drug coverage (Part D), you must sign up on your own.

NOTE

If your birthday is on the first of the month, your initial enrollment period begins a month early. If your birthday is September 1, for example, your IEP will begin on June 1 and your Medicare benefits will kick in one month early on August 1.

It's best to sign up early in your IEP to avoid possible coverage gaps. Also, if you don't sign up during your IEP you may have to pay a late enrollment penalty. Once you've enrolled, your coverage should continue from year to year. You may find that your coverage needs to be changed, and even though Medicare Parts A and B will always stay the same, you can make changes to Parts C and D. If you want to make changes to your Medicare Part C or D coverage, you'll need to do so during Fall Open Enrollment, which runs each year from October 15 through December 7. Any changes you make during that time will go into effect January 1. If you choose a Medicare Advantage Plan during Fall Open Enrollment and find that you are not happy with it, you can change it during the Medicare Advantage Open Enrollment Period that runs each year from January 1 through March 31. The changes you make will take effect on the first day of the next month. So, if you make changes to your Advantage Plan in February, they will go into effect March 1.

As I warned earlier, and I'm sure you have gathered by now, there is a lot to take in concerning Medicare. Thankfully, there is help available. Medicare itself provides a lot of information on its website at Medicare.gov. You also can call Medicare with questions or concerns at 1-800-MEDICARE. Or you can get advice from an organization like Boomer Benefits, a licensed insurance agency for carriers including Blue Cross Blue Shield, Aetna, Mutual of Omaha, and others that provides help at no charge for those looking for a Medicare plan. Licensed in forty-eight states, Boomer Benefits enjoys a five-star rating based on more than 5,500 reviews curated by Shopper Approved, a review collection and syndication tool. You can access and study plans offered by different insurance companies in order to compare what's available, or you can get assistance and free one-on-one counseling through your state's **State Health Insurance Assistance Program** (SHIP). You can find the SHIP number for every state in appendix II of this book.

Medicaid

Medicare is available to those sixty-five and over and to people with certain medical conditions who are not yet sixty-five regardless of income. Medicaid, a jointly funded federal and state program, provides health coverage to those with very low incomes, and it includes adults and children. In some cases, people can have both Medicare and Medicaid. States have a good degree of autonomy in the way they set up and administer their Medicaid programs, so who is eligible and how much they receive fluctuates widely from state to state.

According to the Centers for Medicare & Medicaid Services, in April of 2020 more than 72 million people were enrolled in Medicaid and the **Children's Health Insurance Program** (CHIP), which provides coverage to qualifying children through Medicaid and separate CHIP programs. That compares to 66.7 million people who receive Medicare benefits. One difference between Medicare and Medicaid benefits that many people find surprising is that, while Medicare does not cover long-term care, Medicaid, in many cases, will.

In 2014, the federal government offered expanded Medicaid to all states as part of the Affordable Care Act. In states that expanded their Medicaid program, all people with household incomes under a certain level were covered. However, not all states adopted the expansion, meaning that not all those with incomes below the *federal* poverty level qualify for Medicaid. States that did not expand their programs are Alabama, Georgia, Florida, Mississippi, South Carolina, North Carolina, Tennessee, Wisconsin, Kansas, Texas, South Dakota, and Wyoming. States that adopted Medicaid expansion but as of August 2020 had not implemented it are Nebraska, Oklahoma, and Missouri.

Medicaid eligibility requirements vary depending on where you live, as each state is permitted to set its own. That means someone who qualifies for Medicaid in one state may no longer qualify if they move to a different state. And someone in a state that expanded its coverage may qualify for Medicaid even though their income is higher than that of someone in a state that did not expand coverage. Like Medicare, Medicaid can be complicated. Each state operates its own Medicaid program under the guidelines of the federal government. If you qualify for Medicaid, you may also qualify for nursing home care, which can be a huge advantage. If you have low income and are wondering if you might qualify for Medicaid, you can find a lot of helpful information at the Centers for Medicare & Medicaid Services at Medicaid.gov.

Qualifying for Medicaid

In some unfortunate cases, taking steps to qualify for Medicaid is warranted and necessary, especially when long-term care is required and there are not sufficient resources available to pay for it. The process for doing so, however, can be difficult and time-consuming. Eligibility rules vary, especially pertaining to income and assets. If you begin the process of applying for Medicaid coverage and find out you don't qualify, don't give up—there are steps you can take to increase your chances for eligibility.

Because you can only qualify for Medicaid if your financial assets are extremely limited, you may have to reduce the value of your estate. There are rules regarding how you can do that, however, and you need to be aware of them. If you reduce your assets in a manner that is not within the rules, you can be penalized and your chances for Medicaid eligibility will be jeopardized.

Qualifying for Medicaid can be challenging, but there is help available. Seeking the services of a qualified Medicaid planning professional can help ensure that you or your loved one can become eligible.

The Future of Medicare and Medicaid

Medicare is becoming financially unsustainable. Statistics show that ten thousand baby boomers turn sixty-five every single day, and many of them are retiring. That means they are no longer having payroll taxes—which fund the Medicare hospital insurance program (Part A)—deducted from their salaries. These individuals are now receiving the benefits and not paying for them.

The Medicare Board of Trustees, which oversees the Hospital Insurance (HI) Trust Fund, projects that the trust fund will run out of money in 2026. Even if that happens, the trust fund will continue to take in payroll taxes, but they will only be enough to pay about 90 percent of Medicare Part A (hospital) expenses. If nothing is done before then to cut expenses or increase revenues, another source of funding will have to be found to keep the program fully operational.

While Medicare Part A is funded primarily by payroll taxes, Part B and Part D are funded primarily through general revenue and premiums from people who receive Medicare. The trust fund for parts B and D is called the Supplementary Medical Insurance (SMI) Trust Fund and, because of how it is financed, it is immune from insolvency. Both trust funds are maintained by the Department of the Treasury.

It's a good idea to remain alert for news about changes to Medicare, Medicaid, and Social Security and how those changes could affect benefits. The United States is going to be facing huge debt, partially due to relief spending during the COVID-19 crisis, and will have to figure out how to deal with it. It's not implausible that these programs will be affected and have to be changed.

Like Medicare, the future of Medicaid is also uncertain. Medicaid was expanded in many states under the ACA, but there is ongoing discussion among some lawmakers about repealing and replacing the ACA. So far, their efforts to do so have not come to fruition, but many states are uncertain about what will happen to their Medicaid programs if the ACA is dismantled, and many people who are enrolled in Medicaid are worried they could lose their coverage.

Health Savings Accounts

You read about health savings accounts (HSAs) way back in chapter 1, at which time I suggested that HSAs can be valuable retirement savings vehicles. I like HSAs for several reasons, but especially because they are triple tax-free. The contributions you make to them are not taxed, the growth of the money in the HSA is not taxed, and when you withdraw money from the HSA to cover health care costs, that money is not taxed, either.

Also, an HSA lets you control the money in it. Unlike some health savings plans, you don't have to spend the money in an HSA within a calendar year; it continues to roll over. You can contribute to an HSA until you are sixty-five if you plan to start taking Medicare or Social Security at that age. If you do not enroll in Medicare, you can continue to contribute to an HSA past age sixty-five, assuming you have a high-deductible insurance plan that is compatible with the HSA.

If you opened an HSA as a retirement savings account when you were starting to think about retirement and the money has grown, chances are you will be extremely glad you have it. While Medicare is a good program in retirement, it does not cover all medical expenses, and you must pay premiums as a beneficiary of the program. This often leads to significant out-of-pocket costs, especially if you have a chronic condition that requires extensive care. An HSA can pay for services that basic Medicare doesn't cover, such as vision and dental care and hearing aids.

If you retire before you qualify for Medicare, you normally cannot use money from an HSA to pay private health insurance premiums. There are, however, a couple of exceptions to that rule. If you can extend your employer-sponsored insurance through COBRA, then you can use HSA money to pay the bills (more on COBRA later in this chapter). You can also use HSA money to pay for private insurance if you are getting unemployment compensation. So, if you lose or leave your job, your HSA account may be able to serve as a bridge to Medicare.

Once you turn sixty-five and start getting Medicare, you can use your HSA to pay premiums for Part B and Part D, the medical expenses and prescription-drug coverage portions of Medicare. You cannot, however, use HSA money to pay for Medigap or supplemental plans.

If you have a tax-qualified long-term care insurance policy, you can use funds from your HSA to cover a portion of the premiums. As the premiums increase, you can use the HSA to help offset those increases as you get older.

If you are sixty-five and don't need HSA money to pay for qualified medical expenses, you can take money out to spend on whatever you like without incurring the 20 percent penalty that you'd incur were you to withdraw money for unqualified expenses prior to turning sixty-five. However, you must pay income tax on the money you withdraw.

IN PRACTICE: Even though HSA funds can be taken out for any reason, penalty-free, after age sixty-five, it may be a better idea to use other sources of retirement income for nonmedical expenses and save the HSA money to use tax-free in the event that you do incur medical expenses.

An HSA also has a place in estate planning, which you will learn more about in chapter 13, "Estate Planning."

Private and Supplemental Care

You will need to find your own health care insurance if you retire or lose your job before you turn sixty-five and become eligible for Medicare. This will require some time and effort, but it's important to explore your options, because buying your own insurance can be quite expensive.

If you're very fortunate, the company from which you retire might continue your health care insurance. This isn't an overly common practice, but some companies do it, sometimes as an incentive to get workers to retire early to cut the company's costs. There is usually a time limit on how long insurance will continue, but sometimes it is offered until the retiree is eligible for Medicare.

If your spouse is still working, you might be able to get insurance through their plan. Employers are not required to offer spousal or family insurance benefits, but many do, and it could be a good way to obtain coverage at a reasonable cost.

Another possible option is to get your health care insurance through the ***Consolidated Omnibus Budget Reconciliation Act***, or COBRA. COBRA requires employers to continue the same coverage an employee had before quitting, retiring, or being fired from a job, except if the termination was a result of gross misconduct. The problem with COBRA is that it's expensive.

You'd need to pay 102 percent of what the company pays to the insurer, and that can be a hefty amount. However, it may be better than other options. Comparing options is important.

You can call any insurance company that sells health insurance and purchase a private health care plan, but a potentially better way to go is to find a health care plan on the Health Insurance Marketplace, created in 2010 under the ACA. You can sign up for coverage on the Marketplace from sixty days before retiring to sixty days after.

The Marketplace contains an array of plans with varying prices and coverage levels. Wading through them all to find the right fit for you and your family can be cumbersome, but advice and guidance are available through the Marketplace's call center. You can also find a local insurance agent or broker who is licensed in your state and has signed an agreement to sell marketplace plans.

Some people shy away from seeking in-person help, but I think it's often a good thing to do. There's a perception, more like a myth, that your insurance plan will cost more if you get it through a broker or agent instead of online, but that is not true. Sure, the agent you work with might get a commission from the insurer, but the same commissions are built into plans purchased online.

A good insurance agent will present the plans available to you and explain the advantages and disadvantages of each, leaving you far better equipped to choose the plan that's right for you. Information about finding local help is available on the healthcare.gov website.

Depending on your household income, you might qualify for a tax credit, or subsidy, if you buy a Marketplace health plan. You will need to purchase a plan initially, but the cost could be offset by subsidies.

Regardless of what type of health insurance plan you have, it's important that you understand its terms and conditions. Not doing so could have serious consequences. If you love to travel the world, for instance, it would be especially important for your insurance plan to include coverage for services provided in a different country. Most Medigap plans include that coverage, but most Medicare Advantage plans do not.

Also, remember that insurance plan costs and coverage can change from year to year, so read your plan carefully and contact the company with any questions you might have. Health care is likely to be a substantial part of your budget during retirement, so plan accordingly and keep a close eye on how your money is being spent.

Chapter Recap

» Health care costs generally increase as you get older, making it important to plan for how you will manage them.

» Medicare provides good, basic coverage, but it can leave you with high medical bills if you don't have a supplemental plan.

» Medicaid is health insurance for those with low incomes, and it can also cover the cost of long-term care.

» Like Social Security, the future of Medicare and Medicaid is not guaranteed in their present forms.

» Money in a health savings account can be used to pay for costs not covered by Medicare or another plan.

» If you must procure your own health insurance, consider your options, and compare costs carefully.

| 13 |
Estate Planning

Chapter Overview
» Estate Planning Is Essential for Your Finances
» Everyone Should Have a Will
» Deciding If a Trust Is Right for You
» Understanding Powers of Attorney
» Planning for Your Final Years

Planning is bringing the future into the present so that you can do something about it now.

– ALAN LAKEIN

You've worked hard, saved some money, maybe made some sound investments that appreciated over time, and perhaps acquired some property along the way. If you haven't already done so, now is the time to get an estate plan in place. Whether you are thirty or seventy, now is the time. Some people are put off by the idea of deciding what will happen to their assets after they die, but like they say about death, "talking about estate planning isn't going to kill you." And, while I hope we all live to a ripe old age, no one can foresee the future and it's certainly best to be prepared.

Estate planning is important, and having a plan in place can bring great peace of mind. An *estate plan* is simply a collection of legal documents and strategies outlining what should happen to your assets when you die. The plan also lays out how you want a designated person or persons to make decisions concerning your health and finances if you are unable to do so yourself.

An estate plan benefits your loved ones, which can make you feel good and more confident about what lies ahead. It's far better for you to decide how your assets should be divided than to leave that task to someone else.

NOTE

IN PRACTICE: For a complete estate planning package, I advise my clients to have in place the following: a will, trusts (if applicable), a durable power of attorney for financial decisions, a living will, guardianship appointed for a spouse and all minor children, a medical power of attorney, HIPAA forms, and directions for the disposition of remains. Other legal documents sometimes apply, but these are the most common.

Estate planning can help you achieve numerous objectives, including the following:

> » Deciding how you want your assets to be divided among your heirs
> » Supporting an organization or charity that is important to you
> » Planning for a family member with special needs
> » Maximizing tax benefits for your heirs
> » Setting parameters in the event you believe your heirs may not have the skills necessary to protect or manage your wealth
> » Choosing a guardian for your children in case you die young
> » Minimizing the chances of family strife resulting from lack of clear direction
> » Avoiding possible complications in the event there has been more than one spouse, there is a blended family, or other such factors
> » Designating personal items that have meaning for certain individuals

Some people believe that only people with tons of money and several huge properties need to worry about estate planning, but that's not the case. Your estate includes all that you own, including business interests, your residence and any other real estate, and personal property such as art, vehicles, jewelry, or antiques. Other assets include investments, life insurance policies, annuities, trusts, and more.

It's important to understand the scope and value of your estate. For simplicity's sake, when you add up the value of everything mentioned previously and any other assets you may own, less any debt you have at your death, that's the value of your estate. Some people attempt to accomplish estate planning on their own, and there are many planning documents and guides to help them do that. I would highly recommend, however, that you work with a CERTIFIED FINANCIAL PLANNER™ practitioner to help you design the estate plan and then have an attorney who specializes in estate planning draft and help you execute the documents. Regardless of the size of your estate, I'm sure you want to see it passed along in a safe and thoughtful manner.

In this chapter, we will look at exactly what estate planning entails, the documents you'll need to have, what those documents accomplish, and other considerations, including your wishes for your care in the event it becomes needed. You'll learn about some important aspects of estate planning, including wills, trusts, durable power of attorney for financial planning, medical power of attorney, living wills, guardianship for a spouse and minor children, HIPAA, and the disposition of remains (figure 40).

GRAPHIC

fig. 40

Wills

Durable Power of Attorney

Disposition of Remains

ESTATE PLANNING

Trusts

Medical Directive to Physicians

HIPAA

Guardianship

Medical Power of Attorney

DIGITAL ASSETS

After you read this chapter, download my "End of Life Planning Guide" so you can start developing a plan that fits your situation and will bring you peace of mind. You can find it in your Digital Assets by visiting go.quickstartguides.com/retirement.

Wills

A will is the most common estate planning tool there is, but depending on which survey you look at, less than one third of all Americans have one. It appears that the number of people who draft wills has dropped in the past several years, due to circumstances that include a growing number of people who lack the knowledge and/or resources to get one.

One of the key findings of Caring.com's 2020 Estate Planning and Wills Survey was that 24 percent fewer people reported having a will than did so in 2017. The study also reported that among people who do not have a will, 35.7 percent say it's because they "haven't gotten around to making one," while another 30.4 percent say it's because they "don't have enough assets to leave to anyone." Still others say they don't know how to go about getting a will or they believe it's too expensive to make one (figure 41).

fig. 41

MORE PEOPLE ARE SAYING THEY CAN'T AFFORD OR DON'T KNOW HOW TO GET A WILL

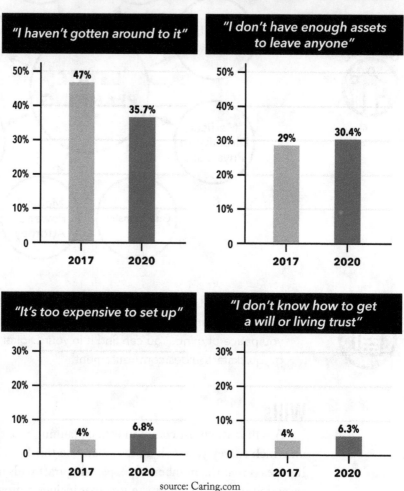

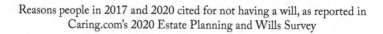

source: Caring.com

Reasons people in 2017 and 2020 cited for not having a will, as reported in Caring.com's 2020 Estate Planning and Wills Survey

A will, sometimes called a last will and testament, is simply a legal document that spells out your wishes about how you'd like your property to be distributed, who the beneficiaries will be, and, in some cases, direction regarding how the assets your beneficiaries receive should be handled. It can also identify an *executor*, who is someone who will manage the disposition of your estate after you die.

NOTE

IN PRACTICE: Your will should not be a once-and-done document. You should review and possibly update your will after a major life change such as divorce, marriage, or death of a beneficiary. You might need to alter your will after you receive an inheritance or buy a beach house. I recommend that my clients review their wills every three to five years along with their beneficiary designations.

You can designate beneficiaries in your will for big items, such as a vacation home, but also for small personal items that hold meaning for you, such as a special photograph, a collection, or even a piece of clothing. You can include these types of items within your will or create an additional document called a letter of instruction that would be kept with your will. A *letter of instruction* can include whatever you wish, such as why it's important to you that your cousin receives your collection of antique postcards.

Once your will has been drafted and executed, you should keep the original copy with your attorney or financial advisor. Another trusted person should keep signed copies in case the original cannot be located. It is not recommended that you keep your will in a safe deposit box that only you have access to, as your family may not be able to get to the will without a court order. Keeping it at home in a fireproof and waterproof box or a safe to which someone else has the combination is preferable.

Having a legal will is extremely important because if you die without one, or without one that is legally recognized in your state, you are said to be *intestate*, and the court can make decisions on your behalf. Yes, you heard me correctly. If you don't execute a will, the state in which you live has one for you, where they decide to whom assets will be distributed. That is not a desirable situation, as the court doesn't know the circumstances of you and your family and could end up acting against your interests.

NOTE

Aretha Franklin, affectionately known as the "Queen of Soul," died in August 2018. She left behind four sons, an estate valued at about $17 million, and no known, legal will. As you can imagine, the situation has caused a lot of angst among Franklin's sons and other relatives. Some handwritten wills were found in Franklin's home, but their contents are confusing, and it was not clear even two years after her death if they would be considered legal. This is just a high-profile example of how not having professionally drafted legal documents can cause turmoil.

Lacking a will, a court-appointed administrator would be directed to gather all the property and assets of the person who has died, pay off any debts, and distribute the remaining assets to beneficiaries, who are determined by the court. In most states, the contents of the estate go to the surviving spouse and children of the deceased. If the deceased does not have a surviving spouse or children, the estate can go to other relatives identified through *intestate succession*, a legal process of distributing assets. If no direct heirs are identified, the contents of the estate can become the property of the state.

While your will contains instructions on the distribution of your assets and other vital information, some assets fall outside the direction of the will. Although the distribution of these assets is not directed by the will, their value will be included in the estate for tax determination.

If you and your spouse own property jointly, such as bank accounts or real estate, that property automatically passes to the surviving spouse if there are rights of survivorship. You cannot direct your portion of the property to someone other than your spouse in this case. If you have a bank account in your name only, however, it will be directed to a beneficiary by the will.

Accounts for which you've designated beneficiaries will not be directed by the will. These typically include IRAs, annuities, transfer-on-death registrations, and life insurance policies. The beneficiary designation on the account supersedes anything written in a will.

Chris named his wife, Lisa, as the beneficiary of his life insurance policy, traditional IRA, and Roth IRA. Unfortunately, Chris and Lisa ended up divorcing. Chris, however, neglected to change the beneficiary designation on his IRAs and his life insurance policy. Three years later he remarried. He and Kristina had been married for ten years when Chris suffered a fatal heart attack. Even though it was indicated in his will and was certainly Chris's wish that Kristina would benefit from his life insurance and IRAs, she did not, because Lisa was still named as the beneficiary, and the designation on the policy took precedence over what was in Chris's will.

IN PRACTICE: I advise clients to make sure they know who they've designated as beneficiaries on all their accounts and to update them as life and preferences change.

Different Kinds of Wills

There are various types of wills, but the most common and frequently used is a *testamentary will*, which is a will that you, the *testator*, (or an advisor or lawyer) prepare and sign in the presence of witnesses. This type of will typically protects against challenges to your wishes from beneficiaries or would-be-beneficiaries after you die, which is one reason it is so widely used.

Other less-often-used types of wills include the following:

» A *holographic will* is one that is written and signed in one's own handwriting, but no one witnesses the signature. Some states recognize holographic wills, but others do not. States that do recognize them typically require proof that it was written willingly by the testator and that they were of sound mind. A holographic will does not provide anywhere near the assurance of a testamentary will and therefore is not recommended.

An interesting example of a case where someone might write a holographic will would be a pilot flying solo in a small plane, which crashes in a remote area. Unsure if he will be rescued, the pilot might express his wishes on paper in hope that they will be acknowledged.

» An *oral will* is one in which the testator verbally expresses their wishes in front of witnesses. This type of will is not widely accepted.

» A *pour-over will* is one used in conjunction with a trust. It ensures that remaining assets of the deceased will automatically transfer to an already established trust at the time of death.

» A *mutual will* is one in which two people, typically spouses, write and execute a will jointly. When one of them dies, the other is bound to the terms of the will. This type of will is typically used to prevent the surviving spouse from passing along assets to a new partner rather than to children of the deceased.

» A *joint will* is another type of will written and executed by two people, typically spouses or partners. It stipulates that all assets be passed to the surviving spouse and then, usually, to children. It's similar to a mutual will, but there are some legal differences.

Guardianship

If you die without a will, the state not only has the right to designate beneficiaries who will receive your assets, but it also gets the right to appoint a guardian to care for minor children or an incapacitated spouse. Normally, a grandparent or other relative is appointed as guardian for children, even if you would have chosen another person to fill that role. A nonrelative, such as a best friend, could petition the court to get custody of the children, but the court may not agree. In the event there are no surviving family members, the child could become a ward of the state and be assigned to the foster care system.

A husband and wife are both killed in a car accident, leaving behind their three small children. They were young and neither spouse had a will. The issue of custody is taken to the court, which decides that the health of the grandparents will not permit them to raise the children. The court appoints custody to the husband's younger sister, who is married to an abusive husband. Because of the parents' lack of wills, the children are placed in an unhappy and perhaps even dangerous situation.

You should also designate a guardian for your spouse in case he or she becomes incapacitated and cannot handle finances or other personal matters after your death. It is better to plan for such a contingency rather than have someone else make that decision for you.

IN PRACTICE: Some people designate guardians within their wills, but I advise my clients to use a separate legal document for matters of guardianship. If for any reason they need to change the designee, doing so will not affect the rest of their will.

Taxes That Can Affect Your Estate and Its Assets

You hear a lot of talk about the federal estate tax, but an exceedingly small percentage of Americans ever pay it. In fact, the Joint Committee on Taxation, a committee of the US Congress, reports that just two out of every one thousand estates pay the tax. An estate tax is a tax on the right to transfer property when you die, and the money is taken from the value of the estate before it's settled. In 2021, much of your estate will be exempt from taxation. If your estate is worth less than $11.7 million, then an estate tax will not be assessed. If your estate is worth $11.7 million or more and you are single or widowed, then the amount over $11.7 million will be taxed. For married couples, up to $23.4 million ($11.7M x 2) will be exempt from the estate tax.

The estate tax exemption is portable between spouses. Let's say that your deceased spouse never gave away any of his allotted $11.7 Million to his heirs. In that case, you, the widow, would inherit the right to give away that money tax free, up to $23.4 million (your spouse's $11.7M + your own).

Twelve states and the District of Columbia levy an estate tax, and most of them with significantly lower exemptions than the federal tax. Connecticut, Hawaii, Illinois, Maine, Maryland, Massachusetts, Minnesota, New York, Oregon, Rhode Island, Vermont, and Washington all have estate taxes, and three of them—Rhode Island, Oregon, and Massachusetts—have tax exemptions of less than $2 million.

Six states charge an inheritance tax, which is different than an estate tax. An inheritance tax is a tax on the assets passed from the estate to an heir, and the heir is responsible for paying the tax. There is no federal inheritance tax, but if the deceased lived in Iowa, Kentucky, Maryland, Nebraska, New Jersey, or Pennsylvania and you are an heir, you may be subject to the tax, even if you do not live in one of those states (figure 42). The tax does not, however, apply to inheritances passed along to the spouse or children of the deceased.

STATES THAT HAVE INHERITANCE TAX OR ESTATE TAX

fig. 42

■ Have estate tax ▨ Have both taxes

■ Have inheritance tax ▨ Have neither tax

Seventeen states and the District of Columbia levy an inheritance tax, an estate tax, or both

NOTE

It's a double whammy if you live in Maryland, as you are subject to both an estate tax and an inheritance tax.

An inheritance does not count as taxable income for state or federal income tax purposes, but there are some tax implications of which you should be aware. If you inherit an IRA, for instance, from someone other than your spouse, then you will be required to take distributions from it over a prescribed period of ten years or less. If it is a traditional IRA instead of a Roth, the money distributed will count as income and be subject to tax.

Capital gains taxes can affect an inheritance in some cases, but they can be largely avoided with inherited real estate, thanks to the ***stepped-up basis rule for inherited property***. If you inherit your parents' home, for instance, which they bought forty years ago for $80,000 and is now worth $300,000, the ***basis*** of the home, which is the combined cost of its purchase price plus any improvements made to it, is automatically "stepped up" to its current date-of-death value. That's good for you, because if you turn around and sell the house for $350,000, you are subject to capital gains on only $50,000. Without the stepped-up basis rule, your capital gains tax would be based on the difference between what your parents paid for the house all those years ago and what you sold it for.

If, however, your parents had given you the house while they were still living and you sold it, you would be responsible for capital gains taxes on the basis of what they had purchased it for, plus any improvements made. Gifting of assets can reduce the value of an estate and result in tax advantages, but most people do not have sufficient assets to make it necessary or advisable to do so. If you are going to consider gifting, I would advise you to consult with a qualified professional and consider carefully.

The stepped-up basis rule also applies to inherited stock. The increase in the stock's value between the time it was purchased and when you inherited it is not taxed. If you sell it, you will only pay capital gains on any increase since the time the stock was inherited.

Capital gains taxes do apply to some inherited property. If you inherit an antique table valued at $5,000 and you sell it for $10,000, you'll be liable for capital gains on $5,000.

IN PRACTICE: The stepped-up basis tax law is not well known but can be greatly beneficial when employed. Unless there is a compelling reason for you to gift a highly appreciated asset while you are living, an action that results in taxes for the heir, I would recommend that you hold onto the asset and pass it along after your death, thereby giving the beneficiary the tax break.

Trusts

Like a will, a *trust* is a method of transferring the assets of your estate to beneficiaries. There are many types of trusts, but generally a trust can be defined as an agreement under which a person or organization, known as the *trustee*, holds property on a temporary basis for the benefit of one or more heirs. A *grantor* is a person who creates the trust and transfers property into it. An individual can be both the grantor and the trustee of a trust, with a successor trustee designated to take over at the time of the grantor's death.

An important distinction is that property can be transferred into a trust while the grantor is still living or after he or she dies. A trust into which property is transferred while the grantor is alive is called a *living trust*. If property is transferred after death, the trust is called a *testamentary trust*. The grantor's wish to transfer property to a trust after their death would be specified in a special type of will.

IN PRACTICE: The type of trust you establish could depend on the state in which you live. If you live in a probate-friendly state, which is one that allows you to streamline the probate process that occurs when a will is filed, you may want to opt for a testamentary trust. If you don't live in a probate-friendly state, a living trust might be a better choice. If you live in one state and have assets in another, choose a living trust, as it will enable you to avoid probate in both states.

Another important difference is whether a trust is a *revocable trust* or an *irrevocable trust*. A revocable trust can be changed whenever the grantor sees fit if he or she is living, but an irrevocable trust is essentially set in stone and cannot be changed.

Trusts can be an asset in your estate planning efforts. They can save time and money and limit tax liability, but they can also be complicated. It's important that they be set up to work exactly how you intended, and for that reason it's important to find someone who is reliable, knowledgeable, and trustworthy to advise you. I will provide some information about trusts in this section, but it is by no means comprehensive. Please seek expert advice if you plan to establish a trust.

Potential Benefits of Establishing a Trust

Establishing a trust can be beneficial in a variety of ways, including potentially providing tax benefits, helping to avoid the probate process that pertains to wills, giving you some control over how your assets are used, and providing flexibility regarding your assets up until the time of your death.

Tax considerations are one of the most common reasons that someone sets up a trust. There are all types of trusts that can help someone reduce estate taxes, many of which are primarily beneficial to large estates. That said, trusts can be used for smaller estates as well as larger ones. I find that they are handy across the board when the family needs to accommodate a special needs child, a spendthrift heir, or a derelict heir. I typically recommend that we use trusts when the assets being allotted are valued at more than $200K.

Trusts can be used to help protect your heirs' money from creditors, litigation, and divorce.

One type of trust commonly established for estate and tax considerations is an irrevocable trust, which, as you read earlier, is a trust that, once set up, cannot be changed. Assets placed into an irrevocable trust are no longer considered part of the grantor's estate. They belong to the trust, not the estate, which reduces the size of the estate and any taxes that must be paid on it. If enough assets are placed in the trust, a grantor can avoid having to pay an estate tax. The income earned on the assets in an irrevocable trust is taxed, but at trust tax brackets, not the grantor's tax brackets.

People who work in professions that make them more susceptible to lawsuits sometimes use irrevocable trusts to shelter money from possible legal creditors and judgments, since the trust cannot be part of a suit. The downside to an irrevocable trust is that it takes your money out of your control. If you set up an irrevocable trust and for some reason determine it was a mistake to do so, the document cannot easily be changed.

Many people establish a revocable trust with the purpose of avoiding *probate*, which is the court-supervised process of verifying the will of a deceased person. Probate is not always necessary, as some states permit property valued below a specified amount to be passed on to heirs without it. If there is substantial property, however, and especially if a will is contested, probate can drag on, extending the time before heirs can receive inheritances and resulting in high legal fees.

NOTE Trust assets are typically distributed by the trustee without having to go through probate. Because a trust is a private agreement, it does not become part of a public record, as a will does. That privacy is important to some individuals and families.

A trust can also help you control how your heirs use the assets you leave them. You can, for instance, leave money to a young grandchild with the stipulation that it not be accessed until the child is eighteen and at that point be used to cover college tuition. You can set up a fund for a family member with special needs or control how money is paid out to someone who is notorious for spending every dime that comes their way.

There are several types of trusts that enable you to contribute to a charity or charities of your choice and also benefit your estate. If there are organizations that support causes that are important to you, using a trust could be advantageous to both the organization and you and your family.

EXAMPLE Don bought a tract of land twenty years ago with the thought of one day building a dream retirement home. He and his family relocated and the home never materialized, but the land greatly increased in value. His $50,000 investment is now valued at $300,000. Don would like to sell the property but is concerned that capital gains taxes would devour a sizeable portion of his profits. His advisor suggests a *charitable remainder trust*, which would enable Don to support a charity he is passionate about while generating income for himself. Don gives the land to the charity, and the charity sells it for $300,000. Because charities do not have to pay capital gains taxes, the charity is able to invest the entire amount in a stock fund, while agreeing to pay Don a percentage of the trust each year for the rest of his life. Assuming the investment makes a return each year, the original principal remains with the charity to be used as needed after Don's death.

If you have a revocable trust and become incapacitated, your trustee can step in and make distributions, pay bills, and take care of other financial considerations for you. If you are both the grantor and the trustee of the trust, the successor trustee can take over. This arrangement can safeguard your family from having to make financial decisions during difficult times.

While trusts have significant benefits, it is particularly important that they are properly established and maintained, especially in the case of an irrevocable trust. Again, I strongly recommend that you find a CFP® practitioner and an attorney with expertise in trusts to assist you.

Power of Attorney

Having one or more powers of attorney is another essential piece of estate planning. A *power of attorney* is a legal document that authorizes an individual to act on your behalf in the event you are unable to do so. The term "power of attorney" can also refer to the person you designate. In legal language, the person who appoints someone to act on their behalf is called the *principal*. The person designated is called the *agent* or the *attorney-in-fact*.

Powers of attorney give certain types of authority to an agent. A *medical power of attorney*, for instance, authorizes an agent to make decisions about your health care and medical considerations. The agent would not be authorized to conduct financial business under the auspices of a medical power of attorney. A *durable power of attorney* grants an agent authority to make decisions concerning your finances.

An often-overlooked document is a *HIPAA release form*, which enables protected health information to be shared with designated family members or others. If you are not sure if you've authorized others to gain access to your health information, you should do so.

Think carefully about who should be able to get that information, and make sure there is a record of it. And, if you have a young adult child who does not have a spouse or significant other, you should request that they designate you on their HIPAA release form. A family in Los Angeles had a college-age daughter who had a serious accident and was in a hospital in San Francisco. Without a HIPAA release form, her parents were unable to get any information about her condition from the doctors, so they had to drive all night to the hospital.

Having a durable power of attorney is crucial because it can protect your and your family's financial interests. If you become suddenly incapacitated and have not designated an agent through a durable power of attorney to attend to your business affairs, tasks such as filing taxes, signing checks, paying bills, and handling bank accounts could remain undone. If you do not have a medical power of attorney, choices regarding your medical condition are left to family members, who may or may not make decisions according to your wishes.

If you don't have a power of attorney and you become unable to make decisions and handle your affairs, the court may appoint one or more individuals to act on your behalf. That person is known as a *guardian* or *conservator*. It's likely that you would have no input regarding who was appointed, and there's no guarantee that the guardian would know enough about your wishes to accommodate them.

If you are retired and do not have a durable power of attorney, or you have an elderly parent, friend, or relative who does not, remember that once someone becomes mentally incompetent, it is too late to get one. You can't authorize one on behalf of someone else; the principal must authorize their own power of attorney.

Some powers of attorney are temporary, while others are permanent. You can assign an agent to handle a specific task, such as trading on a brokerage account for you while you are on an extended trip, or you can assign broader powers at your discretion. If you have both a medical and a durable power of attorney, you can appoint the same person to serve as agent for both.

If your financial affairs are complicated, the agent named by your durable power of attorney can employ a professional, preferably someone who is already familiar with your situation, to help. Those expenses would be paid out of your assets. The agent, who can be a friend or family member, is responsible for carrying out your wishes as specified in the durable power of attorney.

Laws pertaining to powers of attorney vary from state to state, and there is no one power of attorney that is common to every state. If you find an online form and choose to use it to establish a power of attorney, be sure that it complies with the requirements of your state.

Medical Directive to Physicians

In addition to a medical power of attorney, everyone should have a *living will*, sometimes called a "health care declaration" or a "medical directive to physicians." This document provides clear, written health care instructions to your agent, who communicates those instructions to health care providers. Having a living will can be a great relief for family members, who are then able to make difficult decisions based on your expressed wishes. It springs into play when there is an irreversible or terminal medical condition. Most people don't want to be a financial drain on their spouse, so they choose the option of being kept comfortable while not being kept on life support.

Christina and her daughter, Ann, often talked about Christina's wishes regarding her health care, but Christina never drafted a living will. When she broke her hip at age eighty-seven and suffered complications afterward, medical personnel said she would need a feeding tube to survive. Her chances of recovery were unclear, and, knowing Christina's wishes, Ann was reluctant to have the tube inserted, but she felt pressured by the doctors and some family members, and so she agreed. Christina remained in a nursing home with the feeding tube for two miserable years, after which Ann made the heartbreaking decision to have it removed. Her mother died shortly after. Had Christina had a living will, it may have made it possible for Ann to prevent the feeding tube from being inserted in the first place. Doing so would have been honoring what Ann knew to be her mother's wish, but without the living will, she had no basis of proof.

Choosing an Agent

When choosing an agent for a financial power of attorney (not a decision to be taken lightly), it's important that the individual be financially savvy enough to handle everything that will need to be done. The agent does not need to be a financial professional but should be someone with the common sense and humility to know when they need to get some help.

Choosing an agent to handle your medical situation can be even more complex, as not everyone can make difficult decisions concerning health and end-of-life matters. Someone who has never been exposed to medical situations may feel extremely uncomfortable having to discuss medical care with health professionals. While much of the handling of finances can be done remotely, it is a good idea for your medical power of attorney to be local, or at very least possess an intimate knowledge of your health care needs. You will depend on this person to advocate for you in medical situations.

Many people choose their spouse or grown child to serve as the agent for their financial or medical power of attorney. In some cases, the same person is appointed as agent for both. That can work in certain situations, but consider the talents, personality, and temperament of the person you are considering. Some people are better cut out for these roles than others.

And, if you are seventy-eight and name your eighty-year-old husband as your medical agent, consider the possibility that he may not be able to handle that role if you need him to in five or ten years. Above all, choose an agent you trust completely.

Handling End-of-Life Care

End-of-life care is difficult to discuss, and therefore many people simply do not. The Conversation Project, a public engagement initiative that encourages people to plan for and let others know their wishes for the end of their lives, has found that 92 percent of Americans say it is important to discuss what they envision for end-of-life care, but only 32 percent have done so. There are many facets of planning and handling end-of-life care, and it's better to be prepared than unprepared.

Talking about end-of-life care might be difficult, but it is an important part of estate planning and a necessary chore. Will you be able to stay in your current location, or should you consider a retirement community or assisted living facility? Will you be able to continue to drive, do your own yard work, and go grocery shopping? Deciding where to live is an important part of planning for your latter years. If you are able to live on your own, does it make sense to stay where you are, or might you want to get a smaller home with everything on one floor, or look for an apartment where you would not be responsible for upkeep?

Plan for how you will pay for care if you can no longer live on your own. If you have long-term care insurance, review the terms of your contract, and make sure you understand what type and how much care is provided. It's likely that the policy provides a certain number of years of care, after which benefits cease.

If you don't have long-term care insurance, where will the money for assisted living or nursing care come from if it becomes necessary? Research options for what is available in your area. Talk to family members regarding their wishes and concerns. Look into in-home care, which often is much less expensive than assisted living or a nursing home. If your financial resources are sparse, investigate whether you might be eligible for Medicaid, which provides general health coverage and coverage for home health and nursing home services. The process varies from state to state and can be time-consuming, so it's best not to wait to begin.

Other important aspects of planning for end-of-life care include letting others know that your medical wishes are drawn up and shared in your living will, and making sure you have a medical power of attorney and an agent you trust. It can bring you peace of mind and relieve your loved ones of a burden after your passing if you preplan funeral arrangements. You should also make your wishes clear regarding the disposition of your remains.

Regarding the disposition of your remains, basically your choices are to have your body cremated, buried, or donated to science. Thinking about which method you prefer and letting those wishes be known can be extremely helpful to survivors, who will not be forced to guess about what you would have wanted.

IN PRACTICE: If you wish to donate your body for medical research, you will probably need to work with a research hospital or medical school. The process involves getting registered for consideration within the hospital system. If the hospital chooses to accept your body, researchers will perform their work with it and then usually have it cremated and the ashes returned to family members at no cost to the family.

You've already read about the importance of having a living will, which can provide peace of mind for you and your family members. Your medical power of attorney and/or living will should contain the following information:

» Who you want to oversee your medical care if you are unable to do so

» Whether you would prefer to be at home or in a medical facility at the end of your life

» Your thoughts on palliative care and hospice care

» How you feel about certain medical procedures, such as tube feeding, resuscitation, dialysis, and mechanical ventilation

» Your wishes concerning organ and tissue donation after your death

Effective estate planning is an important piece of your financial plan, but it's also a significant personal achievement. Completing a will, setting up a trust (if applicable), getting powers of attorney and advance directives in place, and planning for end-of-life care are necessary tasks that can help ensure you and your loved ones will be secure in the future.

MY TAKE

The two most common mistakes I see relating to financial and retirement planning are not having disability insurance and having no estate planning documents in place. Both of those things are crucial and two of the most important benefits you can provide for your family.

Chapter Recap

» Estate planning is important both financially and for the peace of mind of you and your family.

» A will spells out how you want your assets divided and who should get them.

» A trust is another method of transferring assets; it places property in the hands of a trustee, who holds it on a temporary basis.

» Powers of attorney ensure that your finances will be taken care of and your health care directives will be followed if you become incapacitated.

» Planning in advance for the final years of your life can help your loved ones make informed and measured decisions.

Conclusion

All you need is the plan, the road map, and the courage to press on to your destination

— EARL NIGHTINGALE
American author

Planning for retirement requires time, commitment, attention to detail, and knowledge about managing and investing money. I hope this book has provided a lot of that knowledge and that you feel more confident about taking on your retirement planning than you did before you read it. It was important to me to share my knowledge and experience with you because I don't want to see you make the mistakes many people do. There are some common but serious pitfalls that can cause real setbacks in retirement planning.

I won't list all the mistakes I've seen, but some of the most common include the following (figure 43):

MISTAKES COMMONLY MADE WHEN PLANNING FOR RETIREMENT

fig. 43

⚠ Not setting financial goals in alignment with lifestyle goals	⚠ Not committing to being financially successful
⚠ Not defining a life plan leading up to and including retirement	⚠ Not obtaining education about personal finance
⚠ Not managing credit wisely	⚠ Not confronting one's financial reality
⚠ Not seeking professional assistance	⚠ Not using tax laws to one's advantage
⚠ Not allocating assets properly and adjusting as needed	⚠ Not planning for the unexpected
⚠ Not taking full advantage of employer benefits	⚠ Not choosing the most efficient ways to make distributions from retirement accounts
⚠ Not having an estate planning strategy	⚠ Not creating a comprehensive financial plan

I do not expect you'll remember everything you read in this book. I very much hope, however, that you will take to heart the big ideas, and that by rounding out and expanding your general knowledge base you will avoid the mistakes we've listed. Furthermore, I hope you will begin to understand how all aspects of retirement planning are intertwined.

As you think about and plan for your retirement, I urge you to contemplate these important ideas:

» By setting goals and planning what you want to do with the last twenty or thirty years of your life, you can get an idea of how much money you will need to achieve the lifestyle you desire. You should seek to align your planning with making your money work for you to achieve your goals. And remember, the sooner you begin planning for retirement, the more time you have to grow your money to provide for it.

» Having a budget in retirement is every bit as important as having one before you retire. Work carefully to anticipate what your expenses will be and to prioritize your spending. To assure you'll continue contributing to causes you support, make giving one of your most significant and thoughtful spending commitments. Taxes, debt, living expenses, and investments that keep your money growing at a pace faster than inflation are all also very important, but giving back is the most important thing you can do with your money during your time on this earth.

» Because planning for retirement and managing your finances once you are in retirement take time, skill, and significant effort, you should either commit to doing it well or get a good CFP® practitioner on your team. You can locate all the fine points of crafting and maintaining a comprehensive financial plan on the internet—just google it. Doing so, however, would take hours and hours of your time and a whole lot of effort. In a moment I'm going to explain why it's so important to have a trusted advisor available to guide you, but for now, understand that research has repeatedly shown that the value of an advisor clearly outweighs the associated fees charged for services.

While I understand some readers may be put off by my repeated recommendation that they seek out the services of a CFP® practitioner, I cannot stress enough how important I believe it is to have someone by your side as you manage your financial life and plan for your retirement. Why? Number one, crafting a sound financial strategy plan is not something that everyone has the education, training, and experience to do. I've met exceptionally talented surgeons, IT professionals, teachers, engineers, and others who, though they're experts at their crafts, understandably have little to no knowledge of how to create a financial plan to see them through the next fifty or sixty years of their lives.

A CFP® practitioner will work with you to produce a written plan that will become your guide—your playbook. A financial plan should never be static; it's imperative to have one in place that can be tweaked and adjusted as your circumstances change.

IN PRACTICE: I work with every single new client to produce a written financial plan that states their goals, timeline, and other applicable information. A study among a group of Harvard MBA students revealed that those with written financial goals were faring exponentially better ten years after graduation than those with goals that were not in writing, and far better financially than students who had graduated with no stated goals.

What Your Financial Plan Should Include

A financial plan is a comprehensive picture of what you have, what you'd like to accomplish financially, and how you plan to achieve your financial goals. It should cover all areas that affect your finances, including investments, business interests, real estate, insurance, taxes, estate planning, and everything in between. A financial plan is an ongoing project aimed at helping you plan for the long term and reducing stress concerning your financial future.

Investing is an important part of any financial plan because it is key to accumulating wealth. A savings account with a 0.05 percent interest rate is okay for money you may need to access immediately, but to build a retirement portfolio you'll need to get your money into other types of investments, such as stocks, bonds, and ETFs. And remember, while investing is an important part of a financial plan, it is by no means the only piece. Your plan should also include the following:

> » **Retirement projections.** You'll need a good understanding of what you have and what you will need in retirement, again reinforcing the need for a retirement budget. Know how sustainable the distributions are from your investment accounts. Are you going to

run out of money in five years, or will you have enough if you live to be ninety-five? Assess your lifestyle expectations and ensure that your combined retirement income from sources such as Social Security, a pension, rental income, and portfolio withdrawals will be enough to support those expectations. There are many assumptions that help you make the projections, like inflation, age, and when to take Social Security, to name a few. These can affect your financial projections in retirement, and you'll be wise to take them all into consideration.

» **Insurance coverage.** Having the right insurance plans is important throughout your life, but the types of insurance you need change as you get older. Disability and life insurance are critical during the years you are earning because they replace lost income and enable you to continue providing for yourself or your family, but they may be less important once you are retired and not dependent on earnings. Long-term care insurance probably isn't on your radar when you're in your twenties or thirties but may become a priority as you get into your fifties and sixties. A CFP® practitioner can help you obtain insurance coverage for the right amounts, reasons, and times of your life. It's also quite important not to overlook personal and professional liability insurance.

» **Estate planning.** Although it's an important piece of a financial plan, estate planning is also something you should do to ensure peace of mind. Knowing how your estate, regardless of its size, will be divided and handled after your death is reassuring. In addition to designating heirs, estate planning gives you the opportunity to choose a guardian for minor children, take advantage of tax strategies to save your heirs and estate a lot of money, support a charity that is important to you, or provide for a family member with special needs.

» **Business planning.** If you own a business, it should be front and center in your financial plan, as it likely is responsible for your livelihood. The business piece of your overall financial plan would address factors such as credit, overhead expenses, cash flow, succession planning, employee benefits, tax planning, business structure, and many other moving parts.

» **Tax planning**. As you've read, tax planning is important to your overall financial health. You cannot avoid taxes, but there are methods you can use to minimize what you will need to pay. Tax law flows through every part of your financial plan, so you need to know and take advantage of these laws.

In appendix III of this book, *The Universe of Comprehensive Financial Planning*, I've included a sweeping list of the field's many facets, expanding not only on the categories in the preceding section but others as well.

The Connectivity of a Comprehensive Financial Plan

An important concept to understand is that every part of your financial plan is connected to all the other parts. In my experience, people tend to think of their finances in pieces, or silos. There's the tax piece, the insurance piece, the investment piece, etc. What they fail to understand is how all the pieces of the plan are interconnected (figure 44). Having a big-picture view of your financial plan can help avoid any unintended financial consequences that can occur if you don't understand how each part of the plan works in coordination with the others.

Having the equivalent of three to six months of cash in an emergency fund is an important part of investment management. But what happens if, at the end of the year, you discover you didn't pay enough taxes and you need to come up with $2,500 to make up the shortfall? All of a sudden your emergency fund, from which you withdraw money to pay your taxes, is not only a tool in how you handle your investments, it's also an important piece of your tax planning strategy. Or perhaps you need money from the emergency fund to pay high deductibles on your medical insurance or to finance a three-month waiting period until disability benefits kick in. That would connect the investment management and insurance pieces of your overall plan. Failing to recognize how each part of your overall financial plan is connected to the others can put you one step away from a financial crisis. Picture the scenario of not having an emergency fund and discovering that you owe an additional $2,500 in taxes. You might be forced to take money from an IRA account, encountering taxes and penalties and negatively affecting your overall financial plan.

IT'S ALL CONNECTED

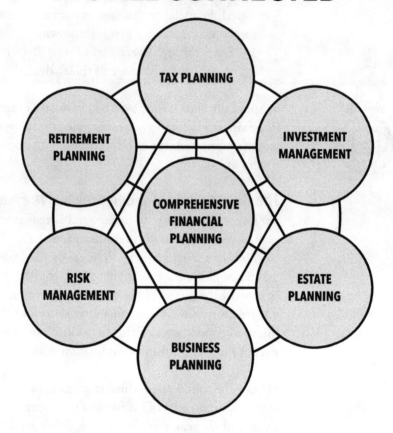

GRAPHIC

fig. 44

Comprehensive financial planning connects all the parts of the plan.

Your CFP® practitioner can explain the workings and details of each part of your overall plan, and how each piece works in connection with every other piece. This will help you to achieve a holistic view of your finances and keep you on track to achieve your goals.

Monitoring and Reviewing Your Plan

Once you have a sound financial plan in place, it's imperative that you review and monitor it regularly. Few things in life remain unchanged, including factors that affect your finances. Changes in tax laws, legislative changes, or external factors can affect your plan. Your health may change, increasing your medical costs and affecting your budget. Market conditions fluctuate, affecting the rate of return on your investments. Perhaps you will decide you want to get your assets into less aggressive investments, necessitating more change.

Monitoring your financial plan is an involved process, but a good CFP® practitioner can work with you to keep the plan on track according to your risk tolerance, life changes, needs, and time frame. Research has repeatedly shown that the value of working with a trusted financial advisor clearly outweighs the associated fees. In fact, the well-regarded "2020 Value of an Advisor Study" from Russell Investments asserts that the value of a financial advisor in the United States creates a benefit to the client of 4.81 percent—an advantageous amount that eclipses the average 1 percent fee charged by an advisor. When you consider that the gain to your portfolio averages roughly five times the fee you pay, it makes a strong case for working with a qualified advisor. If you would like a copy of the Russell Investments study or the "Vanguard Advisor's Alpha" report, which explores similar findings, please email me at tsnow@snowfinancialgroup.com.

Russell's 4.81 percent is based on five areas of value that an advisor brings to a client. These five areas are depicted in figure 45:

A Annual rebalancing of investment portfolios

+ **B** Behavorial mistakes individual investors typically make

+ **C** Cost of basic investment-only management

+ **P** Planning costs and ancillary services

+ **T** Tax-smart planning and investing

fig. 45

THE SUM > THE FEE
The annual advisory fee
charged to clients

source: Russell Investments

Russell Investments' five areas of value a financial advisor brings to a client

Let's have a closer look at each of those five areas.

»   Annual rebalancing helps you to avoid unnecessary risk exposure if markets become unstable and volatile. The Russell study revealed that annual rebalancing of a portfolio has the potential to add 0.32 percent in returns and 0.4 percent in risk mitigation. Compounded over time, those amounts can quickly add up.

» Avoiding behavioral mistakes saves you money, adding as much as 2.17 percent of value to your portfolio, according to Russell. Mistakes such as trading too often, selling winners too early, or holding on too long to losers can happen at any time in the market cycle, making behavior coaching one of the most important services a CFP® practitioner delivers to clients.

» "Basic investment-only management" nowadays typically refers to fully automated portfolio managers, or "robo-advisors." Many people believe that using a robo-advisor can save money, but it's smart to remember that the services offered by a robo-advisor are limited. While a robo-advisor provides basic portfolio management—typically for an annual fee of about .29 percent of the portfolio value—it may not include a financial plan, ongoing service, or guidance. Those additional services, which a CFP® practitioner will always offer, present real value that will often surpass any initial savings on fees offered by robo-advisors.

» A financial plan is imperative, but many people do not have the skills or time to put one into place and shepherd it through to conclusion. The value of having a CFP® practitioner do that for you is set by Russell at 0.72 percent.

» Taxes can significantly eat into returns, making tax management exceptionally important. Tax-smart investing, led by a qualified financial advisor, can result in a 1.31 percent value for a client.

Take a bit of time to consider the value of each of those areas, asking yourself if you would be confident in managing those tasks on your own. When carefully considered, I believe the case for finding a good CFP® practitioner is clear.

When seeking an advisor, remember that while many people offer financial planning services, some are more qualified than others. You can seek financial advice from a stockbroker or insurance agent who solicits potential clients nearing retirement age, but many of these brokers and agents work within a limited scope of services, are not fiduciaries, and don't have the extensive education and continuing education requirements of a CFP® practitioner or a registered investment advisor.

A Parting Thought

As you plan for, enter, and live in retirement, I hope you will strive to create margin in your life. Take time for yourself and to spend with the people you care about. Take time to help others by giving of your time, talents, and resources. Perhaps become someone's mentor or spend time regularly with an underprivileged child.

As you've read numerous times, it is best throughout your life to live well within your means, avoiding unnecessary debt. Avoid the temptation to compare your lifestyle with that of neighbors, friends, or family members, choosing instead to simply enjoy and appreciate what you have and do rather than what you don't have or don't do.

Retirement planning must include both spouses in all financial discussions and decisions; work together to land on the same page as you map out your financial future. More people divorce due to conflict over finances than for any other reason, so work hard to ensure that money does not create friction in your marriage.

Finally, thank you for taking time to read and learn from this book. I hope it has encouraged you to think positively about the possibilities for retirement and to plan well for those possibilities. If you haven't yet, please do take advantage of the tools and resources we've prepared for you as you move forward on your journey. These can be found in your free Digital Assets at go.quickstartguides.com/retirement. I would welcome your comments or questions at tsnow@snowfinancialgroup.com. Meanwhile, I wish you a sound financial future and a satisfying and purposeful life.

REMEMBER TO DOWNLOAD YOUR FREE DIGITAL ASSETS!

 Portfolio Asset Allocator Workbook

 Long-Term Care Need Calculator

 End-of-Life Planning Guide

 Cash Flow/Budget Calculator

TWO WAYS TO ACCESS YOUR FREE DIGITAL ASSETS

Use the camera app on your mobile phone to scan the QR code
or visit the link below and instantly access your digital assets.

SCAN ME

or

go.quickstartguides.com/retirement

VISIT URL

Appendix I
Online Advisors and Robo-Advisors

The popularity of online investment services has increased tremendously in the past several decades, which makes sense, because most trading takes place over the internet. And, while I acknowledge there are many do-it-yourselfers out there who like the ease of investing with online brokers, I would offer a word of caution to anyone who is serious about planning for their retirement.

An online brokerage firm is limited in scope in terms of what it can provide its clients. It is simply a liaison between clients and tradeable securities, not a trusted advisor. And remember that an online broker only handles investments, not other important aspects of retirement planning such as helping you with estate planning or managing insurance accounts.

MY TAKE

If you'll recall my story, as told in the introduction, I worked for Fidelity Investments early in my career. One of the reasons I decided to leave Fidelity and strike out on my own was that I was limited in the advice I was able to offer clients. I could only go so far, and it was frustrating to me, because I knew I was not fully serving my clients' interests. This is true with online brokers, who can only go so far in an advisory capacity.

I'm not saying there is not a place for online brokers. In the whole sphere of retirement planning, however, I believe you would be much better served by a CERTIFIED FINANCIAL PLANNER™ practitioner or a registered investment advisor who could help you with all aspects of your finances as they pertain to retirement.

Despite these caveats, I can't deny that online brokers and robo-advisors are an increasingly pervasive part of the financial services ecosystem. And they are not alike. Here is a list of seven of the best online brokers from StockBrokers.com, an organization that researches and evaluates online brokers (figure 46).

Robo-advisors use sophisticated software and computer algorithms to analyze, build, and manage your investments, based on a risk assessment evaluation and a survey of your investment objectives. Services offered might include automatic *rebalancing of your portfolio*, a practice in which assets are bought or sold so that the portfolio better reflects your risk tolerance or investment objectives.

fig. 46

BEST ONLINE BROKERS 2020

StockBrokers.com's list of best online brokers for 2020

Many robo-advisors also offer tax-loss harvesting services, which is when you sell securities at a loss to offset a capital gains tax liability. This is a standard service with some robo-advisors, but others require that you have a certain amount of money invested before tax-loss harvesting is provided.

Robo-advisors charge clients for their services, but the fees are typically only one-quarter to one-half as much as the standard 1 percent fee charged by a human financial advisor. If you are going to pursue a robo-advisor, look for an account that is easy to set up, contains robust security features, and comes with low fees. Be sure to clarify what type of customer service is available, and how extensive those services are.

If you decide to go with a robo-advisor, it is a good idea to keep an eye on your investments. If your account is through a brokerage that offers its own funds, such as Vanguard or Fidelity, be aware that the algorithms may be configured to favor those proprietary funds, which may hold higher fees.

And again, be aware that robo-advisors cannot assist you with all aspects of your retirement planning, and they do not take the place of a trusted human advisor who can offer a wide and dependable breadth of resources and advice.

Bankrate, a consumer financial services company, released its list of the best robo-advisors in June 2020 (figure 47).

BEST ROBO-ADVISORS
IN JUNE 2020

fig. 47

Bankrate's list of best robo-advisors in June 2020

Whatever your preferences regarding financial advisors, do your homework before deciding with whom to invest your funds. Remain aware and up to date on your portfolio. Do not hesitate to ask questions or seek advice if something does not seem right with your investments or there is something you don't understand.

Appendix II

State Health Insurance Assistance Program Numbers

STATE	PHONE NUMBER
AL	800-243-5463
AK	800-478-6065 or 907-269-3680
AZ	800-432-4040 or 602-542-4446
AR	800-224-6330 or 501-371-2782
CA	800-434-0222
CO	888-696-7213
CT	800-994-9422
DE	800-336-9500 or 302-674-7364
D.C.	202-739-0668
FL	800-963-5337
GA	866-552-4464
HI	888-875-9229 or 866-810-4379 (TTY)
ID	800-247-4422
IL	800-548-9034 or 217-524-4872 (TDD)
IN	800-452-4800 or 866-846-0139 (TDD)
IA	800-351-4664
KS	800-860-5260
KY	877-293-7447
LA	800-259-5301
ME	800-262-2232 or 800-606-0215 (TTY)
MD	800-243-3425 or 410-767-1100
MA	800-243-4636, 617-727-7750, or 800-872-0166 (TDD/TTY)
MI	800-803-7174
MN	800-333-2433
MS	800-345-6347 or 601-359-4929
MO	800-390-3330

STATE	PHONE NUMBER
MT	800-551-3191
NE	800-234-7119, 402-471-2201, or 800-833-7352 (TDD)
NV	800-307-4444 or 702-486-3478
NH	866-634-9412
NJ	800-792-8820
NM	800-432-2080 or 505-476-4846
NY	800-701-0501
NC	800-443-9354 or 919-807-6900
ND	888-575-6611, 701-328-2440, or 800-366-6888 (TTY)
OH	800-686-1578
OK	800-763-2828
OR	800-722-4134
PA	800-783-7067
RI	401-462-4000
SC	800-868-9095
SD	800-536-8197
TN	877-801-0044
TX	800-252-9240
UT	800-541-7735
VT	800-642-5119
VA	800-552-3402 or 804-662-9333
WA	800-562-6900
WV	877-987-4463 or 304-558-3317
WI	800-242-1060
WY	800-856-4398

fig. 48

If you have questions about Medicare or just want some help talking through your options, you can take advantage of free, one-on-one counseling available through your state's State Health Insurance Assistance Program (SHIP). Federally funded, SHIP programs are not connected to any insurance company or health plan. They were established to help beneficiaries choose plans, resolve billing problems, handle complaints about medical care or treatment, and help clarify other issues involving Medicare.

Appendix III

The Universe of Comprehensive Financial Planning

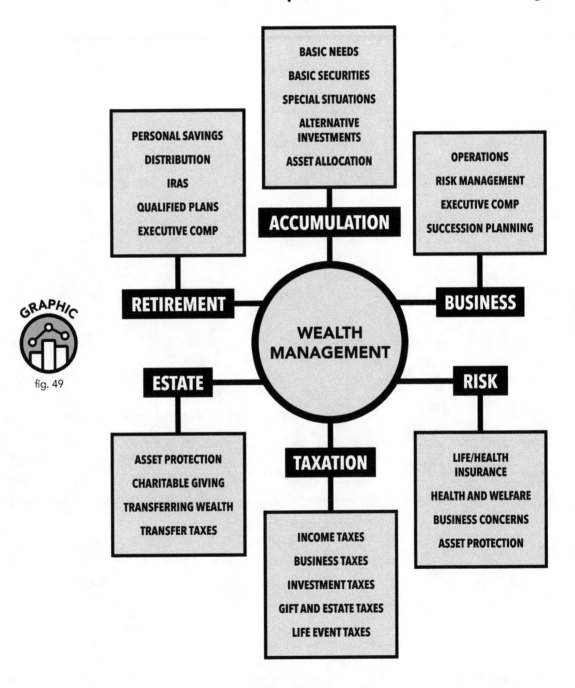

BASIC NEEDS

BASIC SECURITIES

SPECIAL SITUATIONS

ALTERNATIVE INVESTMENTS

ASSET ALLOCATION

PERSONAL SAVINGS

DISTRIBUTION

IRAS

QUALIFIED PLANS

EXECUTIVE COMP

OPERATIONS

RISK MANAGEMENT

EXECUTIVE COMP

SUCCESSION PLANNING

ACCUMULATION

GRAPHIC

fig. 49

RETIREMENT

BUSINESS

WEALTH MANAGEMENT

ESTATE

RISK

ASSET PROTECTION

CHARITABLE GIVING

TRANSFERRING WEALTH

TRANSFER TAXES

TAXATION

LIFE/HEALTH INSURANCE

HEALTH AND WELFARE

BUSINESS CONCERNS

ASSET PROTECTION

INCOME TAXES

BUSINESS TAXES

INVESTMENT TAXES

GIFT AND ESTATE TAXES

LIFE EVENT TAXES

About the Author

TED D. SNOW, CFP®, MBA

Ted is a 34-year veteran investor, money manager, and author of the #1 best-selling *Investing QuickStart Guide* from ClydeBank Media. His written work has been featured in Forbes, U.S. News & World Report, Kiplinger, Yahoo! Finance, CNBC, Investopedia, and the Suit.

Ted's journey as a financial services industry professional began in 1987 when he took a position with a well-known investment firm in Boston. Over the next ten years, Ted honed his craft in the securities industry by providing superior customer service in mutual fund investing, individual securities trading, and financial planning concepts.

After graduating magna cum laude with his MBA in financial planning from the University of Dallas, Ted decided it was time to take a huge leap of faith. He started his own practice with the aim of providing solutions to some of the most prevalent problems he'd observed in the financial services industry. Prior to striking out on his own, Ted had grown uneasy with some of the restrictions that prevented him from offering comprehensive and practical advice to his clients. Too often, as an employee at a large firm, he'd find himself feeling helpless as he watched his customers make emotional and risky financial decisions, choosing to "do it themselves," not knowing what they didn't know. As an independent, Ted would be free to advise his customers with unfettered integrity. Coordination of retirement, investments, insurance, business, estate, and taxes would become the hallmark of Ted's multifaceted, down-to-earth, and detailed approach to financial planning.

After spending eight years with various independent firms and building his own practice in accordance with his values, Ted founded Snow Financial Group LLC in 2006 with the purpose of offering truly personal service to his clients. Snow Financial Group focuses on two primary values: first, offering great client service. The firm's client list is kept small by design so as to provide quick access to Ted and his staff members, all while creating the opportunity for great personal relationships with clients. The second value is best described as "transparency by way of comfort." The idea is to create a friendly and easygoing atmosphere where people feel comfortable being open and honest about their financial lives.

In addition to being a CERTIFIED FINANCIAL PLANNER (CFP)®, Ted is also a former adjunct professor at the University of Dallas, Graduate School of Management. He holds Series 6 and Series 63 Uniform Securities licenses, a Series 7 General Securities license, and a Group I Insurance license. He's a recipient of the Five Star Professional Wealth Manager Award from *Texas Monthly*.

About QuickStart Guides

QuickStart Guides are books for beginners, written by experts.

QuickStart Guides® are comprehensive learning companions tailored for the beginner experience. Our books are written by experts, subject matter authorities, and thought leaders within their respective areas of study.

For nearly a decade more than 850,000 readers have trusted QuickStart Guides® to help them get a handle on their finances, start their own business, invest in the stock market, find a new hobby, get a new job—the list is virtually endless.

The QuickStart Guides® series of books is published by ClydeBank Media, an independent publisher based in Albany, NY.

Connect with QuickStart Guides online at www.quickstartguides.com or follow us on Facebook, Instagram, and LinkedIn.

Follow us @quickstartguides

Glossary

1031 exchange
A concept in real estate that allows someone to exchange one investment property for another and defer capital gains taxes.

Accumulation phase
The period during which one pays money to an insurance company for an annuity.

Additional purchase option
An option in a disability insurance policy that enables the holder of the policy to upgrade it without any additional underwriting qualifications.

Agent
An individual designated in a power of attorney to act on behalf of the principal in the event the principal becomes incapacitated. Also known as the attorney-in-fact.

Annuitization phase
The period during which one gets money back from an insurance company for an annuity.

Annuity
A financial product for which a contract is established between a buyer and an insurance company for the insurance company to provide an income stream to the buyer for a specified amount of time or for life.

Any occupation
A definition in a disability insurance contract that restricts benefits if an employer can find another job within the company for an employee who, because of disability, is not able to perform their usual job.

Asset allocation
A method used to balance different types of investments to ensure diversification and manage risk.

Attorney-in-fact
An individual designated in a power of attorney to act on behalf of the principal in the event the principal becomes incapacitated. Also known as the agent.

Balanced fund
A type of mutual fund that includes both stocks and bonds.

Basis
The combined costs of the purchase price of a property and any improvements made to it.

Bear market territory
A period during which a stock market loses 20 percent or more of its value, resulting in investor fear and widespread sale of investments.

Blue chip stock
Stock of a company that has a well-established reputation for dependability and quality and can generate a profit during both good and challenging economic times.

Bonds
Lending instruments issued by the government or private agencies in exchange for cash. Bondholders are paid interest at prescribed rates and intervals and are repaid the bond's full principal amount when the bond reaches its maturity date.

Bond market
The over-the-counter market on which bonds are traded.

Bull market
A period during which the value of a stock market increases by 20 percent or more over a given period, encouraging investor buying and fueling optimism.

Capital gains
Profit resulting from the sale of a property or investment.

Capital gains taxes
Taxes levied on profit that results from the sale of a property or investment.

Capital losses
Losses that result from the sale of a property or investment.

Cash equivalent
An asset that can be converted into cash immediately. Bank accounts, marketable securities, and money market accounts are considered cash equivalents.

Certificate of deposit (CD)
A financial product offered by banks, thrifts, and credit unions that contains a fixed term of deposit and normally a fixed interest rate.

Charitable remainder trust
A type of trust that enables an individual to support a charity in a manner that generates income for the donor.

Children's Health Insurance Program
A federally administered program that provides matching funds to states to be used to provide health insurance for children who do not qualify for Medicaid.

Cliff vesting
A type of vesting schedule that requires an employee to work for a predetermined amount of time before receiving any employer contributions to a 401(k) plan.

Commission
A portion of the expense of an investment given to the agent or broker who sold it.

Common stock
A type of company stock that usually comes with voting rights for the shareholder.

Compound interest
A powerful financial dynamic created when interest earned on an investment principal begins to earn interest of its own.

Conservator
One or more individuals appointed by the court to manage a person's affairs in the event they are unable to do so.

Consolidated Omnibus Budget Reconciliation Act (COBRA)
A policy that requires employers to allow employees to continue making payments on the same health insurance coverage the employee had before quitting, retiring, or being fired from a job, except if the termination was a result of gross misconduct.

Convertible term policy
A type of term life insurance that enables one to convert the policy to a whole life policy without providing evidence of insurability.

Cost-of-living adjustment (COLA)
An adjustment made to a fixed payment, such as Social Security benefits, intended to help the recipient keep up with inflation.

Cybersecurity
The practice of defending computers, computer systems, mobile devices, networks, data, servers, and other electronic equipment and information from malicious attack.

Cyclical stock
Stock that is negatively affected by downturns in the economy.

Death benefit
A benefit paid to a beneficiary at the time of death of a life insurance policy holder.

Deductible
The amount of money the holder of an insurance policy must pay toward a claim before the insurer begins paying for services.

Defensive stock
A class of stock that is not easily affected by the overall condition of the economy.

Deferred annuity
A type of annuity that does not begin payouts until a post-purchase date selected by the owner of the annuity.

Defined benefit pension plan
A plan in which an employer provides a retired worker with a fixed income from the time of retirement to the end of life.

Defined contribution plan
A plan in which an employee—not an employer—contributes a portion of every paycheck to an account set up to fund retirement.

Delayed retirement credits
Social Security benefits that are delayed past an individual's full retirement age, up until age seventy, when benefits must be taken. Delayed benefits are paid at a higher rate than those taken before or at full retirement age.

Dividends
A portion of a company's earnings distributed to a class of shareholders.

Dividend reinvestment
The process of using dividend proceeds to purchase additional stock.

Dividend reinvestment plan (DRIP)
An automatic investment plan that enables investors to apply dividends they receive from a company to the purchase of additional shares of stock from that company.

Durable power of attorney
A type of power of attorney that grants the agent authority to make decisions regarding financial matters.

Earned income
All income from employment or self-employment, including wages, salaries, tips, royalties, and other taxable employee compensation.

Emergency fund
An amount of money set aside for use when needed in an emergency, such as a job loss.

Emotional vitality
A trait that encompasses enthusiasm, hopefulness, engagement with life, and the ability to face life's stresses with emotional balance. The trait may reduce risk for heart attack and stroke.

Estate plan
A collection of legal documents and strategies that outlines what should happen to one's assets when they die.

Estate tax
A tax levied on the transfer of the estate of a deceased person. The amount of the tax is deducted from the value of the estate before the estate can be divided among heirs.

Evidence of insurability
Proof of good health necessary to secure some types of insurance policies.

Exchange-traded fund (ETF)
An investment instrument that contains a pool of assets and trades on the open market. The value of ETFs fluctuates as they are bought and sold throughout the day.

Executor
An individual designated to manage the disposition of an estate after the death of its owner.

Expense ratio
A fee assessed annually by managers of ETFs or mutual funds. Expense ratios account for administrative overhead and other fixed costs of managing the account.

Federal Employees Retirement System (FERS)
A retirement system under which US civilian employees receive retirement benefits from a pension, Social Security, and the Thrift Savings Plan, which is like a 401(k) plan.

Federal poverty level
A measure of income issued annually by the US Department of Health and Human Services and used to determine eligibility for some government programs.

Fiduciary relationship
A relationship in which one party places a high level of trust and confidence in another party, who bears a duty to act in the best interests of the first party.

Financial independence
The state of being able to support oneself financially in the way one would like to live, without need of help from anyone else.

Financial power of attorney
A type of power of attorney that enables an agent to act on behalf of the principal in matters related to finances.

Fixed annuity
A type of annuity that earns a specified rate of interest over a designated period.

Fully funded pension plan
A pension plan that contains enough assets to cover both the benefits it currently pays and those it will need to pay in the future.

Graded vesting
A type of vesting schedule that enables an employee to gradually take ownership of an employer's contributions to a 401(k) plan.

Grantor
An individual who creates a trust and transfers property into it.

Gross domestic product
The total value of all goods and services produced within a country's border during a specific time.

Growth stock
The stock of a company that is expected to have higher-than-average increases in revenue and earnings.

Guaranteed renewal
A type of disability insurance policy that assures coverage will not be lost if premiums continue to be paid.

Guardian
One or more individuals appointed by the court to take over the affairs of someone who has become incapacitated and has not designated someone to perform that task.

Health savings account (HSA)
An account that offers tax advantages as one saves money for future medical expenses.

HIPAA release form
A legal document that gives permission for protected health information to be shared with designated family members or others.

High-deductible insurance plan
A type of insurance plan that contains high deductibles, meaning the amount the insured person must pay before the insurer starts covering costs.

High-yield bonds
Bonds offered by unreliable companies that are prone to default.

Holographic will
A will that is written and signed by the testator but has no witness to the signature.

Immediate annuity
A type of annuity that begins making payments to the buyer shortly after it is purchased.

Immediate vesting
A vesting schedule that makes an employer's contributions to an employee's 401(k) plan available immediately.

Income stock
Stock that carries a high dividend payout relative to its price.

Index fund
A type of mutual fund or ETF that tracks the performance of a market index such as the Dow Jones Industrial Average or the S&P 500.

Indexed annuity
A type of annuity that contains some features of a fixed annuity but also holds the possibility that one's money can grow if financial markets perform well.

Individual retirement account (IRA)
An account set up with a financial institution into which deposits are made with the purpose of saving money to use in retirement.

Infinite banking
A banking concept that effectively enables an individual to become their own bank to finance their own personal and business transactions.

Inheritance tax
A tax on assets passed from an estate to an heir, which the heir is responsible for paying.

Initial enrollment period
A prescribed period during which someone who wishes to get Medicare can enroll in the program.

Initial public offering (IPO)
The act of offering shares of stock of a private corporation to the public for the first time. A private company that issues stock becomes a publicly held company.

Intestate
The state of dying without a legal will.

Intestate succession
A legal process of distributing the assets of an individual who has died intestate.

Investment-grade bonds
Bonds issued by large reputable companies that have a low risk for default.

Irrevocable trust
A type of trust that, once established, is difficult to alter.

Joint will
A type of will written and executed by two people, typically spouses or partners, stipulating that all assets be passed to the surviving spouse and then to surviving children.

Junk bonds
Bonds that carry a greater risk of default than most bonds issued by governments or corporations.

Large-cap stock
Stock of companies with large market capitalization.

Letter of instruction
A document in addition to a will that provides specific instruction regarding the distribution of assets or other matters.

Leverage
A concept that holds that small amounts of money can be used to exert control over larger amounts of money.

Limited liability company (LLC)
A business structure designed to limit liability to the asset or assets within the LLC and protect one's personal assets in the event they are sued.

Living trust
A type of trust into which property is transferred while the grantor is still alive.

Living will
A document providing health care instructions to an agent who can communicate those wishes if the writer of the living will cannot. Also known as a medical directive to physicians.

Long-term care insurance
A type of insurance purchased to be used if the buyer requires long-term care in the future.

Market capitalization
The total value of all a company's outstanding shares of stock at current prices.

Market timing
A technique employed by investors who buy and sell securities in anticipation of their performance.

Medicaid
A joint federal and state program that provides health insurance coverage to Americans with limited income and resources.

Medical power of attorney
A type of power of attorney that gives an agent authority to act on behalf of the principal regarding medical matters.

Medicare
A federal health insurance program for Americans who are sixty-five or older and for those with certain disabilities.

Medicare Advantage Plan
An alternative to original Medicare that is sold through private insurers who determine premiums. It often is called Medicare Part C.

Money market fund
A type of mutual fund that purchases short-term securities such as cash or cash-equivalent securities.

Money market mutual fund
A type of mutual fund in which the value of one's original investment doesn't change and on which investors have historically earned higher interest than with a savings account.

Mutual fund
An investment in which investors pool their money and a fund manager uses the money to buy a variety of investment vehicles, likely including stocks, bonds, cash equivalents (like T-bills), and real estate.

Mutual fund provider
A financial institution that owns a mutual fund family.

Mutual will
A will in which two people, typically spouses, write and execute a will jointly. Upon the death of one, the other is bound to the terms of the will.

Net asset value
The value of one share of a stock, ETF, or mutual fund.

Noncancelable policy
A type of insurance policy assuring that if premiums are paid, the policy will be renewed each year without an increase in the premium or a reduction of benefits.

Online broker
A broker, or brokerage firm, that interacts with customers online rather than in person. Online brokers can also offer resources to enable clients to conduct their own trading.

Open-end mutual fund
A type of mutual fund that has no size limit and can continually issue shares in response to demand.

Oral will
A will in which the testator verbally expresses their wishes in front of witnesses.

Original Medicare
Parts A and B of Medicare, which cover hospitalization and medically necessary services.

Own occupation
A definition in a disability insurance policy that assures that benefits will be paid in the event the holder of the policy becomes disabled and is not able to perform the precise job for which they were hired, even if a different job is available at the same company.

Penny stock
A low-priced stock, usually traded at less than five dollars per share and sometimes traded outside of the major stock exchanges.

Periodic investment plan
A plan set up with a broker that draws a dollar amount from one's cash account at regular intervals to be reinvested in designated securities.

Phishing
A form of cybercrime in which cybercriminals attempt to steal personal information by sending a text, email, or other form of correspondence intended to trick a user.

Pour-over will
A will used in conjunction with a trust that ensures the remaining assets of the deceased will automatically transfer to a designated trust at the time of death.

Power of attorney
A legal document that authorizes an individual to act on behalf of another if the other becomes incapacitated. Power of attorney can also refer to the person authorized to act on another's behalf.

Preferred stock
A type of company stock that normally does not offer voting rights to the shareholder.

Premium protection
An optional plan or rider with an insurance policy that guarantees the insured will not lose their original investment.

Premium
The amount of money an individual, family, or company pays on a regular basis, usually monthly, for an insurance plan.

Primary insurance amount
The amount of Social Security benefits one receives if they start taking benefits at their full retirement age.

Primary market
A market where stocks and bonds are offered for the first time, such as stock that is offered in an initial public offering.

Principal
The individual who appoints someone to act on their behalf as power of attorney if they become incapacitated.

Probate
The court-supervised process of verifying the will of a deceased person.

Public sector exemption from Social Security
A stipulation that excludes public employees in fifteen states from contributing to Social Security, which excludes them from receiving Social Security benefits when they retire.

Qualified distributions
Money that can be withdrawn without penalty from a 401(k) or IRA when the owner of the plan turns fifty-nine and a half.

Qualified dividends
Dividends that are taxed at the capital gains rate instead of the higher rate levied on ordinary dividends.

Rebalancing of portfolio
The process of buying or selling assets within a portfolio to ensure that the balance remains at its original target allocation.

Regular income
Also called ordinary income, it is the income generated through salaries and wages and taxed at ordinary rates.

Required minimum distributions
Withdrawals that are required to be taken from a retirement account when one reaches a certain age.

Revocable trust
A type of trust that can be changed after it is established by the grantor.

Roth 401(k)
A variation of a traditional 401(k) for which contributions are taxed up front and do not reduce taxable income. Assuming certain criteria have been met, money is not taxed when it is taken out of the account, regardless of how much the account has grown.

Secondary market
A market where investors buy assets from other investors on an exchange instead of from issuing companies.

Self-directed brokerage window
An option with a 401(k) plan that allows for additional investment opportunities via the buying and selling of securities through a brokerage platform.

Series LLC
A type of limited liability company (LLC) designed to cover a series of assets, keeping them siloed off from one another's potential liabilities. Series LLCs are not available in all states.

Simple LLC
A type of limited liability company (LLC) designed to limit liability to a single asset.

Simplified employee pension (SEP) IRA
A type of IRA that enables a business owner to make pretax contributions for herself and her employees. A self-employed person who does not have any employees can also save with a SEP IRA.

Small-cap stock
Shares of stock of companies with small market capitalization values.

Social Security Administration (SSA)
An independent agency of the United States government that administers the Social Security program.

Social Security Trust Fund
A United States Treasury fund that holds money not needed to pay Social Security benefits and administrative costs in the current year. The money is required by law to be invested in Treasury bonds that are guaranteed by the US government.

Spousal benefit
A Social Security benefit based on the work history of an individual but paid to the individual's spouse.

Spousal IRA
A type of IRA that allows a spouse to contribute money on behalf of the other spouse, who does not have earned income.

State Health Insurance Assistance Program
A federally funded program established to help individuals choose plans, resolve billing issues, handle complaints about medical care or treatment, and help clarify other issues involving Medicare.

Stepped-up basis rule for inherited property
A readjustment of the value of an appreciated asset for tax purposes when a property is passed along to an heir.

Stock exchange
A platform used by investors to buy and sell investments, mainly stocks.

Stock option
A form of compensation that gives employees the right to buy shares of their company's stock.

Stock
An asset class used as a tool for a company or other entity to raise money. Owning stock in a company represents partial ownership of that company.

Supplemental insurance plan
An insurance plan used to supplement another plan, such as Medicare, which covers some but not all of an individual's medical expenses.

Surrender period
The period during which money cannot be withdrawn from an annuity without incurring a penalty. It is sometimes called the surrender charge period.

Systematic withdrawal plan
A strategy in which regular withdrawals are taken from a mutual fund or other account with the intent of lowering the tax rate of long-term gains.

Tax-loss harvesting
A method of offsetting capital gains with capital losses incurred by selling an investment for less than the purchase price.

Tax-deferred
A tax feature that prevents the money in an account from being taxed until the savings are withdrawn.

Term life insurance
Life insurance that covers a certain period, often ten, twenty, or thirty years.

Testamentary trust
A type of trust into which property is transferred after the death of the grantor.

Testamentary will
A will that is prepared and signed by the testator in the presence of witnesses. It is the most common and frequently used type of will.

Testator
An individual who prepares and signs a will.

Thrift Savings Plan
A defined contribution plan for United States civil service employees and retirees. Members of uniformed services, which include military and some other corps, also participate in the plan.

Tolerance for risk
The degree to which an investor is willing to risk loss to the value of an investment.

Trust
An estate planning tool with which a person known as the trustor gives another person, known as the trustee, the right to hold title to property or assets on behalf of one or more beneficiaries.

Trustee
A person designated to hold title to property or assets on behalf of a beneficiary.

Underfunded pension
A pension that does not contain enough assets to fund its obligations.

Unfunded plan
A pension that uses company income to make pension payments as it becomes necessary to do so. Also known as a pay-as-you-go plan, as there are no assets set aside.

Unqualified dividends
A type of dividend that is taxed at the standard income tax rate, which is higher than the capital gains rate at which qualified dividends are taxed.

Value stock
Stock that is undervalued compared to that of similar companies.

Variable annuity
A type of annuity that gains or loses value depending on the performance of the subaccounts on which it is based.

Vesting schedule
A schedule that determines when a benefit, such as an employer-matched 401(k) plan, becomes available to an employee. Usually tied to an employee's length of employment.

Whole life insurance
A life insurance policy that, as one pays premiums, enables them to accumulate a cash value in the policy that can be accessed prior to their death.

Disclosures

Securities offered through Kestra Investment Services LLC (Kestra IS), member FINRA/SIPC. Investment advisory services offered through Kestra Advisory Services LLC (Kestra AS), an affiliate of Kestra IS. Snow Financial Group LLC is not affiliated with Kestra IS or Kestra AS. Kestra IS and Kestra AS do not provide tax or legal advice.

The opinions expressed in this book are those of the author and may not necessarily reflect those held by Kestra IS or Kestra AS. The information contained in this publication is for general information only and is not intended to provide specific investment advice or recommendations for any individual. It is suggested that you consult your financial professional, attorney, or tax advisor regarding your individual situation. Mathematical illustrations presented in this book do not predict likelihood of investment outcomes. Comments concerning past performance are not intended to be forward-looking and should not be viewed as an indication of future results. Please note, all investments involve varying levels and types of risks. These risks can be associated with the specific investment or with the marketplace. Loss of principal is possible.

Mutual funds and variable insurance are sold by prospectus only. Before investing, investors should carefully consider the investment objectives, risks, charges, and expenses of a mutual fund or a variable insurance product and its underlying investment options. For mutual funds, the fund prospectus, and for variable insurance, the current contract prospectus and underlying fund prospectuses, provide this and other important information. Please contact your representative or Snow Financial Group LLC to obtain a prospectus. Please read the prospectus(es) carefully before investing or sending money.

For exchange-traded funds (ETFs), investors should consider carefully information contained in the prospectus, including investment objectives, risks, charges, and expenses. Please read the prospectus carefully before investing. ETFs do not sell individual shares directly to investors and only issue their shares in large blocks. ETFs are subject to risks like those of stocks. Investment returns will fluctuate and are subject to market volatility, so that an investor's shares, when redeemed or sold, may be worth more or less than their original cost.

References

Adamczyk, Alicia. 2020. "Here's Exactly How to Pick Investments for Your 401(k)." *CNBC make it.* January 9. https://www.cnbc.com/2020/01/09/exactly-how-to-pick-investments-for-your-401k.html.

—. 2019. "The Average Employer 401(k) Match Is at an All-Time High – See How Yours Compares." *CNBC make it.* June 10. https://www.cnbc.com/2019/06/10/this-is-the-average-401k-employer-match.html.

Aldeman, Chad. 2019. "Why Aren't All Teachers Covered By Social Security?" *TeacherPensions.org.* August 14. https://www.teacherpensions.org/blog/why-aren%E2%80%99t-all-teachers-covered-social-security.

Anderson, Steve. 2019. "A Brief History of Medicare in America." *MedicareResources.org.* September 1. https://www.medicareresources.org/basic-medicare-information/brief-history-of-medicare/.

Andrews, Michelle. 2017. "Why a Long-Term-Disability Policy Is More Important Than Pet Insurance." *NPR.* October 11. https://www.npr.org/sections/health-shots/2017/10/11/556946744/why-a-long-term-disability-policy-is-more-important-than-pet-insurance.

Ashworth, Will. 2020. "24 Dividend Cuts and Suspensions Chalked Up to the Coronavirus." *Kiplinger.* July 14. https://www.kiplinger.com/slideshow/investing/t018-s001-15-dividend-cuts-and-suspensions-coronavirus/index.html.

Backman, Maurie. 2019. *The Motley Fool.* August 28. Accessed June 29, 2020. https://www.fool.com/retirement/9-retirement-expenses-every-senior-should-plan-for.aspx.

Beattie, Andrew. 2019. "The History of Insurance in America." *Investopedia.* December 11. https://www.investopedia.com/articles/financial-theory/08/american-insurance.asp.

Bomey, Nathan. 2019. "'It's Really Over': Corporate Pensions Head for Extinction as Nature of Retirement Plans Changes." *USA Today.* December 31. https://www.usatoday.com/story/money/2019/12/10/corporate-pensions-defined-benefit-mercer-report/2618501001/.

Borzykowski, Bryan. 2018. "The Trillion-Dollar ETF Boom Triggered by the Financial Crisis Just Keeps Getting Bigger." *CNBC.* September 14. https://www.cnbc.com/2018/09/14/the-trillion-dollar-etf-boom-triggered-by-the-financial-crisis.html#:~:text=While%20ETFs%20first%20arrived%20in,trillion%20today%2C%20according%20to%20Statistica.

BrightScope. 2019. "BrightScope/ICI Data Show Diverse Range of 401(k) Investment Options." *BrightScope.* June 19. https://blog.brightscope.com/2019/06/19/brightscope-ici-401k-report-2019/.

Brockman, Katie. 2019. "This Is How Much the Average American Household Saves Each Year." *The Motley Fool.* October 27. https://www.fool.com/retirement/2019/10/27/this-is-how-much-the-average-american-saves-each-y.aspx.

Caplinger, Dan. 2018. "Why Does Social Security Leave Out Teachers in These 15 States?" *The Motley Fool.* October 7. https://www.fool.com/retirement/2018/10/07/why-does-social-security-leave-out-teachers-in-the.aspx.

Caring. n.d. "2020 Estate Planning and Wills Study." *Caring.com.* Accessed August 19, 2020. https://www.caring.com/caregivers/estate-planning/wills-survey#:~:text=In%202017%2C%20almost%20half%20(42,25%25%20in%20just%20three%20years.

Centers for Medicare & Medicaid Services. n.d. "National Health Expenditure Data Fact Sheet." *CMS.gov*. Accessed June 15, 2020. https://www.cms.gov/Research-Statistics-Data-and-Systems/Statistics-Trends-and-Reports/NationalHealthExpendData/NHE-Fact-Sheet.

Congressional Research Service. 2020. "Medicare: Insolvency Projections." *Federation of American Scientists*. May 29. https://fas.org/sgp/crs/misc/RS20946.pdf.

Crane, Casey. 2019. "3 Cyber Fraud Tactics Targeting Seniors and Why They're So Effective." *Cybercrime Magazine*. September 13. https://cybersecurityventures.com/3-cyber-fraud-tactics-targeting-seniors-and-why-theyre-so-effective/.

Dimensional Fund Advisors LP. 2016. "Performance of Premiums in the Equity Markets."

Duke University. n.d. "How Attitude Can Reduce Your Stress." *Duke Human Resources*. Accessed August 6, 2020. https://hr.duke.edu/wellness/mental-health-stress/success-over-stress/outsmart-stress/how-attitude-can-reduce-your.

eHealth. 2020. "How Much Does Health Insurance Cost Without a Subsidy?" *eHealth Insurance*. November 23. https://www.ehealthinsurance.com/resources/affordable-care-act/much-health-insurance-cost-without-subsidy.

Elder Law Answers. 2020. "Medicare Part A: Hospital Coverage." *ElderLawAnswers*. March 11. https://www.elderlawanswers.com/medicare-part-a-hospital-coverage-12188.

Elkins, Kathleen. 2017. "A Brief History of the 401(k), Which Changed How Americans Retire." *CNBC make it*. January 4. https://www.cnbc.com/2017/01/04/a-brief-history-of-the-401k-which-changed-how-americans-retire.html.

Fidelity Viewpoints. 2020. "How to Plan for Rising Health Care Costs." *Fidelity*. August 3. https://www.fidelity.com/viewpoints/personal-finance/plan-for-rising-health-care-costs#:~:text=It%20is%20estimated%20that%20the,the%20largest%20expenses%20in%20retirement.

Fisker, Jacob Lund. 2019. "Early Retirement Extreme: The Ten-Year Update." *Get Rich Slowly*. October 2. https://www.getrichslowly.org/early-retirement-extreme/.

Flitter, Emily and Karen Weise. 2019. "Capital One Data Breach Compromises Data of Over 100 Million." *The New York Times*, July 29.

Folger, Jean. 2019. "The Most Popular States to Retire to in the U.S." *Investopedia*. August 4. https://www.investopedia.com/articles/retirement/020117/most-popular-states-retire-us.asp.

Friedman, Zack. 2020. "Student Loan Debt Statistics In 2020: A Record $1.6 Trillion." *Forbes*. February 3. https://www.forbes.com/sites/zackfriedman/2020/02/03/student-loan-debt-statistics/#996e3e6281fe.

Gallup. n.d. "Social Security." *Gallup*. Accessed July 3, 2020. https://news.gallup.com/poll/1693/social-security.aspx.

Genworth. 2020. *Cost of Care Survey*. March 30. https://www.genworth.com/aging-and-you/finances/cost-of-care.html.

Grandstaff, Mark. 2016. "This Is How Much It Really Costs to Own a Dog Per Year." *USA Today*. August 24. https://www.usatoday.com/story/money/personalfinance/2016/08/24/how-much-costs-own-dog-per-year/88449800/.

Hannon, Kerry. 2019. "How Working in Retirement Became a Reality." *Forbes*. September 6. https://www.forbes.com/sites/nextavenue/2019/09/06/how-working-in-retirement-became-a-reality/#7375bc3873fc.

Harrison, Jonathan. 2018. "Is Generosity the Secret to Wealth?" *Sound Stewardship*. January 30. https://www.soundstewardship.com/generosity-secret-wealth/.

Hartman, Rachel. 2020. "Companies With the Best Retirement Plans." *U.S. News and World Report - Money*. February 5. https://money.usnews.com/money/retirement/401ks/articles/companies-with-the-best-retirement-plans.

Harvard Women's Health Watch. 2016. "How Your Attitudes Affect Your Health." *Harvard Medical School, Harvard Health Publishing.* May. https://www.health.harvard.edu/mind-and-mood/how-your-attitudes-affect-your-health.

Horan, Stephanie. 2020. *SmartAsset.* January 22. Accessed August 26, 2020.

Howard, Jacqueline. 2016. "Your Parents Hold Clues to Your Life Expectancy, Heart Health." *CNN Health.* August 15. https://www.cnn.com/2016/08/15/health/parents-life-expectancy-heart-health/index.html.

Huddleston, Tom Jr. 2020. "How Many Recessions You've Actually Lived Through and What Happened in Every One." *CNBC make it.* April 9. https://www.cnbc.com/2020/04/09/what-happened-in-every-us-recession-since-the-great-depression.html.

Iachini, Michael. 2020. "ETF vs. Mutual Fund." *Charles Schwab.* January 28. https://www.schwab.com/resource-center/insights/content/etf-vs-mutual-fund-it-depends-on-your-strategy.

Insurance Information Institute. n.d. "Facts + Statistics: Industry Overview." Accessed June 24, 2020. https://www.iii.org/fact-statistic/facts-statistics-industry-overview#:~:text=The%20U.S.%20insurance%20industry%20employed,and%20reinsurers%20(28%2C500%20workers).

Jastra. 2020. "Robo-Advisors to Become $1.4T Industry This Year." *Traders Magazine.* February 5. https://www.tradersmagazine.com/news/robo-advisors-to-become-1-4t-industry-this-year/.

Jefferson, Elana Ashanti. 2020. "7 Ways Cyber Criminals Target Seniors — and How to Stop It." *Property Casualty 360.* June 26. https://www.propertycasualty360.com/2020/06/26/7-ways-cyber-criminals-target-seniors-and-how-to-stop-it/?slreturn=20200724100306.

Kenton, Will. 2020. "Lump Sum vs. Pension: What Is the Better Option?" *NewRetirement.* June 1. https://www.newretirement.com/retirement/lump-sum-vs-pension-which-is-the-better-option/.

Kurt, Daniel. 2020. "How Good a Deal Is an Indexed Annuity?" *Investopedia.* July 29. https://www.investopedia.com/articles/personal-finance/051214/how-good-deal-indexed-annuity.asp.

—. 2019. "Retirement and Depression." *Investopedia.* August 11. https://www.investopedia.com/articles/retirement/120516/retirement-and-depression-6-ways-overcome-it.asp.

—. 2014. "The Best Time to Get Long-Term Care Insurance." *Investopedia.* May 20. https://www.investopedia.com/articles/personal-finance/052014/whats-best-time-get-longterm-care-insurance.asp#:~:text=The%20Best%20Age%20to%20Buy,in%20their%2070s%20or%2080s.

LaPonsie, Maryalene. 2020. "How Living Longer Will Impact Your Retirement." *U.S. News.* April 22. https://money.usnews.com/money/retirement/articles/how-living-longer-will-impact-your-retirement.

Leonhardt, Megan. 2019. "Here's What the Average American Typically Pays in 401(k) Fees." *CNBC make it.* July 22. https://www.cnbc.com/2019/07/22/how-much-the-average-american-typically-pays-in-401k-fees.html#:~:text=Financial%20experts%20agree%3A%20Employer%2Dsponsored,to%20the%20Investment%20Company%20Institute.

Levine, David. 2017. "Can Retirement Be a Depression Risk?" *U.S. News.* July 28. https://health.usnews.com/health-care/patient-advice/articles/2017-07-28/can-retirement-be-a-depression-risk.

LIMRA. 2020. "Secure Retirement Institute: U.S. Annuity Rankings Reveal New #1 in 2019." *LIMRA.* March 16. https://www.limra.com/en/newsroom/news-releases/2020/secure-retirement-institute-u.s.-annuity-rankings-reveal-new-1-in-2019/.

Lohmann, Raychelle Cassada. 2017. "Achieving Happiness by Helping Others." *Psychology Today.* January 29. https://www.psychologytoday.com/us/blog/teen-angst/201701/achieving-happiness-helping-others.

Luscombe, Richard. 2017. "Life Expectancy Gap Between Rich and Poor US Regions Is 'More Than 20 Years'." *The Guardian*, U.S. Edition. May 8. https://www.theguardian.com/inequality/2017/may/08/life-expectancy-gap-rich-poor-us-regions-more-than-20-years.

Macrotrends. n.d. "U.S. Life Expectancy 1950-2020." *Macrotrends*. Accessed June 30, 2020. https://www.macrotrends.net/countries/USA/united-states/life-expectancy.

Malkiel, Burton G. 2003. *The Random Walk Guide to Investing*. New York: W. W. Norton & Company.

Medicaid. 2020. "July 2020 Medicaid & CHIP Enrollment Data Highlights." *Medicaid*. July. https://www.medicaid.gov/medicaid/program-information/medicaid-and-chip-enrollment-data/report-highlights/index.html.

Mental Health Minnesota. n.d. "Mental Health and Physical Health." *Mental Health Minnesota*. Accessed November 12, 2020. https://mentalhealthmn.org/learn-more/mental-health-and-physical-health/.

National Academy of Social Insurance. n.d. "Who Gets Social Security?" *National Academy of Social Insurance*. Accessed July 6, 2020. https://www.nasi.org/learn/socialsecurity/who-gets.

National Association of Chronic Disease Directors. n.d. "The State of Mental Health and Aging in America." *CDC*. Accessed November 12, 2020. https://www.cdc.gov/aging/pdf/mental_health.pdf.

Nerdwallet. 2016. "When Hybrid Long-Term Care Insurance Makes Sense." *NerdWallet.com*. June 22. https://www.nerdwallet.com/blog/insurance/hybrid-long-term-care-insurance-makes-sense/#:~:text=While%20many%20factors%20can%20influence,or%20until%20care%20is%20needed).

Next Insurance. 2018. "How to Survive a Small Business Lawsuit." *Next Insurance*. May 13. https://www.nextinsurance.com/blog/survive-small-business-lawsuit/.

Norris, Louise. 2020. *healthinsurance.org*. July 8. Accessed August 31, 2020. https://www.healthinsurance.org/obamacare-enrollment-guide/who-should-help-me-enroll-in-a-health-plan/.

Novotney, Amy. 2019. "The Risks of Social Isolation." *American Psychological Association*. May. https://www.apa.org/monitor/2019/05/ce-corner-isolation.

Owaida, Amer. 2020. "FBI: Cybercrime Losses Tripled Over the Last 5 Years." *welivesecurity*. February 13. https://www.welivesecurity.com/2020/02/13/fbi-cybercrime-losses-tripled-last-5-years/.

Parker, Tim. 2020. "What Is the Federal Employees Retirement System (FERS) and How Does It Work?" *Investopedia*. October 30. https://www.investopedia.com/articles/personal-finance/062513/what-federal-employees-retirement-system-fers-and-how-does-it-work.asp.

Pension Rights Center. 2019. "How Many American Workers Participate in Workplace Retirement Plans?" *Pension Rights Center*. July 15. https://www.pensionrights.org/publications/statistic/how-many-american-workers-participate-workplace-retirement-plans.

Puchalski, Christine M. 2001. "The Role of Spirituality in Health Care." *National Institutes of Health*. October 14. https://dx.doi.org/10.1080%2F08998280.2001.11927788.

Rapacon, Stacy. 2020. "Top 25 Part-Time Jobs for Retirees." *AARP*. March 5. https://www.aarp.org/work/job-search/info-2020/part-time-jobs-for-retirees.html.

Reed, Chuck. 2017. "Think Public Pensions Can't Be Cut? Think Again." *Governing*. April 26. https://www.governing.com/gov-institute/voices/col-public-pension-cuts-unsustainable-retirement-systems.html.

Russell Investments. 2020. "2020 Value of an Advisor Study." *Russell Investments*. Accessed October 12, 2020. https://russellinvestments.com/Publications/US/Document/Value_of_an_Advisor_Study.pdf.

Sarandeses, Rafael. 2018. "A Guide to the Science of Giving." *Medium.com, Better Humans.* May 7. https://medium.com/better-humans/a-guide-to-the-science-of-giving-ba007d9304ff.

Schnaubelt, Catherine. 2018. "Social Security: Past, Present and Future." *Forbes.* May 30. https://www.forbes.com/sites/catherineschnaubelt/2018/05/30/social-security-past-present-and-future/#627d8e0059ab.

Segal, Troy. 2020. "Lump-Sum Vs. Regular Pension Payments: What's the Difference?" *Investopedia.* February 28. https://www.investopedia.com/articles/retirement/05/lumpsumpension.asp.

Seligman, Martin E. P. n.d. "Perma Theory of Well-Being and Perma Workshops." *Penn Arts & Sciences, Positive Psychology Center.* Accessed November 13, 2020. https://ppc.sas.upenn.edu/learn-more/perma-theory-well-being-and-perma-workshops.

Sergeant, Jacqueline. 2020. "Total Annuity Sales Reach Highest Levels In More Than Decade." *Financial Advisor.* February 19. https://www.fa-mag.com/news/total-annuity-sales-reach-highest-levels-more-than-a-decade-54160.html#:~:text=Total%20annuity%20sales%20climb%20to,Quarter%20U.S.%20Annuity%20Sales%20Survey.

Silverman, Lauren. 2014. "Learning a New Skill Works Best to Keep Your Brain Sharp." *NPR.* May 5. https://www.npr.org/sections/health-shots/2014/05/05/309006780/learning-a-new-skill-works-best-to-keep-your-brain-sharp.

Smith, Kelly Anne. 2020. "The 9 FIRE Blogs You Should Read." *Forbes.* March 25. https://www.forbes.com/advisor/retirement/the-9-fire-blogs-you-should-read/.

Social Security Administration. n.d. "Life Expectancy for Social Security." *Social Security.* Accessed July 2, 2020. https://www.ssa.gov/history/lifeexpect.html.

Stark, Caitlin. 2012. "By the Numbers: Social Security." *CNN.* August 17. https://www.cnn.com/2012/08/17/politics/btn-social-security/index.html.

Stepler, Renee. 2017. "Led by Baby Boomers, Divorce Rates Climb for America's 50+ Population." *Pew Research Center.* March 9. https://www.pewresearch.org/fact-tank/2017/03/09/led-by-baby-boomers-divorce-rates-climb-for-americas-50-population/.

Tepper, Taylor. 2018. "How Much Will You Need to Retire? Most Americans Have No Idea." *Bankrate.* June 7. https://www.bankrate.com/retirement/survey-how-much-needed-to-retire/.

Terrell, Kenneth. 2019. "Who's Working More? People Age 65 and Older." *AARP.* November 22. https://www.aarp.org/work/working-at-50-plus/info-2019/surging-older-workforce.html.

The Conversation Project. n.d. "About Us." *The Conversation Project.* Accessed August 23, 2020. https://theconversationproject.org/about/.

U.S. Census Bureau. 2020. *U.S. Census Bureau.* April 28. Accessed July 25, 2020. https://www.census.gov/housing/hvs/files/currenthvspress.pdf.

White, Ed. 2020. "Detroit Lawyer Tapped to Take Over Aretha Franklin Estate." *ABC News.* March 3. https://abcnews.go.com/Entertainment/wireStory/detroit-lawyer-tapped-aretha-franklin-estate-69370410.

Williams, Rita. 2019. "3 Ways Inflation Affects Your Retirement Savings." *The Motley Fool.* March 3. https://www.fool.com/retirement/2019/03/03/3-ways-inflation-affects-your-retirement.aspx#:~:text=1.,diminish%20their%20value%20over%20time.

Index

GET YOUR NEXT
QuickStart Guide®
FOR FREE

Leave us a quick video testimonial on our website and we will give you a **FREE *QuickStart Guide*** of your choice!

RECORD TESTIMONIAL

SUBMIT TO OUR WEBSITE

GET A FREE BOOK

TWO WAYS TO LEAVE A VIDEO TESTIMONIAL

Use the camera app on your mobile phone to scan the QR code or visit the link below to record your testimonial and get your free book.

SCAN ME

or

go.quickstartguides.com/free-qsg

VISIT URL

SAVE 10% ON YOUR NEXT

QuickStart Guide®

USE CODE: QSG10

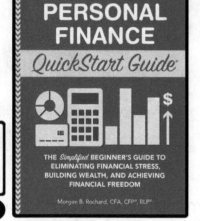

www.quickstartguides.shop/finance

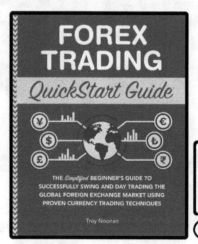

www.quickstartguides.shop/forex

www.quickstartguides.shop/investing

www.quickstartguides.shop/trading

Use the camera app on your mobile phone to scan the QR code or visit the link below the cover to shop.

Get 10% off your entire order when you use code 'QSG10' at checkout at www.quickstartguides.com

LISTEN TO *QuickStart Guides* ON THE GO

NEW AUDIBLE MEMBERS
GET THEIR FIRST AUDIOBOOK
FREE!

DIGITAL MARKETING *QuickStart Guide*

FOREX TRADING *QuickStart Guide*

FLIPPING HOUSES *QuickStart Guide*

REAL ESTATE INVESTING *QuickStart Guide*

INVESTING *QuickStart Guide*

TWO WAYS TO SELECT A FREE AUDIOBOOK

Use the camera app on your mobile phone to scan the QR code
or visit the link below to select your free audiobook from Audible.

or

www.quickstartguides.com/free-audiobook

 SCAN ME

 VISIT URL

Terms: Your free Audible membership will rebill at up to $14.99 after the end of the 30-day trial period and is subject to Audible's terms and conditions. There are no commitments, and you can cancel your Audible membership at any time, including before the end of the trial period. Free monthly credits can be redeemed for audiobooks from the Audible catalog and are yours to keep. This promotion is provided by Audible and is restricted to US and UK customers only. ClydeBank Media QuickStart Guides are not affiliated with Audible. Any devices depicted on this page are for illustrative purposes only and are not included in this promotion. ClydeBank Media QuickStart Guides may receive affiliate compensation should you choose to start a paid Audible membership using any of the links we provide.

CLYDEBANK MEDIA

QuickStart Guides®

PROUDLY SUPPORT ONE TREE PLANTED

One Tree Planted is a 501(c)(3) nonprofit organization focused on global reforestation, with millions of trees planted every year. ClydeBank Media is proud to support One Tree Planted as a reforestation partner.

Every dollar donated plants one tree and every tree makes a difference!

Learn more at www.clydebankmedia.com/charitable-giving or make a contribution at onetreeplanted.org.